Žižek and Communist Strategy

ŽIŽEK AND COMMUNIST STRATEGY
ON THE DISAVOWED FOUNDATIONS OF GLOBAL CAPITALISM

∞

Chris McMillan

EDINBURGH
University Press

© Chris McMillan, 2012, 2013

First published in hardback in 2012 by
Edinburgh University Press Ltd
22 George Square, Edinburgh EH8 9LF
www.euppublishing.com

This paperback edition 2013

Typeset in 11/13 Sabon by
Servis Filmsetting Ltd, Stockport, Cheshire

A CIP record for this book is available from the British Library

ISBN 978 0 7486 4664 7 (hardback)
ISBN 978 0 7486 8233 1 (paperback)
ISBN 978 0 7486 4665 4 (webready PDF)
ISBN 978 0 7486 5549 6 (epub)

The right of Chris McMillan to be identified as author of this
work has been asserted in accordance with the Copyright, Designs
and Patents Act 1988 and the Copyright and Related Rights
Regulations 2003 (SI No. 2498).

The author would like to thank the editors of *The International
Journal of Žižek Studies* for allowing the reproduction of sections
of 'The Communist Hypothesis; Žižekian Utopia or Utopian
Fantasy?', originally published in vol. 5, no. 2, 2011.

Contents

Acknowledgements

Writing can often appear to be a solitary pursuit. Long hours are spent with one's head in a book or hunched over a silent computer. Large periods can pass without a word being uttered. Yet constructing this book has been anything but a lonely experience for me. I have been accompanied and encouraged by a range of characters throughout the journey, without whom this document might not have come to completion.

Much of this book enjoyed its first life as a PhD thesis while I studied at Massey University in New Zealand, where I was supervised by Warwick Tie and Grant Duncan. I began working with Warwick in my honours year and this project has been a culmination of several years of debate and discussion which I have found to be nothing less than a pleasure. Warwick has been a constant sounding board and a great mentor for whom I have massive admiration. For this reason, I owe Warwick, along with Grant, a huge debt of gratitude. I would also like to thank Colin Cremin, Glyn Daly and Chamsy el-Ojeili for their very useful critiques of my project.

The process of writing this text would certainly not have been the same without the companionship and camaraderie of my fellow students in the PhD room at the School of Social and Cultural Studies. Being able to share this experience with you all is something I will never forget. Also, to those within the school who provided resources, guidance or a friendly smile, I thank you also.

I would also like to thank Edinburgh University Press for their patient support and encouragement throughout this process, in particular Nicola Ramsey and Eddie Clark, and their copy-editor Jonathan Wadman.

To my good friends – Marty, Drakie, Doddy, Ange, Thames and Leon – most of whom I have known since high school, I thank you for putting up with my political rants and my strange habits, my lack of funds and increasing withdrawal from 'real life'.

To my family – Mum and Dad, James and Melanie, and Grandma and grandparents lost – as well as my 'new' family, the Maynes, I thank you for being the ongoing foundations of my life. If I have faith in anything, it is faith in the love and support of my family. From my early years to this day, this has never wavered and I'm sure this book would have not have been possible without your support.

Most of all, to my wife Victoria, who has stuck by me through thick and thin, from my days as an aspiring undergraduate business tycoon, to scholarly communist, through breakdowns – academic, financial or 'other' – and adventures. Victoria, you have been my constant companion throughout this journey, riding the ups and downs as much as I have. You have tolerated the (occasional) long hours, (constant) financial sacrifice and my increasing detachment from everyday life as this project lurched its way towards completion. I love you: I dedicate this book to you.

Introduction

The dust jackets for Slavoj Žižek's books often announce him as 'Elvis of Cultural Theory' or 'The greatest intellectual high since *Anti-Oedipus*'.* Whilst these conceptions no doubt irk Žižek as mechanisms that subvert his radicalism by emphasising his popularity, they aptly capture the excess of his appeal. Regularly drawing audiences in their hundreds, if not thousands, Žižek appears to hold a position of mastery for many radical Leftists. Despite repeated attempts to subvert this position, Žižek is continually positioned as the subject who is supposed to know, and then derided when his latest book fails to provide a utopian blueprint (or even a concrete conclusion). Everyone knows who Žižek is, but nobody knows what he stands for – including Žižek, if his critics are to be believed. In this manner, for many Žižek represents the failure of radical Leftist political theorising to respond to the sustained and semi-permanent crisis of Marxism and the contradictory failing, and continued thriving, of global capitalism.

There is no need to be reticent: I shall lay my cards on the table. This tragic positioning of Žižek and Žižekian theory is not the position taken in this book. Against the predominant production of Žižekian theory as 'good theory, bad politics', I come to argue that his work identifies the path towards a regeneration of Marxist political practice and an effective disruption of global capitalism in the name of a better future.

Žižek is certainly an outstanding theorist of culture, of ideology and of subjectivity, but his influence goes beyond this superstructural analysis. Žižek's renewal of Marxist analysis, thoroughly coloured by Lacanian psychoanalysis and Hegelian dialectics, offers a critique of capitalism that highlights the path to a communist future. This restoration does not come with an idealist manifesto, or the detailed

---

* While these two quotes come from the *Chronicle of Higher Education* and the *Village Voice* they are so ubiquitously clichéd that it hardly seems to matter: indeed, it is difficult to source the original sources.

confession of once-hidden ethical principles. Instead, the reading of Žižek produced in this book highlights a return to a classical Marxist approach, both identifying the material contradictions of capital that will prevent its infinite reproduction and distinguishing the mechanisms for political action stemming from these contradictions.

The unique value of Žižekian theory lies in understanding the economies of enjoyment that mediate against these contradictions and perpetuate the circuit of capital, as well as the potential for subverting these mechanisms by evoking the trauma of the excluded Real. Whilst Žižek does not produce a detailed manifesto for a future society (Žižek is a sorry, comedic figure for a Master. His positioning in this manner is worthy evidence of the tragedy of our times), Žižekian theory is of vital importance in the battle against the disembodied evil of global capitalism.

Being Slavoj Žižek

To regular readers of continental philosophy or political theory, Slavoj Žižek requires no introduction – if only because at least fourteen introductory titles and readers have been written so far (all 'critical', of course).* Each of these introductions recounts a series of required attributes: Žižek comes from a small Eastern European nation (Slovenia), once part of Yugoslavia, formed as part of the fall of communism across the region. His struggles as a dissent academic removed from the traditional centres of analysis have defined his contrarian theory, if the psycho-biography of the likes of Ian Parker (2004) is to be believed.

Most significantly, however, Žižek's work is fun, if only because most contemporary philosophy remains entirely in the abstract. By contrast, Žižek's work commands the reader to enjoy. Combining the highest of theory with the most obscene of observations and jokes, fans of Žižek are subjected to deft analyses of culture, popular or otherwise, as we earnestly search for clues the Master has left about our political salvation.

Further into these introductions readers learn that Žižek's reworking of ideology and subjectivity, where he combines his Lacanian

---

* See Wright & Wright (1999); Kay (2003); Myers (2003); Žižek & and Daly (2003); Parker (2004); Sharpe (2004); Butler (2005); Boucher et al. (2006); Dean (2006); Pound (2008); Sharpe & Boucher (2010); Kul-Want (2011); Sheehan (2012); Irwin & Motoh (forthcoming); Lu (forthcoming).

dogmatism with his own brand of German idealism, produces startling insights into culture and the role of enjoyment in politics. Of this, few critics are in doubt. Against the dry analysis of deconstructionism and post-Marxism, Žižek has brought the body, materiality and political enjoyment back into focus, whilst reigniting debate around the status of the Cartesian subject.

Moreover, even if Žižek is too heterodox to inherit the Freudian/ Lacanian psychoanalytic mantle, he is certainly regarded as its primary contemporary populiser. Early works such as *Everything You Wanted to Know about Lacan (But Were Afraid to Ask Hitchcock)* (1992), *Enjoy Your Symptom* (1993a) and *Looking Awry* (1993b) reached a wide audience. Certainly few theorists have been regarded as so enjoyable and in utilising these concepts, Žižek's analysis extends to an incredible range of subjects: his works appear across the fields of philosophy, politics, sociology, cultural studies, psychology, media studies and theology.

The breadth of Žižek's work is revealed in both his own scholarship and the critical reflection around this work. Producing around twenty-five books (depending on our method of measurement) and numerous articles and critical interventions in the mainstream press, the pace of Žižek's writing is reflected in a constantly developing and differentiated critical field. In addition to frequent articles and reviews, an internationally referred journal, *The International Journal of Žižek Studies*, has been created along with the Centre for Ideology Critique and Žižek Studies at the University of Cardiff, and now two documentaries, *Žižek!* and *The Pervert's Guide to Cinema*. Outside Žižek's scholarship and the attempts to introduce and explain his rapidly shifting ideas, a number of theorists have sought to utilise Žižek's ideas for social and political analysis. Here we can include texts by the likes of Colin Cremin (2011), Jodi Dean (2010), Heiko Feldner (Vighi & Feldner 2007), Adrian Johnston (2005; 2008; 2009), Paul Taylor (2011) and Fabio Vighi (2010). It is these texts that form the basis of the field of Žižekian studies.

Mapping Žižekian Studies

Whether there exists a field of 'Žižekian studies' is not a manner of objective concern: one does not apply to the international board of philosophical classification to gain official membership. It cannot be anything other than a subjective wager that the work of a theorist is of sufficient interest and influence to have moved beyond the boundaries of their works. In this book I take the position that there is a field of Žižekian theory: indeed, this text is part of that field. Holding Žižek as the central inspiration, the argument contained within engages with ideas developed by Žižek without taking them as self-evident. The argument does not rest upon the validity of these concepts but, rather, seeks to develop beyond Žižek's work. My focus lies on *using* ideas developed within Žižek's eccentric and often inconsistent oeuvre, rather than engaging in an immanent critique of Žižek's work.

Žižekian studies is a burgeoning field, encapsulating a wide range of interests across the academic world. As well as his base in Ljubljana, Slovenia, where Žižek has close associations with Mladen Dolar and Alenka Zupančič, his influence has spread across the spheres of continental Europe, the United Kingdom and the United States. Whilst this influence is often located in single scholars rather than institutional identifications, in addition to the Centre for Ideological Critique and Žižek Studies at the University of Cardiff, there has been considerable critical engagement from the School of Government at the University of Essex, which has housed Ernesto Laclau. Here theorists such as Mark Devenney, Glyn Daly, Jason Glynos, David Howarth and Aletta Norval, whilst tending to be in the realm of discursive analysis and ideological critique, have sought to engage and expand upon the political consequences of Žižekian analysis.

Žižek's influence has also spread 'down under', with a number of texts and critical engagements stemming from Australasian theorists. Here Geoff Boucher and Matthew Sharpe (Sharpe 2004; Boucher et al. 2006; Sharpe & Boucher 2010; Boucher 2008) have been particularly influential, but there have also been edited volumes produced by Rex Butler and Scott Stephens (Žižek 2005b; 2006e), and further interventions from the likes of Colin Cremin (2011), Laurence Simmons (2008) and Warwick Tie (2004, 2009).

The scope of Žižek's influence is symbolic of the age in which he writes, both in terms of the content of his theory, which provides a level of enjoyment and radical incitement particularly attractive to graduate students, and the flows of information which disregard geographical territory. Ironically, it is the expansion of capitalism that has allowed for the expansion of Žižek's influence, although his critics would no doubt suggest that this is symptomatic of the commodification of the Žižek brand and his inclusion within the order he rails against.

Žižek's role as a theorist of enjoyment is a central element of engagement for the likes of Jodi Dean (2006; 2010) and Fabio Vighi (2010), who have utilised Žižek's work as a theory of enjoyment, ideology and subjectivity. Dean has been supportive of Žižek's critical reading of democracy, and of capitalism as a society of enjoyment (2006; 2010), whilst developing Žižekian theory to consider subjectivity in regards to (post)modern uses of media technology, an engagement extended by Paul Taylor (2011).

Taking a more expressly theoretical approach Vighi, particularly in his recent work with Heiko Feldner, has constructed Žižek as a theorist of political freedom, one capable of conceptualising potential breakthroughs from our contemporary ideological deadlock (Feldner & Vighi 2010). Likewise, Adrian Johnston (2005; 2008; 2009) undertakes a philosophical reconstruction of Žižek's theoretical underpinnings, particularly in relation to Žižek's ontological commitments and his theory of the political act, contrasting it with Alain Badiou's associated notion of the event in order to develop Žižek's work as a theory of political change.

By contrast to these largely supportive interpretations, the Žižekian field is bordered by a number of highly critical positions. Whilst often sympathetic to some aspects of his programme, some of the criticism of his work, and indeed Žižek himself, is amongst the most vitriolic in contemporary philosophy. Ian Parker, for instance (2004: 23; 2007: 158), has cited 'personal' examples to accuse Žižek of a number of crimes, primarily insinuating that Žižek's political actions do not match his theoretical positions. Likewise, the combative collection of essays entitled *The Truth of Žižek* (Bowman & Stamp 2007) contains a number of polemical and often personal contributions, a point not missed on Žižek, who responded:

> The first feature that should be noted is the frequent brutality of the attacks – *anything goes*, from hints at my personal pathology and claims that my texts do not satisfy even the requirements of an undergraduate paper, up to lies pure and simple about my political engagements ... The question to be asked here (but which I have no will or patience to engage in) is: why am I so often selected as a target about which one can write things that would otherwise immediately provoke an indignant politically correct rebuke? (Žižek 2007b: 199)

The decline of Žižek's (public) relationship with Ernesto Laclau is particularly instructive of the controversy he evokes. Laclau wrote an encouraging preface to Žižek's first English language text *The Sublime Object of Ideology* (1989), although in hindsight his remarks that Žižek's work 'possesses highly original features' (Laclau 1989: x) can be seen in a different light. Yet, by the end of their collaborative discussion (with Judith Butler) in *Contingency, Hegemony and Universality* (Butler et al. 2000), Laclau had accused Žižek of a number of sins, having suggested that Žižek's work was 'not organised around a truly *political* reflection' (Butler et al. 2000: 289) and that 'I cannot even know what Žižek is talking about – and the more this exchange progresses, the more suspicious I become that Žižek himself does not know either'. Laclau's (2006) strong response to Žižek's critique of his work on populism – in which he describes Žižek's argument as 'dinosaurean', 'undergraduate' and 'pure delirium', amongst other things – appears to have severed intellectual ties entirely.

Beyond the symptomatic enjoyment evident in these accounts, two strong themes have emerged in the critique of Žižek's work. Both, however, come to argue that problems within Žižek's theoretical approach result in intractable difficulties in the political application of his work. The first suggests that the style and structure of Žižek's theory simultaneously prevents the development of feasible political positions and allows him to conceal the very emptiness of his work. On the other hand, some critics have suggested that Žižek's dogmatic commitment to a Lacanian ontology and Marxist politics produces too narrow an understanding of the potential for political analysis and action.

In Žižekian Style

Žižek's style, considered primarily in terms of his method of argumentation, has also been the subject of concerted critique from the likes of Leigh Claire La Berge (2007), Paul Bowman (2007), Ian Parker (2004) and Richard Stamp (2007), principally because it subverts the expectations of academic philosophy. As Laclau states in the preface to *The Sublime Object of Ideology*:

> This is not a book in the classical sense; that is to say, a systematic structure in which an argument is developed according to a pre-determined plan . . . It is rather a series of theoretical interventions which shed mutual light on each other not in terms of the *progression* of an argument, but in terms of what we could call the *reiteration* of the latter in different discursive context. (Laclau 1989: xii)

This subversion of 'classical' expectations, both in stylistic composition and in structural arrangement, has led to harsh criticism. Jeremy Valentine (2007: 188), for example, in critiquing Žižek's reading of *Anti-Oedipus*, contends: 'Instead he arrives at a confirmation bias ... or what is more usually called a complete load of bollocks.' In the same collection, Jeremy Gilbert (2007: 62) argues that Žižek displays 'a level of scholarship which would be considered pitiable in an undergraduate student'.

The overriding concern with Žižek's style of argument is that its popular focus and Žižek's own 'celebrity' status elides the essential emptiness of his provocations. Indeed, some have argued that, as could be expected from a theorist who seeks to combine Lacan, Schelling and Marx, Žižek's work is without a core trajectory such that there is not a true Žižek but, in an ironically postmodern analysis to which Žižek would stand in staunch disapproval, there are multiple Žižeks to be constructed. Sarah Kay, for example, states that 'as with Lacan, every reading of a Žižek text is only a possible trajectory' (2003: 16). Likewise Denise Gigante more harshly contends that Žižek

> is unique, and where he makes his radical break with other literary theorists who take up a position, any position at all that pretends to some notional content or critical truth, is in the fact that he fundamentally has no position. His recent outpouring of critical texts – ranging from ideologico-psychological film theory, such as *Everything You Always Wanted to Know about Lacan (But Were Afraid to Ask Hitchcock)*, to the politico-philosophical *Essay on Schelling and Related Matters* (matters which include, and why not, quantum physics) – describes a hybridized critical identity that is almost impossible to pin down. Rather than importing interdisciplinary texts and events to his own theoretical perspective, he functions as a 'vanishing mediator', mediating between various theoretical points of view. (Gigante 1998: 153)

Certainly, Žižek's work displays a number of political stances, or perhaps strategies: from an initial implicit support of Laclau's radical democratic project; calls to traverse the fantasy and repoliticise the economy; a controversial affair with the Lacanian act (one that still lingers today); a rejection of immediate political action through the notion of 'subtractive politics'; contentious support for the 'communist hypothesis'; and, as I write, a developing engagement with the Occupy movement. Moreover, he does not appear to consider any subject outside his discipline (if discipline is the correct term) and infamously moves between them at rapid pace. A joke by the Marx brothers can appear to hold the same analytic value as a quote from the *Communist Manifesto*. In this sense, a different Žižek can be constructed within any number of discourses – as a film theorist, a reader of political or cultural enjoyment, a Marxist or a cantankerous communist with a nostalgic bent.

For some critics this plurality is evidence of a fundamental lack of consistency. Those less sympathetic to Žižek, such as Parker, have suggested that there are no specific Žižekian concepts. Consequently, 'you cannot be a "Žižekian" and only Žižek can be Žižek' (2004: 10) because 'there is no theoretical system as such in Žižek's work' (2004: 115). Within this construction there is no core to Žižek's work: it is without any kind of philosophical system and instead consists of a number of provocative points masquerading as a coherent philosophy.

As an extension of this critique Matthew Sharpe and Geoff Boucher (2010: 21) suggest that Žižek's unsystematic approach is built into the form of argument. Critically describing Žižek's method as an example of parataxis, 'a rhetorical style that suppresses the logical and causal connections between clauses in a sentence, paragraph, chapter or work', Sharpe and Boucher argue that this leaves the reader to infer what is missing within this logical break. This critique implies that Žižek's method suggests that more exists to his argument than is immediately apparent: part of the mystery of his approach is that despite his overtly radical analysis, Žižek makes very few direct political positions, but by leaving open gaps in the analysis he leaves space for the reader to draw independent conclusions. In doing so Žižek subverts the position of the Master and the (ultimately pointless) desire for activity without regard for the limitations imposed by capital.

Although there are valid reasons to doubt both Parker's and Sharpe and Boucher's readings, Žižek's style is certainly worthy of discussion. Little has changed from Laclau's initial observations (except for the tone in which these observations can be viewed). Žižek rarely moves directly towards the object which is the direction of his enquiry. His is not a discourse of desire but, rather, a drive in which his writing moves around the Real element of the discourse. For this reason, as Kay (2003: 6) notes, 'at the level of the chapter, and still more of the book, his writing can seem chaotic'.

Žižek often begins with a single proposition or question but his response makes its way through a series of examples, none of which have, at first glance, anything to do with their explicit subject. Yet, at the end of this apparently chaotic discourse, we find our position has been inexplicably altered as the examples act to demonstrate the argument being posited. As Kay suggests, this can be attributed to the struggle of writing on, or around, the Real: the object of enquiry cannot be encountered directly but must instead be discussed through its effects (Kay 2003: 6–8). Indeed, she quotes Žižek with regard to Lacan, when Žižek states: 'The only way to comprehend Lacan is to approach his work . . . as a succession of attempts to seize the same persistent traumatic kernel' (Žižek 1994: 173).

Žižek's approach can thus be regarded as an exemplary case of Lacanian political enquiry, utilising Hegelian dialectics to reveal the hidden inconsistencies within an ideological apparatus. His style is not evidence of a poorly developed argument or a façade masking the essential nullity of his politics, but results from the requirements of writing around the edges of the Real. Yes, this can led to some frustrating encounters with his work, particularly for the graduate student seeking to pin down a Žižekian position, but it is also the great value of his method of enquiry. Whilst it is true that Žižek breaks the rules of traditional scholarship – one could easily imagine critically marking an undergraduate essay written in the same style, regularly demanding to see more evidence or a clearer structure – this is not a flaw in his argument, although it can lead to regular frustration for the reader. Conversely, these conventions are not necessary elements of productive philosophical works. It need not be universally celebrated – not all writing needs to tarry with the Real – but critics do often miss the value of this approach when highlighting the limitations of Žižek's political interventions, which have themselves proved immensely controversial.

Žižek's Politics

In the foreword to *The Truth of Žižek* (Bowman & Stamp 2007), Simon Critchley (2007a: xvi) recalls that Žižek once commented to him at a conference, 'I have a hat but I have no rabbit.' Correspondingly, as articulated by Critchley in response to criticism of his own work, the predominant criticism of Žižek-as-Lacan is that Žižek's 'radical' politics are inherently conservative because they are unable to occupy any concrete position. Critchley asks: 'What does one *do* with this insight at the level of prescription, action and the rest?' Žižek's work is deadlocked and his only way out is radical calls for utopia and violence that are nothing but whistling in the dark (Critchley 2007a: xv–xvi).

Certainly there is nothing in Žižek's work to inspire policy wonks. There does not exist a singular reading of Marxism or psychoanalysis that would translate into a radical alternative to global capitalism. Indeed, Žižek has often suggested that no such alternative currently exists and we should instead focus on forcing upon space within capitalism where alternative thinking (and action) could flourish. Recently responding to the Occupy Wall Street movement, Žižek (2011b) states:

> We don't know where we are. But I think that this openness is precisely what is great about these protests. It means that precisely a certain vacuum open the fundamental dissatisfactions in the system [sic]. The vacuum simply means open space for thinking, for new freedom, and so on. Let's not fill in this vacuum too quickly.

Nonetheless, few critics are prepared to accept the limits of Žižek's work, rather searching through his work for a hidden essence. Too many theorists and critics look to Žižek as a distorted form of the Master, constantly demanding answers from his work. Laclau, for example, contends:

> Žižek had told us he wants to overthrow capitalism; now we are served notice that he wants to do away with liberal democratic regimes – to be replaced, it is true, by a thoroughly different regime which he does not have the courtesy of letting us know anything about. . . . Only if that explanation is made available will we be able to start talking politics, and abandon the theological terrain. Before that, I cannot even know what Žižek is talking about – and the more this exchange progresses, the more suspicious I become that Žižek does not know either . . . I can discuss politics with Butler because she talks about the real world, about strategic problems people face in their actual struggles but with Žižek it is not possible to even start to do so. (Laclau 2000a: 289–90)

Likewise, the title of Jeremy Gilbert's contribution to *The Truth of Žižek*, 'All the Right Questions, All the Wrong Answers' (Gilbert 2007), suggests the predominant political reading of Žižek's work: Žižek provides an interesting form of critique, provoking exciting questions but providing disappointing answers, the implication being that it is possible to provide the right answers to these questions. Undoubtedly, theorists looking for 'the right answer' within Žižek's work will be sadly disappointed. Perhaps symptomatic of this demand to the Master is the tendency to allow Žižek some form of a 'right of reply' in publications critical of his work, including the *International Journal for Žižek Studies*, and a number of critical and introductory texts (Bowman & Stamp 2007; Eagleton 2009; Johnston 2005; Kay 2003; Sharpe 2004; Stavrakakis 1999, Zupančič 2000).

If Žižek's style is thought to mask his ultimate lack of a political position and his false radicalism, so too his commitment to Lacanian psychoanalysis, along with Marxism, is often said to excessively limit the scope of his political interventions. Against the positioning of Žižek as a pluralist without any kind of position, this discourse suggests that Žižek's adherence to Lacanian orthodoxy prevents the development of a coherent or productive form of politics.

Although often invoked as a supplement to political analysis, psychoanalytic discourse has seldom inspired hope in the hearts of the hungry and disenfranchised. From Freud's proto-Hobbesian conservatism in *Civilisation and its Discontents* to Lacan's dismissal of the 1968 French student protestors, this current of psychoanalysis seems more likely to dissuade potential revolutionaries than to inspire them. Not surprisingly, Žižek's application of psychoanalytic insights in the name of revolution has been controversial.

Is Psychoanalysis Street Savvy?

It is through this reading of psychoanalytic politics that we strike the alternative to the pluralist reading of Žižek: an attempt to identify a singular commitment within his work. Most often, as is the case with Sean Homer (2001: 7), who claims that Žižek's Lacanianism rules out any validity to his Marxist appeal, Žižek's work is rejected because of a fundamental commitment to either Lacan or Marx, a commitment that distorts the influence of the other. By the same reasoning, Laclau (2000a: 289) claims that Žižek's reliance upon Lacanian psychoanalysis prevents him from developing any sense of politics, stating, 'Žižek's thought is not organised around a truly *political* reflection but is, rather, a *psychoanalytic* discourse which draws its examples from the politico-ideological field.'

Resonating with Homer's and Laclau's sentiments, psychoanalysis in relation to politics remains intensely controversial. This is the case even though, as Yannis Stavrakakis (2007: 1) reports, it has become second in influence only to analytical liberalism.* Psychoanalysis,

---

* Anthony Elliott too remarks, 'Indeed, for some considerable period of time, it seemed that theory just wasn't theory unless the name Lacan was referenced' (2004: 1).

first through Freud and then through Lacan, has been a major influence in the turn to culture and language that redefined Marxism and Leftist politics. In doing so, it has come to represent many of the difficulties with this turn, reinventing our understanding of shared social life without producing any significant institutional mode of political engagement.

The prospects for a psychoanalytically inspired mode of politics have been a point of considerable debate, with a number of strands emerging. Whilst these discussions have led to several philosophical advances in politics, or what Glyn Daly (2009) calls the 'politics of the political', no stable political frontier has emerged. Indeed, Žižek's Lacanian reading of the political rejects any possibility of advancing a psychoanalytic ideal of shared social life, as such an ideal stands in contradistinction to Lacan's own work on ethics. Because of this rejection, Žižek's adherence to Lacan is often positioned as the cause of his supposed political conservatism.

Whilst Lacan has been accepted as a theorist of cinema or sexuality, his influence has not been as welcomed within political theory. Indeed, Anthony Elliott (2004: 2) contends, 'At its bleakest, the Lacanian symbolic was deployed to underscore the inevitability of social order and political domination as a fundamental state of human desire.' Moreover, Andrew Robinson and Simon Tormey (2005; 2006) argue that the negativity inherent in Lacanian thought reproduces the antagonism, domination and violence of capitalism, the very things they believe Leftist politics should seek to revoke.

As a consequence, Homer (1996: 109) states that although psychoanalysis can engage in a 'continuing critical dialogue with political and social theory', its constitutive inability to develop a positive sense of ideology means that more reactionary positions will fill this gap, and for this reason psychoanalytic discourse is an inappropriate partner for Leftist political practice. Likewise, Elizabeth Bellamy (1993) comes to argue that whilst psychoanalysis has tremendous analytic potential, it does not offer any more fruitful opportunities for political action than had already been developed in the discursive turn. Psychoanalysis, it seems, has explained the hopelessness of culture and the domination of capitalism a little too well.

It is the translation between clinical analysis and political interventions that has proven particularly troublesome. Whilst Žižek has dismissed claims that psychoanalytic categories cannot be easily applied to sociological concerns as 'boring' (2006b: 5–6), for Sharpe and Boucher (2010: 27, original emphasis), Žižek's use of psychoanalytic theory for political analysis means that '*at base, Žižek is committed to the notion that all these theoretical fields have the same basic structures, which can all be analysed using the same terms and methodology*'. As a consequence, Žižek is unable to generate a convincing political theory because he views all objects through the same lens, one that cannot account for the multiplicity of societal interactions. The structure to which the authors refer is the 'big Other', which they locate as the core of Lacanian theory, suggesting that Žižek posits Capital as this God-like point that comes to mediate all social relations.

Ultimately, Sharpe and Boucher argue that, for Žižek, people and political systems have the same structures, allowing psychoanalytic theory to be transposed directly to political analysis. Because, however, psychoanalytic categories were not constructed for this kind of task, the range of Žižek's analysis is limited, and, as a consequence, he is able to satisfy his radical desires only with naïve political demands that have no regard for concrete circumstances.

The difficulties of articulating a psychoanalytic form of politics become particularly apparent in Žižek's attempts to rehabilitate a form of Marxism in the name of a renewed critique of global capitalism. If Lacanian theory has been accused of nihilism, the opposite is true of Marxism. Against the turn to language that dominated continental philosophy in the latter half of the twentieth century, the essentialism and economism of classical Marxism appear positively embarrassing. Equally discomfiting, however, has been the resultant impotence of the political Left either to posit an alternative to capitalism or to reconstruct a viable mode of the critique of political economy. It is within this context that Žižek's work, and this book, operate.

ŽIŽEK'S MARXISM

Despite the increasingly apparent contractions of global capitalism, the political Left remains largely impotent. At best, it offers a softening of the injustices of capitalism. If 'What is to be done?' was the prototypical Leftist question, at least for those able to bear the presence of Lenin, today those who cannot do so appear to be reduced to asking 'How can we help?'

The twentieth century witnessed both the theoretical overrunning of Marxism, as alternative explanations about the continuous flourishing of capitalism and the prospects for human freedom came to the fore, and then its political fall as many Marxist-inspired socialist movements collapsed. These difficulties pre-empted the development of a hegemonic movement that focused on culture and language, rather than the economy. Seeking at first to expand Marxism's explanatory appeal, but ending up with the dismissal of the idea of emancipation entirely, much of what began as an innocent attempt to rethink Marxism ended up with the politics of Warhol or the 'radicalism' of Live Aid. As a result, both the essentialism of the Marxist class narrative, and the hope of emancipation for those suffering from capitalism, have become unattainable. Lessons have been learned, but the focus on the particularity of cultural expression is pathetically inappropriate in an era of financial crisis, mass famines and floods, and the apparent allure of Rodeo Drive.

In the face of this breakdown of Marxist politics, a number of theorists have attempted, against the grain of postmodern plurality, to reconsider the prospects of universality and truth in relation to Marxism after the turn to language. The most seminal of these attempts stems from Laclau, initially in conjunction with Chantal Mouffe. In their breakthrough text, *Hegemony and Socialist Strategy* (1985), Laclau and Mouffe attempted to reread Marxism and socialism 'beyond the positivity of the social' and the turn to language. Here all links to essentialism are dropped – except the primacy of language – and Marxism becomes little more than an interpretative tradition. Nonetheless, by returning to the question of universality in response to the particularism of cultural identity politics, Laclau and Mouffe's work remains a decisive theoretical event.

This new post-Marxist horizon has come at a cost, however, as the materialist politics of class struggle were dropped in favour of the contingency of hegemony and the battle to hold the empty place of the democratic signifier. Whilst Laclau and Mouffe's restoration of the concept of universality proved to be a significant advance over hegemonic modes of cultural Leftism, it also banished notions of materialism, economy and class struggle in favour of discourse, democracy and contingency: although the title of the text suggested a revival of socialism, it was democracy that held the transcendental position for Laclau and Mouffe.

This book operates in the same conceptual terrain as *Hegemony and Socialist Strategy*, considering the prospects for Marxism after the turn to language. However, the Žižekian argument presented in this text diverges from Laclau and Mouffe's project in a number of important respects. First, it turns to psychoanalysis as an explanatory

14

device, arguing that Laclau's discourse theory does not adequately explain the fixity of language. By reference to psychoanalysis – embodying the discursive turn as being an effect of symbolic castration rather than of differential contingency – and, in particular, the categories of *jouissance* and the Real, we are better positioned to understand the appeal of capitalism and character of the difficulties associated with bringing about a fatal disruption to its operation. Moreover, I seek to return to political economy and the question of class struggle: rather than envisioning democracy as the ultimate category of human freedom, I posit that under contemporary circumstances it is capitalism that is more worthy of our critical attention. In positing global capitalism as the necessary centre of Leftist critique, Marxism, and in particular Žižek's construction of Marxism, becomes vital. As such, a reading of Žižek's embrace of Marxism in the context of the discursive turn shall be the subject of Chapter 2.

Žižek's Marxism embodies many of the difficulties associated with both Marxism and postmodernism. His work appears to fit in the same category as those readings of Western Marxism that have sought to reengage the descriptive dimension of Marxism without reference to a prescriptive politics. Indeed, this is the central critique of Žižek's work – that he produces a reading of capitalism and a form of politics which, although intriguing, leads to a political deadlock and ultimate conservatism (Robinson & Tormey 2005: 102).

Whilst this criticism has a certain validity – Žižek offers nothing like a restored sense of normativity or party politics that would revive the saliency of Marxist politics – his work entirely rethinks what it means to practise Marxist politics in the twenty-first century. Not only does Žižek's reject both past Leftist essentialist positions and the contemporary ethics of contingency associated with the likes of Derrida and Laclau, but he refuses to posit any substantive alternative. Although his critics argue that Žižek is thereby not far divorced from various forms of political conservatism – acknowledging the intractable character of the symptoms of capital without positing any alternative – Žižek comes to argue that the shape of his politics is a historically appropriate response to the deadlock that characterises global capitalism and liberal democracy.

For critics, however, the combination of Žižek's dual embrace of Lacan and Marx results in a dogmatic politics that paints him into a corner in which the politics of the impossible are the only feasible response – specifically the impossible notion of the Lacanian act (Sharpe & Boucher 2010: 127–9). Mark Devenney, for instance, argues that because Žižek fails to articulate a conception of capitalism, he lies blind to strategic opportunities within it, creating a deadlock for which his own solution is the act (2007: 59). This act is conceived to elide any political calculation, rejecting any possibility for subtle action or political reform in favour of total revolution without any sense of the future. This is not the kind of pitch which tends to attract many devotees. What then, is the appeal of Žižekian theory for Marxist political practice?

Taking a Žižekian Path

I have thus far established and rejected two possible readings of Žižek: Žižek as an empty pluralist and Žižek as a Lacanian–Marxist essentialist. The first suggested that no singular sense of politics has emerged from Žižek's work, the second that his commitment to Lacan and to Marx is excessively dogmatic, and consequently ignores wider strategic opportunities for political action. Both these interpretations of Žižek hold some value, with each suggesting that no singular reading of the content of Žižekian politics is possible. This is a premise shared by this text: critically, however, this lack is taken to be at the core of Žižekian interpretative strategy and his response to capitalism.

In distinct contrast to Matthew Sharpe and Geoff Boucher's claim (2010) that Žižek orientates his work around the God-like status of the big Other, I hold that Žižek's work is ultimately a response to the Lacanian Real, a position that is explored in detail in Chapter 4. Whilst this orientation is defiantly psychoanalytic, albeit with a Hegelian–Marxist edge that has no place within the clinic, it does not determine any positive content within shared social life. Instead, by locating the Real as the core of human existence, in regard to both subjectivity and ideology, Žižek provides a unique insight into human existence. Žižekian theory can provide an analysis of the multi-dimensional nature of social life not because the content of these elements, be they sexual relations, tribal cultures or financial markets, is reflected in clinical analysis, but because their particularities are a response to the universal dialectic exchange between the lack of the Real and excesses of *jouissance*.

Thus, following an earlier reading by Sharpe (2004: 4), this interpretation holds that there is a singular 'Truth of Žižek' provided by the Real, but that this singularity has no necessary content. Here, Žižek can be considered to be a comedic philosopher. His work is often supplemented by jokes which serve as illustrative examples; however, the comedic logic goes beyond these witticisms, pervading the deepest logic of his theory. Žižek is a comedic philosopher because he is a meta-philosopher – a philosopher of everything – of the Real, that which does not exist: Žižek is a meta-philosopher of nothing. Žižek's work is not tragic, in the sense that it points to the existence of something that was had, authentic Marxism for example, and is now lost but, rather, comedic: the thing that we were looking for was never present to begin with.

This basic logic of humour, as ably illustrated by Alenka Zupančič (2008; 2006a), marks the Hegelian logic of universality upon which much of Žižek's work relies. The standard doxa of the discursive turn is that the universal is made impossible through humanity's constitution by language. It is the tragedy of this loss that leads to many of the limitations of postmodernity, whereby both ideals and emancipation are dismissed as dangerous illusions. Yet, for Žižek, whilst the universal is indeed impossible, it was never possible to begin with: human life is constituted as a search for a lost object that was never possessed. Moreover, Žižek suggests that because humanity continues to search for the universal, installing various signifiers in its image, it is this failure which constitutes the universal in what Žižek, following Hegel, labels concrete universality.

This understanding of Žižek can be best illustrated by a regularly cited example within his own work, that of French anthropologist Claude Lévi-Strauss's interpretation of a tribal village (Žižek 1994: 25; 2008: 287). Here the villagers were asked to draw a ground map of their village. Two groups emerged – one represented the village as two concentric circles, the other showed it divided by an invisible linear frontier. The question Žižek asks, following Lévi-Strauss, is how to interpret this discrepancy. Within contemporary social science, there are two dominant positions, which can be broadly identified as modernist and postmodernist. The postmodernist position conceives that there is no true village layout – reality exists only in the manner in which it is constructed by the villagers – implying that there is no singular truth to be told about any social construction. By contrast the modernist perspective takes an opposite, scientific, approach to truth. Here there is a Truth to be had and it is one that can be discovered empirically, perhaps by obtaining some aerial photographs of the village. By contrast, the Lacanian/Žižekian approach locates Truth in the cause that is producing the effect of the split, that cause being the Real. If social life is divided around a certain point, for Žižek that antagonistic kernel is the Truth of any given form. Within our example village this kernel might be antagonistic class divisions that divide the representations of the village around ideas of justice: the linear division considers there to be no injustice, whereas the concentric circle field identifies a division between the elite and the masses.

This interpretation can be applied to Žižek, where a division exists between an attachment to the plurality of his work and its fixity on Lacan. What both these positions miss, however, is the antagonism that is causing the division in representation. Žižek suggests that it is this antagonism which holds the Truth in any given situation and provides the dislocating force to which discourse is a response. This antagonism is nothing but the Real, which provokes both singular attempts to label that 'thing' that Žižek's work is doing and the plurality of positions which emerge from the failure of these attempts.

There is not, however, any necessary translation of this understanding into politics – Žižek does not produce a singular 'Politics of the Real' that is transportable between horizons. Although Žižek is committed to a Lacanian/Hegelian ontological reading, what emerges is a number of different relationships with the impossibility of the Real that can be considered within a Marxist orientation. As such, Žižek's politics are constituted by different strategic interpretations of the political, which can be deployed depending on the political circumstances. These strategic alternatives shall be debated in Chapter 6.

Thus, rather than attempting to develop a singular reading of Žižekian politics, this text is unique in suggesting that Žižekian theory produces a number of strategic alternatives in regard to the dialectics between the Real, enjoyment and ideology. Each of these positions – here I identify the act, subtractive politics and the practice of concrete universality as foremost amongst Žižek's work – produces a particular method for evoking the Real within an ideological matrix.

Žižek does not, however, produce any ideal sense of shared social life. If you are reading Žižek, or this book, in order to find out how we should best live, you are reading for the wrong reasons. This is not to suggest that the question of normativity is invalid, belonging to a bygone era. There is certainly a very interesting encounter between psychoanalysis, Žižek and ethics, one that shall be explored in Chapter 3. In this book I do not seek to dismiss the question entirely; instead I suggest that it is not where the value of Žižek's work lies. Instead, my central argument is that Žižek's work should fundamentally be read as a particularly effective response to global capitalism in the twenty-first century.

There are two reasons for constructing the value of Žižek's work as a response to capitalism. Firstly, capitalism has become the limit to all political action such that any form of emancipatory politics must tarry with this limit. If Žižekian theory has significant limitations, many of these limitations can be attributed to the political constriction of capital. Arguing that capital has become a self-revolutionising force, Žižek rejects the prospect of reforming and revolutionising capitalism from the inside. Political movements can only change so much before they hit a hard, Real, limit established by capital. Social movements can be included within capitalism so long as they do not hinder the circuit of capital and the return of profits: whilst offering recyclable shopping bags promotes the 'green' image of a company without increasing costs, the prospects of restricting consumption in order to halt ecological catastrophe appears to be impossible.

Secondly, Žižek's rehabilitation of Marxist critique through Lacanian psychoanalysis and Hegelian dialectics is uniquely able to understand both the continual functioning of capitalism and the opportunities for its destruction. Žižek's superstructural understanding of the 'success' of capitalism is not limited to the structural dominance of capitalism noted above, but includes the manner in which the agents of capital have co-opted the processes of desire to naturalise the fetishism of consumption and of the commodity, as well as the mediating function of ideology in smoothing away the increasingly apparent contradictions of capitalism. Against this dominance, however, Žižek introduces a number of antagonisms that threaten capitalism, in particular the operation of class struggle and the presence of what he labels 'new forms of apartheid' (2008: 423–4), and, I will suggest, the universal class of the repositioned lumpenproletariat.

Žižek and Global Capitalism

Conversely, that Žižek's work is directed at capitalism or the economy is neither universally accepted nor endorsed. Geoff Boucher and Matthew Sharpe (2010: 177), for example, suggest that despite Žižek's valid call for the return to economic critique in Leftist analysis, he fails to accomplish this act. Laclau has been quite forceful on this point, arguing that Žižek's notion of capital-as-Real is both nonsensical and incompatible with the Lacanian concept of the Real (Laclau 2000a: 291; 2006: 9–10). Similarly, Devenney (2007: 47) argues that 'Žižek fails to give an adequate account of capital or of political economy' both because he does not identify the fundamental fantasy of capitalism and because he reads the economy through the Lacanian Real, rather than the traditional structures of political economy. As a consequence, for these critics Žižek leaves himself with only the radicality of the act and total transformation because his psychoanalytic critique of political economy is unable to see room for action within capitalism. Ceren Özselçuk and Yahya Madra (2005; 2007) present a similar argument in suggesting that Žižek's conception of class struggle allows him to only conceive of specifically capitalist conditions of class struggle.

By contrast to this position, in Chapter 5 of this text I come to argue that Žižek does have a theory of capitalism, and one that is capable of altering the way of we think and act in relation to capitalism. This does not mean that Žižek is an economist, nor that he is repeating Marx's *Capital*, or the *Communist Manifesto*. Žižek's work has profound consequences for the theory and practice of Marxism, but in producing a Lacanian–Hegelian reading of Marxism and 21st-century capitalism, Žižek does not engage directly with economic practice or the normative aspects of our material reproduction. Instead, his critical reading of the dialectics of ideology and enjoyment, class struggle and the contradictions of capital allows us to understand the methods through which capitalism continues to flourish and the opportunities to halt its infinite reproduction.

Fundamentally this book argues that the value of Žižek's work lies in his reading of global capitalism. This reading is an intervention in itself, based upon Žižek's unique form of politics that combines a Lacanian understanding of enjoyment and the Real with Hegelian dialectics and Marxist economics to identify both the underlying contradictions of global capitalism and the economies of enjoyment which keep these contradictions under wraps.

Žižekian theory is uniquely able both to identify the seductive appeal of capitalism, with its historically unprecedented manipulation and perpetuation of desire, and to specify the hard systematic limit that thwarts Leftist political ambition. It is for this reason, identified but not determined by his Lacanian foundations, that Žižek rejects the kind of 'rabbits' that Critchley would ask for. These positions, whether through the abstract ideals of justice and equality or through the concrete pragmatism of recycling and ethical consumption, are disparaged not because they are inherently unworthy, but because they only seek to soften and reproduce capitalism more efficiently.

As Cremin (2011) posits, whilst we can see that capitalism is 'naked', its contradictions exposed to the world, the effect of this trauma is mediated by ideological mechanisms and discourses of (consumptive) enjoyment. Most pertinently, in the absence of any possible alternative to capitalism – any government positing anti-capitalist measures to the recent finance crisis, for instance, would only have been doubly punished by the markets – the Left and its citizens tend to focus on smaller 'rabbits' that reduce the problems of capitalism to more manageable pieces. Here class inequality becomes union wage demands, and the ecological crisis sustainable fishing and recycling programmes.

Rejecting these rabbits, Žižek instead insists upon an adherence to the Real as the only way of disrupting the reproduction of capital-ism. Here he has increasingly sought to identify class struggle as a modality of the Real. Whilst there are several objections that will be mounted against Žižek's conception of class, by utilising this identi-fication, along with the presence of those excluded from capitalism, we are beginning to see the shape of a Žižekian–Marxist politics that rehabilitates determinate negation within global capitalism. These politics operate by identifying the positioning of the effects of this Real exclusion within the hegemonic ideologies of capitalism and by seeking to disrupt the mediating effects of ideology such that the full trauma of the Real is felt. These strategies do not hold a singular purpose but, rather, can be deployed depending on the political cir-cumstances. Identifying the operation of the Real within capitalism, along with the strategic politics of manipulating these antagonistic points, is the subject of the latter half of this text.

In producing this critique of capitalism, Žižekian theory does not stay in a negative key. Most recently, as part of a wider return to communism, Žižek has engaged with a 'communist hypothesis' that offers a renewed hope for a beyond to capitalism. Here, by refer-ence to the inherent impossibilities within global capitalism itself, the question of a utopian imaginary is rejuvenated in Chapter 7. The utopia of the communist hypothesis is not a fantasmatic utopia but, rather, the utopian urge that occurs when we are forced to reimagine a new way of being, as has been suggested by Fredric Jameson (2005; 2009). That is, if capitalism is unable to mediate against its increas-ingly rampant contradictions, in particular the lumpenproletariat, who are unable to be included within capitalism, our response should not be to formally construct new modes of being but, rather, to insist on the embodied presence of this impossibility in order to force open space for a reinvention of shared social life.

Such hope is not often associated with Žižek's work. Although he is often constructed as a theorist of violence and lack, Žižekian theory has much potential. Nonetheless, we should not place all our hope in the Žižekian basket. One day we will need the rabbits that Žižek professes to lack. Just because Žižek does not speak of policy programmes or good governance, this does not mean they should not be part of a renewed future, a point that he himself acknowledges (2011b). Conversely, they do not feature within this analysis, as focusing on such forms of politics is to remain within the realm of capitalism. The focus of Žižekian analysis is to engage with the Real of an ideological formation in order to produce radical change. This does not mean that radical change should be fetishised in itself, nor that there is no place for normativity, just that we should stop looking to Žižek for answers to all our problems.

2

Marxism after the Discursive Turn

If Žižek's work is fundamentally a response to capitalism, then it is also a reaction to the dilemmas of Marxism today. Yet, Žižek is not a Marxist in the sense that he is a Lacanian. Žižek's reading of Lacanian theory is sufficiently orthodox that for many contemporary theorists, Žižek's Lacan *is* Lacan. Indeed, Žižek has rarely been critical of Lacan, although his is certainly an interpretation rather than a strict reproduction. Žižek's Marxism, however, is more of an orientation than a strict disciplinary commitment. Žižek has not sought to engage in the kind of empirical analysis that filled Marx's *Capital* and is overtly aware of the problematic history of Marxist theory and practice.

What Žižek does seek to do is to inhabit the spirit of the Marxist critique of political economy, entering into the critique of capitalism and analysing the potential for halting the reproduction of the circuit of capital. In doing so, however, Žižekian theory is entrapped within the darkest difficulties of Leftist political theory. As such, in order to understand the Marxist influence upon his politics, in particular in regard to psychoanalytic theory and the critique of capitalism, in this chapter I shall engage in a detailed analysis of the difficulties of Marxist theory after the 'turn to language'.

If Marxism has dominated Leftist political practice since its conception, today Marxism dominates predominantly by virtue of its absence. Marxism has been dealt some traumatic blows, both intellectually and politically. These difficulties have been defined by a loss of faith in essentialist interpretations of history and the revolutionary destiny of the proletarian subject. Without the presence of an actually existing communism, or the hope provided by a revolutionary subject, Marxism appears as dead as Francis Fukuyama's sense of history, with its existence now often defined by passing references to the bad old days, or, for some, the good old days of certainty.

In this chapter I shall return to the losses and gains for Marxism after its invasion by analytic concerns about the signifier. Rejecting a positivist or scientific reading of Marxism, I consider the 'turn to language' that has called into question the fundamental tenets of Marxism. This discursive turn found a willing participant within Marxism itself as a way of explaining the failure of history to bring about its own consummation, and of the revolutionary subject to advance that progression. In identifying with this discourse, the dominant strands of thought within Marxist theory moved away from the economic determinism of historical materialism and into culture. What began as a supplement, however, has ended up colonising the entire approach such that the signifier 'Marx' appears to be no longer required in Leftist political practice.

Such a dismissal has been a major loss for global politics. The withdrawal from the universal and emancipationist dimension of Marxism has allowed for circumstances in which global capitalism has become more widely influential than any mode of politics in history. Today it seems the only feasible alternative to the market is a withdrawal into various religious fundamentalisms, themselves a reaction to the instability of capitalism and of its attendant social inequality.

Whilst a move away from essentialism in favour of a focus on culture, on language and on the politics of enjoyment might generally be applauded as a response to real problems within the Marxist tradition, the losses have been more significant. In terms of the ideological direction of Leftist politics, forms of postmodern thought have sought to distance themselves from any sense of widespread emancipation, revolution and certainly any notion of the collective Good. Moreover, these discourses have moved away from the economy as the primary target of Marxist analysis.

Towards the end of the twentieth century, however, Ernesto Laclau's rereading of the Marxist category of hegemony offered the possibility of returning to the question of universality within the realm of discourse. Yet, although Laclau's work provided a break from the flighty dominance of postmodern thought, his post-Marxism operates through a distancing of analysis from the economy. For Laclau and other post-Marxists, the economy was an element of discourse and thus could not be distinguished from the political. Whilst we might agree that the economy could not be anything but discursive, it is nonetheless vital to insist upon its role.

As a consequence of Laclau's conflation of politics and the economy he ends up largely ignoring capitalism in favour of democracy and the freedom provided by dislocations in the symbolic order. Furthermore, he reduces politics to discourse at the expense of materiality. Laclau's ontology does not specify a driving source, as such; if language is only held together by reference to itself and politics is purely discursive, then fundamental political change should be relatively commonplace.

It is against this framework, and the difficult history of psychoanalytic Marxism, that Žižek's Marxism has developed. Although highly controversial, Žižek has sought to rehabilitate both the descriptive and the prescriptive elements of Marxism, albeit within the limitations of contemporary political practice. This rethinking occurs within a Lacanian framework, itself a response to the discursive turn. Against the differential contingency of discursive approaches, Žižek's Lacanian reading of language returns to materiality, enjoyment and the fixity of political discourse. Conversely, if Žižek's Lacanian reading of Marxism offers the possibility of a return to the body and to the economy, it is unclear what kind of politics stems from this rehabilitation and we are left to consider whether Žižek's conception of shared social life offers any prospects for the redevelopment of that life beyond capitalism.

Absolutely, Positively, Marxist

Marx's work is often assumed to be the quintessential example of essentialism, from his grand explanation of the laws of history to the inalienable good represented by communism. Certainly, much of postmodernity is built upon a rejection of this image in favour of the contingency of language. The consequence of the discursive turn, in which language is thought to create a barrier between objects and the symbols used to represent them, has been a tendency to reject both the quasi-scientific determinism and the scale of Marx's theory of history. As a result, both the Marxist critique of capitalism and the transition to communism have been found lacking.

Marx's work was a fusion of description and prescription as he sought to develop a philosophy which changed what it sought to understand, an 'Emancipationist Philosophy' that attempted to develop a relationship between epistemology and politics. Marx argued that an understanding of the true contours of capitalism by the proletariat, who both suffer most from capitalism and are most able to act against it, would invoke the revolutionary class transformation destined by the laws of history. Of course, mere awareness does not bring change in the way Marxists imagined.* Indeed, much of the history of Marxism after Marx has considered why knowledge of exploitation under capitalism either remains hidden or has no effect upon those who are exploited and, as I shall expand on throughout the remainder of this book, much of this explanatory duty has fallen to psychoanalysis.

Marx's emancipatory politics was thought to rest upon two essential premises: that the 'iron laws' of history would bring about the transition from capitalism to communism and that this revolution in the mode of production was wholly desirable. As we shall see, the prescriptive aspect of Marxism remains deeply problematic, in Marx if not subsequent forms of Marxism. Whilst Marx was highly suspicious of abstract morality, the theory and practice of communism is attached to essentialist narratives of the Good that have come under sustained critique.

Similarly, the laws of history that structured Marx's critique of capitalism have been charged with both determinism and economism (Hunt 1977b: 7). Moreover, that capitalism continues to expand and become more deeply embedded in human being than ever before, despite increasingly apparent global crises, belies the thrust of Marx's understanding of history and of political economy. Although Marx had argued that historical change required a revolutionary subject rather than a teleological sense of itself, he very much relied upon a deterministic theory of history based around the materiality of production. This determinism is often referenced to the supposed 'base–superstructure' model, through which Marx had suggested that the mode of production came to determine political affairs. This model is derived from Marx's contention, in the Preface to *A Contribution to the Critique of Political Economy*, that

> in the social production of their life, men enter into definite relations that are indispensable and independent of their will, relations of production which correspond to a definite stage of development of their material productive forces. The sum total of these relations of production constitutes the economic structure of society, the real foundation, on which rises a legal and political superstructure and to which correspond definite forms of social consciousness. The mode of production of material life conditions the social, political and intellectual life process in general. It is not

---

* This is not a problem specific to Marxism; today's strongest public critics of globalisation, Noam Chomsky, Naomi Klein and John Pilger, seem to have the same sense of objective emancipation.

the consciousness of men that determines their being but on the contrary, their social being that determines their consciousness. (Marx & Engels 1980: 11–12)

Here the productive forms of society are thought to determine the relations of production in that society, which then shape the political superstructure. There is certainly room for interpretative manoeuvring within this statement, both in Marx's work and in subsequent readings. Indeed, the interactions between the base and superstructure have been a point of conjuncture throughout the history of Marxism (Eagleton 2011: 148–59). Nonetheless, the general thrust of economic determinism is evident: for Marx it is the method of our material reproduction that holds the trump card.

From this idea, Marx argued that social change comes from contradictions in the mode of production* as the laws of capitalism, and of history, would bring about the destruction of the former and the end of the latter. Within a certain version of Marx, the revolutionary overhaul of capitalism appears inevitable as politics is reduced to contradictions in the mode of production. Change appears to be linear as the very economic existence of a proletariat class is enough to produce a revolutionary politics (Hall 1977: 20–1).

Here, in a sweeping grand narrative, Marx argued that history before communism had been the story of class struggle as the forces and relations of production come into contradiction. It is through this narrative that Marx explained what he conceived to be the major epochs of history: from primitive communism or tribal production to ancient, feudal and finally the capitalist modes of production. Each revolution in production was caused by a breakdown in the relationship between those that control production and those who produce, a process that proceeds, according to Marx, by way of the 'iron laws of history'.

Likewise, within capitalism, capital expands through the appropriation of surplus value from labour. As capital grows it is concentrated into fewer hands, and workers, the key to the production of surplus, become increasingly impoverished. As this division grows stronger, the working class become the majority and have the capacity to overthrow the owners of production. In creating

---

* Although this chapter is directed at establishing the hegemonic interpretation of Marx's work, it is worth noting the presence of alternative readings of Marxism, based upon texts such as *Capital* and the *Grundrisse*, which refute the determinism evident in the infamous passage above.

value, therefore, capital also plants the seeds of its own inevitable destruction.

Moreover, Marx had conceived that the human essence could be derived from the materiality of production, 'production' here going beyond the strictly economic. If postmodernity – and to an extent late modernity – has rejected any sense of foundationalism, Marx argued that 'species being' is the material ground for the human condition. Species being embodies both Marx's deterministic view of materiality and production, and his conflation of description and prescription. For Marx, species being – how we are – determines how we should be.

Species being, otherwise known as 'species essence' (depending on the translation of the German *Gattungswesen*) attempts to capture the social yet materialised nature of the human condition. What is essential to our species being is the recognised interdependence of human beings, a social bond required by the necessity of material production. Through the specialisation of labour that characterises production under capitalism, Marx argued that the worker is alienated from this human essence, a condition that would be avoided under communism.

Nonetheless, although Marxism appears to affirm a grand explanation of the existing, whether it offers a sense of morality beyond this is a matter for debate (Marx & Engels 2004: 18). Terry Eagleton (1997: 43) asserts that Marxism is structured not around an abstract idealism but around a rejection of the apparent contradiction between the ideals of modernity and the practicalities of capitalism. Marx rejects capitalism in the name not so much of the full expression of species being under communism but, rather, of the end of the contradiction within capitalism whereby, according to Eagleton, 'in accumulating the greatest wealth that history has ever witnessed the capitalist class has done so within the context of social relations which have left most of its subordinates hungry, wretched and oppressed' (Eagleton 1997: 44).

Therefore, Marx did not suggest that communism represented any sense of the 'Good' beyond a refutation of the ills of capitalism. Indeed, he rejected abstract moral explanations, refusing to critique capitalism in these terms. Marx argued that morality was just the ideology by which the ruling elite justify the existing relations of production (Wood 2004: 127–42). As such, morality is never entirely abstract but results from the existing material conditions of our reproduction. Thus, by contrast to utopian socialists of his time,

Marx did not specifically argue that the wage-labour system was an injustice; instead it was the only form of economic justice available within capitalism. Moreover, although he might have used the term 'exploitation' to describe the vulnerability of labour to capital that produces surplus value and the conditions of the worker, he did not use it pejoratively (see Wood 2004: 242–64).

As a consequence, although Marx's work is certainly directed towards instigating the end of capitalism and bringing forth the coming age of communism, it does so by reference to the material progress of history, rather than any ideal. Marxism has certainly relied upon a foundation, but only in a descriptive conception of the path of history. For Marx the descriptive merged into the prescriptive such that he did not require a moral foundation – history provided it for him.

Nonetheless, although Marx did not explicitly reference his critique of capitalism to an abstract moralism, there does appear to be an underlying morality implicit in his work. One does not implore people to 'throw off their chains' in the name of history alone. Not only is Marx's work often full of deprecatory terms such as 'robbery', but his understanding of the alienated subject of capitalism as at odds with its 'species being' implies an understanding of the Good, even if Marx was unwilling to prescribe it any further in his conception of communism. Moreover, statements like 'From each according to their ability, to each according to their needs!' from Marx's *Critique of the Gotha Program* appear to be as much of a moral imperative as anything we might find in the likes of Kant. If the laws of history predicted the coming of communism, for Marx this was something to be celebrated.

Nonetheless, the problem of Marx's essentialism is not so much the utopianism of communism – this came after Marx – but his belief in the scientific laws of history that made any essentialism redundant. It is these laws that have also failed to explain the continued functioning of capitalism, as economics and history failed to turn into politics and the end of class struggle. Thus, the failure of Marx's theory of history to realise itself has left Marxism with two problems: explaining the continuation of capitalism and defending an implied sense of normativity without the guarantee of history.

In responding to these problems, Marxism has become profoundly split between what might be deemed its (classical) 'scientific-structuralist' and 'critical-cultural' schools (Gouldner 1980). Whilst the former remains committed to the objective necessity of the collapse of capitalism, the latter sensed that social transformation requires a subjective embodiment of a revolutionary positioning and a rethinking of the relationship between the economic and the political. As Stuart Hall (1977: 24, original emphasis) notes, 'There is no *necessary immediate correspondence* between the "economic" and "political" constitution of classes.' Although we might assert that the proletariat have a revolutionary position in the economic structure, there is no necessary correspondence between this position and a revolutionary politics (Hall 1977: 27).

The rethinking of Marxism initially emerged through what came to be known as 'Western Marxism'. Beginning with the likes of György Lukács, Antonio Gramsci and the Frankfurt School, this label emerged largely as a way to distinguish between the 'messy' political practice of Marxism in the USSR and more critical and philosophical forms which emerged in the global West. Attempting to explain the historical failures of Marxism, Western Marxists turned to culture, philosophy and politics to critique the economism of historical materialism (Anderson 1976; Schecter 2007).

Though this culturalist rejection of scientific objectivity and economic determinism has proven to be a productive platform for explaining key elements of contemporary capitalism, it has given birth to a number of academic disciplines that now appear entirely divorced from the economic concerns upon which Marx's work was formed. This rethinking largely occurred under the auspices of the 'turn to language' that came to dominate continental philosophy in the latter half of the twentieth century.

Turning to Language

If for Marx it was our material being that determined the world of consciousness and ideas, the turn to language was indeed revolutionary. Otherwise known as the discursive turn, this seminal movement stemmed from the structural linguistics of Ferdinand de Saussure but was dominated by the likes of Derrida and Lacan and the emergence of cultural studies, arguably replacing Marxism as a hegemonic force amongst Leftist political philosophy.

Giving ontological primacy to the domain of language, the discursive turn suggests that rather than meaning being derived directly from an object, meaning develops via differential chains of signifiers. Here the signifier is considered arbitrary, contingent upon a history of relationships with other signifiers. Because meaning is differential, there are no positive meanings – there are no signifiers which mean in and of themselves – and language is inherently negatively charged.

This rejection of the correspondence between language and truth is not necessarily idealist. We do not have to go down the road of Bishop Berkeley, conceiving that only what is constructed in the mind exists. A tree does indeed fall in the woods despite no one being around to hear it crash. This is a problem Laclau dealt with effectively in debates with traditional Marxists such as Norman Geras (1987), who were unwilling to accept the consequences of his rereading of Marxism through the notions of hegemony and discourse. Laclau states:

> The discursive character of an object does not, by any means, imply putting its *existence* into question. The fact that a football is only a football as long as it is integrated within a system of socially constructed rules does not mean that is thereby ceases to be a physical object. (Laclau & Mouffe 1990: 100–1, emphasis in original)

Nonetheless, language – or, in Laclau's terms, discourse – provides the lens through which things appear meaningful. As the meaning of objects comes from cultural understandings, or ideology, rather than the object itself, meaning can never be fully determined: there is no essential kernel to any particular element. In considering human nature, for instance, this essence cannot be said to stem from nature, from our bodies or from the laws of history. Instead, every conception is ideological and political, differentially derived by the articulation of signifying chains. As a consequence, social life is negatively charged: there are no positive meanings (meanings in themselves) but, instead, social life is defined by a constant ontic lack.

This ontological positioning has had significant political consequences, at a theoretical level at least. Political theory could no longer make appeals to something outside itself, such as God, rationality or human nature. Those transcendental signifiers that once provided a guarantee were now seen as differential elements in a chain of infinitely deferred meaning.

Nonetheless, attempts to access an essentialist anchoring point have not ceased. Indeed, as political liberalism began to question what were once considered the foundations of a good society, various fundamentalist narratives have fought back. Many who would consider the concept of a 'transcendental signifier' to be academic mumbo-jumbo still believe in the transcendental status of God and are willing to bring a gun to a town hall meeting on health care reform to prove it.

The overarching value of the turn to language, however, has

been the capacity to understand political movements as ideological attempts to fix the chain of meaning. Ideological critique became not a matter of revealing a concealed concrete truth – that there is no God, perhaps, or the contradictions in the mode of production – but, rather, a critique of the abstract manner in which ideological constructions are named. It did not matter what proper name was given to God, only that a God-like signifier can have a structuring role at all. Negative ontological political theory did not seek to substitute one truth with another – the proletariat being a superior Truth than God – but instead began to consider what we meant by 'truth'. It is this move from Truth to the meaning of 'truth' that signalled a transition from traditional modernism to late modernism and postmodernism.

The turn to language, however, is not a paradoxically homogenous Truth in itself, somehow outside history. Rather, it is itself a historical discourse, the fundamental elements of which continue to be a focus of debate. There was not some official announcement of a 'turn to discourse' at a conference of philosophers. Nonetheless, it has been a substantial move within continental philosophy and within those seeking to rethink Marxism. As we shall see in this chapter and the next, there are substantive differences between and within poststructuralist or postmodern ontologies and that of psychoanalysis. Moreover, these differences relate to significant distinctions both in what it means to practise politics and in political performance itself. Nonetheless, it is vital to note that the turn to language was a significant moment in political theory. In terms of Marxism, this ontological movement marked a change from culture as a supplement to the economy to culture as a determinant in itself. The turn proved a significant threat to Marxism, already challenged by historical events, the link between which was only just becoming clear. What began as an attempt to supplement Marxism and restore the critique of political economy ended up rejecting them altogether. Both moves occurred within the framework of postmodernism.

The Postmodern Challenge

Postmodernity is, according to Eagleton,

> the contemporary movement of thought which rejects totalities, universal values, grand historical narratives, solid foundations to human essence and the possibility of objective knowledge. Postmodernism is sceptical of

truth, unity and progress, opposes what it sees as elitism in culture, tends towards cultural relativism, and celebrates pluralism, discontinuity and heterogeneity. (Eagleton 2003: 13)

Rejecting any possibility of a political anchor that would provide the basis for the kind of essentialism that once defined Marxism, post-modern discourses have emphasised the contingency of language and the differentiality of meaning. Without any metaphysical ambitions, postmodernism suggests a philosophical relativism that at best provides support for diversity, for difference and for a flowering freedom of identity positions. At worst this form of social constructivism leads to cultural support for a cynically debauched wallowing in consumerism and for an administrated hedonism quite divorced from the political economy – and political consequences – of its construction.

The strongest blow to Marxism was the first. When Jean-François Lyotard rejected any sense of grand narrative, the primary narrative to which he referred was Marxism (Eagleton 2003: 38). The death of the grand narrative signals perhaps the most fundamental element of postmodernism: the rejection of foundationalism and essentialism. Awareness that the referentiality of language left social life without any ultimate guarantee meant there could be no grand narrative on which to support a vision of politics; any such narrative would have to rely upon a signifier that did not rely upon another. Language proved to be a poor substitute for God or transcendental rationality.

Yet, if postmodernity has rejected the essentialism of classical Marxism, it nonetheless looks suspiciously like 'a new epic fable of the end of epic fables', as Eagleton put it (2003: 45). This deterministic narrative about the rejection of deterministic epistemology has led to something of a normative crisis:* if the grand narrative is dead, then everything and nothing is possible.† Postmodernism, in this sense, can be regarded as deeply conservative, both because the rejection of all foundations has led many to search for even deeper

---

* Given Marx's own rejection of morality, there is something quite comedic about this normative crisis which followed the downfall of the hegemony of Marxism.
† This is the paradox of the death of 'God', otherwise known as the transcendental signifier. If the original fear of the theists (linguistic or otherwise) was that the dismissal of this guarantee would mean the end of order, then perhaps the opposite has occurred; we have invented new signifiers to fill this lack. Moreover, because they are self-imposed they have an even stronger disciplinary effect. We see this change in the move from a sovereign authority to the all-seeing discipline of panoptical control; if God is dead, then nothing, rather than everything, is permitted.

foundations – hence the rise of fundamentalisms in the twenty-first century – and because of the dismissal of emancipation that became associated with the death of determinism.

Whilst only the most vulgar forms of postmodernity – generally found in cultural practice rather than political theory – have dismissed ethics altogether, nothing resembling the politics of communism has emerged. Postmodern thinkers began to reconsider what it meant to live the Good life, a large part of which included the rethinking of what 'Good' meant and whether it was still appropriate to speak of it with a capital G. Much of the ethical thinking of those of a negative ontological bent is itself negative, a critique of those unities that should be differences. For these postmodernists, any hint of the normative or unity is immediately repressive. Benevolent as it might be to invoke the concept, it immediately restored the primacy of God: etymologists in search of the origins of meaning were the ultimate theists. As language is naturally repressive, because it narrows down differences by turning them into a categorical unity,* the task of postmodern ethics was to open up this unity in a celebration of difference.

The removal of the emancipationist drive can be regarded as the biggest loss from the postmodern response to Marxism. Emancipation is incommensurable with postmodern thought, as it invokes unfashionable universal constructions and collective movements whose rationale depended upon grand narratives. Most importantly, without the support of history or the science of historical materialism, emancipation brought up the awkward question of the auspices under which it would occur.

Yet, aspects of postmodernity and the discursive turn have been welcomed by Marxist discourse. Not only has the turn to language provided the theoretical resources to understand the cultural dimensions of capital, but the danger inherent in essentialism has been brought to the fore. No longer can we hold innocently to any sense of ideology, longing for the annihilation of an enemy who is nothing but an ideological construction. Marxism should be more than reluctant to forget the horrors that have been committed in its name.

---

* For instance the concept of 'tree' collapses a number of different types of tree into a singular meaning. Likewise, the signifier 'women' is repressive because it ignores the difference between different categories of women, such as black women, black working women, black working homosexual women, all of which are themselves repressive concepts . . .

There is certainly value in a form of ethics that supports difference and breaks down barriers closed by essentialist anchors.
Nonetheless, although the expansion of ethics and normativity provided by postmodernity should be applauded, we should not mistake
the celebration of personal or cultural identifications as the political
horizon of our time (Žižek 2000a).* Indeed, the postmodern rejection of meta-narratives is intimately linked with the positioning of
capitalism as *the* unacknowledged grand narrative of our time and
a movement away from production as the source of antagonism to
consumption. This move brought a dispersion of the place of power
from the working class to a fractured identity-based consumer
culture (Bauman 2005; Cremin 2011: 111). In doing so, resistance to
capitalism, at least within the West, became particularly difficult to
organise as the injustices of production moved off-shore, leaving only
the haunting underfulfilment of consumer desire.

We can consider that postmodernism, instead of being a radical
form of emancipation from identity, is just the latest articulation of
capitalism. If early modernity had considered capital to require the
parochial discipline that characterised the industrial era, modernity's
combined and uneven entry into a postmodern era was considered
to be a mortal threat to the interests of capitalism. For Fredric
Jameson, however, postmodernity has actually saved capitalism
from its own inherent contradictions (1991; 1996). He postulates
that the burgeoning development of social identities that came with
the birth of postmodernism became a seamless cure for the ills of
overproduction, as, along with the financialisation of capital, new
social identities were ideal for the development of new products and
new markets.

These markets were generated by the 'new social movements' and
cultural identifications that developed alongside the turn to language
and emphasis upon cultural differentiation amongst Leftists. Whilst
these movements have provided the impetus for the liberation of very
real limitations upon subjective expression, they cannot be considered to be subversive. Rather than acting as a threat to capitalism,

---

* Identity politics, rather than being an exemplary element of postmodernism,
embodies the position of cultural studies between modernism and postmodernism.
Although a form of particularism concurrent with postmodernism, it is an attempt
to establish an essential unity that is quite opposed to the celebration of difference
which characterises postmodernity. Nonetheless, in terms of political positioning,
identity politics and cultural studies have much in common.

working women, racial enlightenment and sexual reform allowed the development of new and profitable markets. Postmodernism might have been experienced as liberation for those outside the hegemony of the white man within Western nations, but this expression has come to mean little more than the commodification of cultural difference: Westerners may have a more diverse range of restaurants at which to eat, but for those who experience eating as an infrequent necessary, postmodern liberation remains entirely other. As Jameson (1991: 5) ominously states:

> This whole global, yet American, postmodern culture is the internal and superstructural expression of a whole new wave of American military and economic domination throughout the world: in this sense, as throughout class history, the underside of culture is blood, torture, death, and terror.

Thus, whilst postmodernism acts as a valuable reminder of the dangers of totalising forms of modernist practice, it provides no answer to either the contradictions of contemporary capitalism or the pragmatic attempts to restore the smooth functioning of capital. Ultimately there is something a little tragic about postmodernity; the Left appears gun shy, unwilling to take power in any radical sense lest the mistakes of the past be repeated. It is, as Eagleton states in regard to the foundations of the Western empire; 'a rather awkward moment in human history to find oneself with little or nothing to say about such fundamental questions' (2003: 102).

For this reason we must insist, as Žižek does, that Marxism remains *the* radical alternative form of political economy with the potential to resist the meta-hegemony of capitalism. The difficulty lies in proceeding with a Marxist approach without the materialist guarantee of history that supported both the critique of political economy and the subsequent mode of normativity. We must consider how one can hold to class exploitation as the ultimate form of capitalism, or communism as the unquestionable form of the Good, whilst accepting the ontological differentiality of the signifier.

Laclau and the Shrinking Hegemony of Socialist Strategy

Against these difficulties, a return to universality has provided the impetus for a restoration of Marxist theory. For theorists such as Laclau, the discursive turn is not a threat but a vital moment in the renewal of the Marxist project. Here, rather than restoring the primacy of economic analysis and the revolutionary subject, Laclau comes to suggest that politics involves the development of strategic coalitions that come to hold the place of universality. In doing so, he manages to merge an effective mode of politics with an understanding that 'society doesn't exist'. Conversely, communism, class struggle and materialism fade away so as to leave Marxism without the critical edge provided by its theoretical foundations, such that Laclau's is often defined as the seminal work in the 'post-Marxist' project.

Post-Marxism has been defined by Laclau and Mouffe's breakthrough text, *Hegemony and Socialist Strategy* (1985). Introducing both discourse theory and its political dimension, radical democracy, Laclau and Mouffe began from within the Marxist tradition – the work attempts to rearticulate *socialist strategy* (emphasis is required on both these terms) and uses Antonio Gramsci's reading of the Marxist concept of hegemony to do so – but they establish a strong break with Marxism, attempting to articulate a new form of Leftist politics based around political struggles for the place of universality.

For Laclau and Mouffe the focus on particularism, as well as being philosophically inept, is also a form of political defeatism. If movements are to grip the polis they must appeal to a sense of universality which, whilst impossible, is also necessary (Laclau & Mouffe, 1985: 189). Here Laclau suggests that if language constructs the social field, this construction is never complete, such that 'society does not exist'. The battle of politics – a battle of hegemony – is the ultimately impossible struggle to fix meaning around certain nodal signifiers. These points, which Laclau labels empty signifiers, structure 'chains of equivalence' that define the ideological terrain through an appeal to universality. Here politics becomes a matter of strategy, with particular groupings forming coalitions housed under a single signifier. In turn that signifier holds the place of universality by standing in for the point of lack in society and becoming a point of identification for multiple ideologies.

Freedom, for instance, acts as an empty signifier within American political discourse. Structurally empty, it stands for nothing in itself, but acts as a central point of identification for political groups who fill it with competing meanings as part of extended chains. Freedom might be attached to national security within Republican ideology, or the right to civil liberties for Democrats. If at the moment a globally hegemonic Leftist signifier is 'green', then chains of equivalence have built around this signifier, with the result that green groupings, whether political parties or otherwise, come to hold the multiple demands which characterise contemporary Leftist politics, most notably the politics of anti-discrimination (Stavrakakis 2000b). Thus, Laclau (2006) argues that there is no privileged objective agent of political transformation. Instead, politics becomes a matter of holding the place of universality through strategic battles for political hegemony.

Moreover, Laclau not only designates a formal matrix of political performance but, like Marx, derives a normative vision from his ontology. Unlike Marx, however, Laclau's political ideal does not hold onto any foundation. Instead, for Laclau it is the contingency of language that allows for the possibility of human freedom from ideological subjugation and containment. As such, the early Laclau suggested that this freedom is best represented by what he, amongst others, labels 'radical democracy'. Radical democracy celebrates the contingency of politics in the name of universality. Laclau argued that 'true liberation does not therefore consist in projecting oneself towards a moment that would represent the fullness of time but, on the contrary, in showing the temporal – and consequently transient – character of all fullness' (1990: 193) and goes on to state, 'A free society is not one where a social order has been established that is better adapted to human nature but one which is more aware of the contingency and historicity of any order' (Laclau 1990: 211). As a consequence, he comes to suggest, with an increasingly loose reference to socialism, that the best strategy for Leftist politics is the development of an articulated coalition of what has come to be known as new social movements.

If, however, for Laclau the society that is most free is that which is aware of its dependency upon discourse, one must consider what this means for those bodies which have been excluded from the material fruits of society. One could perhaps expand Laclau's thesis to suggest that the exclusion of these bodies is entirely contingent and can thus be altered. Moreover, this awareness of the contingency of societal construction could be extended by including the previously excluded within a democratic chain of equivalence, such that the world's poorest inhabitants became included within a global demand for justice. Most importantly, perhaps, despite the apparent benefits of his rereading of Marxism, there is nothing in Laclau's theory that suggests a more productive reading of capitalism, one that is more able to explain its continual development, its ills or how capital might be overturned.

Thus, if Marx attempted to circumvent the problem of normativity with his 'scientific' historical materialism, which did not rely upon an ideological morality as much as a faith in the progress of history, then the post-Marxist critique of this determinism has left Marxism without any reason to be 'Marxist'. Without a transcendental support for class struggle and political practice, either from a descriptive reading of history or from abstract moral prescription, there appeared little reason for post-Marxist thought to continue to reference itself to Marxism or to a critique of capitalism. Marxism, it seems, had been reduced to an empty signifier around which the Left could rally to establish their radical credentials. In terms of political practice, the only difference – with the exception of some institutional tweaking – between the politics of radical democracy supported by the early Laclau and the liberal democracy practiced under late capitalism is their theoretical reference point.

For this reason, for those who still hold to both a strident critique of capitalism and the validity of Marxist discourse, Laclau's work has come under attack. The primary motivation behind post-Marxism is that the economy cannot be an object in itself and thus cannot determine social relations other than through the contingency of hegemony. The economy is not economic in and of itself but, rather, just another element of political discourse. Arguing that there is no difference between postmodern struggles and class struggle, Laclau rejects any sense of the primacy of the economy, contending that 'class struggle is just one species of identity politics, and one which is becoming less and less important in the way we live' (Laclau 2000b: 203). In a sense, Laclau is correct; class struggles are becoming less apparent in the way we (the West) live. If for Laclau this is a point of celebration, those on the wrong end of this struggle may have cause to disagree.

Ultimately, the difficulty with Laclau's post-Marxism is that it has struggled to develop a conception of the economic away from his rejection of Marx's essentialist notion of the economy (Devenney 2002: 18). If classical Marxism – and, as we shall see, Žižek – attributed a causal positioning to class struggle and political economy, this cannot be held within a purely discursive approach. Laclau's theory of hegemony allows for an element to hold a determining position but this cannot be determined *a priori* – rather it is achieved through a battle for hegemony. Without this prioritising of the economy, Marxism loses much of its political edge. Laclau's position reminds us of the 1970s feminist slogan 'The personal is political' and its infamous rejoinder 'The personal is personal too, so piss off'. Yes, the economy is political, but it is also economic: the economy is always the *political* economy.

Finally, despite acknowledging an initial affinity with psychoanalysis, particularly in regard to the institutionalisation of lack in the struggle for hegemony (Laclau 1990), Laclau has struggled to integrate his reading of discourse with the materiality of psychoanalysis. As a consequence, it is difficult to conceptualise why universal signifiers would have any more hold over the subject than particular elements – an issue I shall respond to in some detail in the following chapter.

In response to these criticisms (Laclau 2003), Laclau has subsequently moved away from Chantal Mouffe and radical democracy to a form of politics which focuses more upon the potential for identification, rather than differentiation, provided by his conception of contingency. Laclau's contemporary thought attempts to construct a theory of populism and 'the construction of the people' (Laclau 2005; 2006), moving away from the institutionalisation of lack to focus primarily on the role of affective identifications in the determination of hegemony. For Laclau, populism is a 'pure' form of politics that coincides with his theory of hegemony. There are few remnants, however, of the reliance upon contingency which dominated his conception of radical democracy. Instead democracy now accounts for one 'moment' within populist discourse.

Laclau conceives of populism as a neutral movement, like that of hegemony, as opposed to the proto-fascism attributed to it by liberals. Preferring populism to class struggle because it keeps open the space of power rather than offering a privileged content as the general equivalent of all other struggles, Laclau contends that populism exists only in form without suggesting any content: just as he opined that society does not exist, neither do the people. By standing as the universal equivalent of all struggles, 'the people' act as a historically contingent mode of the revolutionary subject.

If any construction of the people is a hegemonic one, it also requires the exclusion of an antagonistic enemy from the chain of equivalence. In this way, Žižek suggests, not only is fascism a form of populism – 'Jew' is the ultimate signifier of lack constructed to fill the lack in the big Other – but populism entails a naturalisation and a potential suspension of the political (Žižek 2008: 276–85).

Perhaps a more symptomatic example of Laclau's understanding of populism comes from a 2010 report of British football hooligans uniting to protest against Islam. Normally composed of violently opposed groups associated with individual clubs – the groups included the Cardiff City Soul Crew and Bolton Wanderers Cuckoo Boys – the hooligans have begun protesting together under the title of the English Defence League, becoming mobilised against the presence of the Islamic religion within the United Kingdom (Briggs 2010). Here we have otherwise opposed groups – what Laclau would call particular elements – forming a chain of equivalence under an empty signifier, the English Defence League, in a battle for hegemony over the meaning of 'British'.

Laclau's move from radical democracy to populism has thus maintained his descriptive ontology, but his politics have flipped from the negative to the positive register. Both radical democracy and populism rely upon the identification of a constitutive impossibility within linguistic structure. This point of impossibility signals the empty place of universality; the element which comes to hold this position is regarded as universal. For the early Laclau, politics should be directed towards holding this place open to allow the inherent dislocatory freedom of language to operate. By contrast, Laclau's populism now suggests that the key task of any political movement is to hold the place of hegemony. This move suggests a radical transition from the politics of lack to the politics of *jouissance*, although Laclau does not use the term, which I shall expand upon in the next chapter.

Although his notion of populism appears a more powerful political device, in relying upon the positioning of an antagonism to create 'the people', Laclau appears to be returning to the same positivising sense of the social against which he initially rallied. Populism may reject the historical naturalism of the revolutionary subject, but in accepting that the place of the 'people' can and should be held, Laclau's politics are not markedly different from forms of Marxism before the discursive turn – his populism is Marxism without the critique of political economy.

Thus, whilst Laclau's political applications of his theory of hegemony – in both its radical democratic and populist guises – are effective across a limited range, his work does not restore Marxism in any manner which provides a response to the contradictions of the global economy. Although Laclau's attempt to restore the dimension of universality to Marxist discourse should be welcomed, his politics, whether radical democracy or populism, operate through the exclusion of class struggle and the economy. Laclau's work may mark an advance on the contingent ethics of particularity and difference that characterise the divergent realm of postmodernity, but it has not been able to compensate for the losses associated with the denunciation of historical materialism. In rejecting economic determinism, Laclau has rejected the economy altogether and in doing so no longer engages with global capitalism. Instead Laclau's work reads as a critique of the difficulties of the politics of modernity. By contrast, interactions between psychoanalysis and Marxism have tended to engage with political economy. Moreover, psychoanalysis, particularly in its Lacanian variety, has been able to return to materiality in its reading of the discursive turn. As we shall see, Žižek has been at the core of this movement.

Psycho-Marxism

Since its development, psychoanalysis has had a major impact on social theory. An engagement with psychoanalysis has enlarged understandings of ideology, of subjectivity, of the role of culture and enjoyment in politics and of the relationship between the individual and society (Elliott 2005: 175). Freud's *Civilization and its Discontents* (1930) exemplified the use of psychoanalysis as a sociological pursuit as Freud developed an understanding of the manner in which the demands of civilised society required a level of repression in the subject that is expressed in a destructive manner.*

Freud was reread by Lacan – who maintained he was only supplementing Freud's work – reworking psychoanalysis in light of Saussure's structural linguistics, famously stating that the unconscious is structured like a language (Lacan 2006: 416), so that 'language, as a system of differences, constitutes the subject's repressed desire' (Lacan 2006: 182). In this sense, unconscious desire, like language, constitutes an intersubjective space between and within individual subjects (Lacan 2006: 183). Moreover, intersubjectivity – with the impossibilities associated with its constitution as a differential linguistic system – offers a mediating background for subjectivity. As Anthony Elliott (2004: 11) states:

> For many, the theoretical advantages of Lacan's Freud concerned, above all, his inflation of the role of language in the construction of the psyche, an inflation which happened to fit hand in glove with the 'linguistic turn' of the social sciences.

* This is a line of thought further developed by Marcuse (1956) in particular.

Lacanian theory, it seemed, had come along at just the right moment, speaking to the analytic dilemmas that came to be associated with postmodernism whilst responding to the problematic to which postmodernism became a response. Against the postmodernists but within the linguistic turn, Lacanian psychoanalysis achieved an alternative hegemony by responding to several of the problems which haunted postmodernism. In particular, Lacanian theory sought to rehabilitate the categories of subjectivity, structure and the body, each of which shall be expanded on in much more detail in the following chapter. Through the rejuvenation of these concepts, Lacanian theory offered a new way to understand (Western) Marxism and its relationship to the discursive turn.

The difficulties of combining psychoanalysis and Marxism are intertwined with the collective hope and traumatic failure of Leftist emancipation. Following the unease felt towards the halted progress of Marxist practice and theory, psychoanalysis has long been looked upon as both the saviour and the failure of radical Leftist politics. Yet no stable theoretical fusion has developed between the two traditions, and contemporary theory has come to regard the notion of collective emancipation as rather pathetically passé.

Psychoanalysis was initially attached to Marxism as part of the cultural turn which sought to explain the perceived shortcomings of Marxism in response to the continued presence and development of capitalism. In this initial relationship, characterised by the Freudian Marxism of Wilhelm Reich and the Frankfurt School theorists, psychoanalysis was used to add a theory of subjectivity to Marxism in the face of the failure of the Marxist 'revolutionary subject'. These theories of subjectivity focused mainly on the role of culture in mediating the effects of capitalism and preventing a true class consciousness from emerging.

The second phase of 'psycho-Marxism' was dominated by Louis Althusser's structuralist revision of Marxism (Miklitsch 1998: 85). Althusser's return to Marx through psychoanalysis was the first to be dominated by Lacan, rather than Freud. As such, Althusser was perhaps the first to politicise Lacanian thought in his reworking of Marxism and ideology. Using Lacan's notion of the mirror stage to exemplify (mis)recognition in ideology through what he called 'interpellation', Althusser's work had a strong influence upon efforts to reformulate both Marxist determinism and the role of culture and ideology in maintaining the dominance of capital.

The movement from Freud to Lacan proved to be both a threat

and an opportunity for Marxist theory. Lacan's emphasis on the structuring role, and ultimate failure, of language dismissed the foundations of Marxist essentialism and previously assumed forms of political action associated with communism. Communism may have remained as a reference point, but the essentialist justifications had long disappeared, dispatched to a theoretical attic to allow for occasional bouts of nostalgia. Importantly, however, this dimension was not dismissed altogether. Althusser and those that followed remained committed to Marxism for a reason, although others, such as Laclau, may not have been so sure. The problem was that whilst psychoanalysis did not fall prey to the transgressive particularism of postmodernity, it did share a deep suspicion of politics, utopianism and revolution. If many theorists have found psychoanalysis woefully inadequate as a political torch-bearer, Marxists held no further optimism.

Although Marxism and psychoanalysis share several theoretical similarities – a committed engagement to reducing the gap between theory and practice, an analogous notion of causality (in terms of class struggle and the unconscious respectively) and a radically divergent focus on generating change – in both their underlying ontology and their optimism towards the prospects of political change they have proved radically incompatible.

A Žižekian Marx?

Much, if not all, of this criticism is aimed at Žižek, not only because he is the most significant scholar within the field but also because his work relies heavily upon a reading of Marxism that both re-establishes and circumvents the central currents of traditional Marxist politics – most notably class struggle and communism. Operating as an antagonistic answer to the dilemmas of universality, truth and language without wanting to reoccupy any nostalgic sense of Marxist essentialism, Žižek demands that the Left respond to the dominance of capitalism.

Whilst not a new addition to Žižek's work, Marxism has become an increasingly influential partner. If his initial work was often directed against totalitarianism (Kay 2003: 130; Sharpe & Boucher 2010: 112–36), Žižek's Marxism has come to the fore only with his increasingly radical critique of global capitalism. Nonetheless, this Marxist current has been evident from the very beginning of his work. Indeed, *The Sublime Object of Ideology* (1989) begins by suggesting that it was Marx who invented the Lacanian symptom, as well as providing detailed considerations of commodity fetishism and ideology within the opening chapter.

Žižek's Marxism is certainly difficult, making no attempt at orthodoxy and often being highly critical of the Marxist tradition and in particular its utopian implications. Suggesting that the downfall of Marxism lies in the assumption that the end of private property will bring about the end of alienation and the disjuncture between individual desire and the requirements of the collective, Žižek evokes Lacan to argue that alienation is an inherent aspect of the human condition, generated by our 'symbolic castration' by language rather than by the mode of production. Moreover, ideology is not a partial discourse that hides the true nature of our existence; rather it acts as a fantasmatic totality that hides the essential lack in existence. As I will build on in the following chapter, this reading of ideology (and enjoyment) has substantial consequences for political practice.

More pertinently, Žižek produces a definitive critique of the Marxist reading of the role of contradiction within capitalism. Žižek posits that capitalism is in essence a system in crisis, but a constitutive crisis that produces the upward spiral of productivity that is the basis of the capitalist production of surplus. Whilst he is not alone in developing this point, Žižek builds upon Lacan's identification of the analogous relationship between surplus value and surplus *jouissance* (an analogy I will examine in the following chapter), suggesting that the dynamics of lack and excess in human subjectivity are mirrored by the logic of capitalism. If Marx had considered that the productivity of capitalism could be harnessed for a communist future in which abundant surplus would be equally distributed and the working day shortened, for Žižek Marx's hopes were ultimately fantasmatic. What Marx did not consider was the Lacanian logic of *jouissance* – that there is no *jouissance* without the obstacle that propels it – a central tenet of the following chapter. Marx believed that by removing the obstacle (the private appropriation of surplus value) the productivity generated by surplus value would remain and could be utilised for communal good. What Marx missed, however, is that without the inner contradiction in capitalism the economy loses its drive: without this contradiction, the productivity upon which communist ideals were reliant dries up.

Conversely, Žižek offers a rehabilitation of the notion of an objective or privileged social agent within the realm of negative ontological politics. Žižek's social agent (a point of particular conjecture for Žižek's critics) is not scientifically determined by the laws of history, but is a necessary consequence of the operation of capital. Žižek breaks down the barrier between scientific objectivity and contingent hegemonic struggle by way of his Hegelian reading of universality, which suggests that the important element of universality is not the abstract point of identification but, rather, what must be excluded to create this point. Because it is this point of exclusion that establishes the field of universality, it is also this point that holds the greatest threat to that order: its intrusion into the symbolic order threatens the coherence of that order. Žižek's notion of universality, therefore, offers a potential rereading of Marxian class struggle and the disruption of capital. Moreover, his critique of capitalism and in particular the economies of enjoyment that maintain it establishes the dialectical equation for a renewal of Marxist politics.

I shall discuss this idea in much greater detail in regards to universality, class struggle and the Real throughout the remaining chapters. For now, however, it is worth noting the value of Žižek's contribution, despite its characteristically critical reception. In rejecting the inevitable development of communism and rejuvenating class struggle, amongst other things, Žižek's Marxism remains immensely controversial. As noted in the introduction, critics such as Devenney, Homer, Laclau, Parker and Sharpe and Boucher have severe reservations about the viability of Žižek's Marxism, suggesting that Žižek does not engage in the kind of sustained analysis of the economy that would justify the reference to Marxism, and that his Lacanian orthodoxy prevents any rehabilitation of Marxian politics. This text is built upon a refutation of the former notion. In Chapter 5 I will argue that Žižekian theory does inspire a theory of capitalism that both explains its continued functioning and identifies opportunities and methods for disrupting its reproduction. Before turning to this reading, however, it is necessary to engage with the charge that Žižekian theory, and Lacanian psychoanalysis, is unable to provide any viable substitute for Marxian politics.

Žižekian theory can be considered a response to the problematic set out in this chapter, in which both the descriptive and prescriptive elements of Marxism have come under attack by the turn to language, but Žižek remains too heterodox to be strictly deemed a Marxist. Nonetheless, the reference to Marxism and the critique of political economy is inseparable from his critique of capitalism and, as such, critiques of his reading of Marxism in concepts such as ideology (Chapter 3), class struggle (Chapter 5), and communism (Chapter 7) occur throughout this book.

Although I have thus far introduced psychoanalytic discourse as a positive contributor to Marxism, psychoanalytic theory has a complex relationship with its Marxist counterpart. Through its conception of symbolic castration, psychoanalysis allows for a reading of the discursive turn which is rooted in the body. In doing so it is better able to materialise discourse and explain the apparent fixity of the symbolic order. Moreover, primarily through Žižek's work, a return to the economy is possible without reverting to a strict determinism. In doing so, we see that, following the rejection of historical materialism and the political vacuum which followed, psychoanalysis adds to the explanatory power of Marxism, providing an understanding of the difficulty of shifting capitalism and hence the possibilities for doing so without the inevitability of history.

Whilst this 'psycho-Marxism' may be able to better explain why the contradictions of global capitalism prove to be obdurate, in the next chapter we shall see that no form of politics – certainly in terms of the material reproduction of shared social life – stems naturally from the combination of Lacan and Marx. If historical materialism produced not only a reading of capitalism but the inevitable progression of the revolutionary subject, Žižek's dialectical materialism provides little such confidence. Indeed, Lacanian theory may act as the ultimate dismissal of traditional Marxist politics, leaving the question of politics and normativity in the rebellious hands of psychoanalytic discourse and its central troublemaker, Žižek.

3

Jouissance and Politics

Psychoanalysis has often been looked upon as a discourse of emancipation. Just as Marxist theory both explains the present and seeks to explain how to change it, psychoanalysis is rooted in the idea that if the body can come to an understanding of its mental pathologies, it can be induced to change. Vitally, however, where Marxism has sought to critique and change capitalism in the name of a better future, psychoanalysis has not been so optimistic. Although Freud had hoped to allow his patients to function 'normally', Lacanian psychoanalysis sought only to bring the analysand a greater degree of enjoyment from their symptoms. This normative division, between the prescriptive normativity of classical Marxism and the almost cynical restrictions of psychoanalysis, provides perhaps the strongest difficulty within Žižek's work.

Lacan appears an unlikely hero for the destitute populations of the world or for those unreconstructed Marxists still intent upon a communist future. If Lacanian psychoanalysis is able to offer an alternative reading of the discursive turn, one which does not wholly reject materialism or universality, this reading puts any restoration of communism inspired by historical materialism to bed. Instead, psychoanalysis appears more equipped to understand the flourishing appeal of capitalism than to provide a new revolutionary hope for the working class.

By contrast to Marx, for Lacan alienation is neither contingent nor political but, rather, an ahistorical condition of being. The subject of language is alienated not only by the differential separation of the concept from the thing but also by the material separation of the body from itself, otherwise known as symbolic castration. We humans, unlike our fellow animals, cannot purely react upon instinct or enjoy our bodies. Instead, upon entry into the symbolic order, the subject loses access to total materiality.

Nonetheless, Lacanian theory suggests that whilst language produces a fragmentation to social life from which there is no possibility of recovering, an excessive, materialist, remainder of existence persists. This materiality is not the determining stuff of historical materialism but, rather, a dialectical materialism driven by the impact of language upon the body. Where Marx suggested a commonality to human existence based around the shared conditions of production, for Lacan intersubjectivity is based around the shared grip of language and its remainder, *jouissance*. If for postmodernists all that was solid had melted, Lacan suggested that the signifier does not melt social life into thin air but, rather, into a bodily substance called *jouissance* which ensures that politics is not just a matter of signification.

Here, the human condition is constituted by a complex dialectic between lack and excess: lack in the sense of the negativity being caused at heart by the subject's essential separation from *jouissance* through the operation of the signifier, excess because of the compensation the subject receives for this sacrifice, a surplus *jouissance* located in the object cause of desire (*objet a*). Žižek, following Lacan and Freud before him, defines this movement between lack and excess as the death drive. Being is never just being, such that 'human life is never "just life": humans are not simply alive, they are possessed by the strange drive to enjoy life in excess, passionately attached to a surplus which sticks out and derails the ordinary run of things' (Žižek 2006b: 62).

As such, by conceiving of the problem of signification as one of symbolic castration – an issue as much of the body as the psyche – Lacanian theory has been able to restore universalism, materialism and fixity as key elements of theory once lost by Marxism to postmodernity and the discursive turn. In restoring these dimensions, Lacanian psychoanalysis (through Žižek in particular) has been able to rehabilitate Marxism as an explanatory device beyond any deterministic sense of history.

What Lacanian psychoanalysis has not been able to restore, however, is the emancipationist demand at the heart of the Marxist approach. Indeed, psychoanalytic theory – including its Freudian forebear – can be considered perhaps more sceptical about the prospects of revolution and emancipation than postmodern thought. If postmodern ethics hold some optimism about human freedom, although dismissive of the universality required for widespread political change, psychoanalysis holds no such optimism: the death drive is not a concept for the sunshine theorists of the human mind. As we shall see throughout the remainder of this chapter, however, this is not the last word on the role of psychoanalysis in politics.

Whilst Lacan orientated his psychoanalytic treatment around an ethical imperative, that imperative was to loosen the grip of morality upon the subject rather than reformulate the normative foundations of a more just political order. As with Freudian analysis, the ethical pursuit of Lacanian theory was orientated at the body of the individual rather than the interactions of a community of bodies: Lacanian ethics is a response to the guilt experienced by the subject from having to forgo its bodily instincts upon entry into the symbolic order.

According to both Freud and Lacan (in different variants), ideological notions about what it means to live well, to match up to moral standards imposed by the collective, are nothing but the imposition of the superego upon the body. This imposition creates perverse forms of *jouissance* (enjoyment) that move the subject away from the kind of behaviours notionally encouraged by these ideologies. Any notion of how we should live must tally with the dialectics of enjoyment that structure social life.

Thus, the question I shall consider in this chapter is whether the Lacanian foundations of Žižekian theory offer any conception of political practice. Certainly, psychoanalysis is not purely a clinical pursuit, but, as Freud made clear in *Civilization and its Discontents*, nor does it offer significant hope for a progressive future. Instead, the focus of the Lacanian mode of clinical practice is on releasing the subject from the binds of morality. This release does not offer the subject a hedonistic utopia but, rather, a more satisfying relationship with the limitations of their bodily enjoyment.

For the likes of Yannis Stavrakakis, this relationship with limitation signals the possibility for a Lacanian informed theory of democracy. This psycho-democracy attempts to steer clear of the twin imposters of total ideological *jouissance* and the dry formalism of administrative Leftism, arguing that Lacan's understanding of feminine enjoyment best informs a non-exclusive form of social life. However, not only is Stavrakakis's work based upon a misreading of the Lacanian feminine, but it also seeks to institutionalise what is fundamentally an anti-institutional practice. It is this failure which speaks to the heart of the difficulty in mobilising psychoanalysis as a political practice. Psychoanalysis cannot become a form of the Good in itself: psychoanalysis is fundamentally directed as a response to the Good and any attempts to subvert this structure are found wanting. This leaves the political prospects for Žižekian theory on difficult ground, entirely unable to make a normative commitment except for that implied by a strident opposition to capitalism. For critics, this is where the story ends: Žižek as an increasingly hysterical conservative, calling for more and more radical political acts without any mechanism to achieve such change or purpose for starting the process at all.

Ultimately, in this chapter I will not deny that Žižekian theory does not provide a normative foundation for political practice: there is no Žižekian ideology. Nonetheless, Žižek's work remains significantly productive in spite of these limitations, producing a theory of shared social life that informs an understanding to the continued functioning of global capitalism. In this chapter and those that follow, I suggest that Žižek's work is a highly productive form of contemporary political practice not because it offers an alternative to capitalism, but because it is capable of disrupting capitalism by evoking its disavowed foundations.

Psychoanalysis and the Discursive Turn

Jouissance is Žižek's ultimate (Lacanian) answer to the question he poses in *The Sublime Object of Ideology*: 'What creates and sustains the *identity* of a given ideological field beyond all possible variations of its positive content?' (Žižek 1989: 87, emphasis in original). Žižek begins to answer this question by suggesting that Ernesto Laclau and Chantal Mouffe's *Hegemony and Socialist Strategy* provides an answer in their conception of the nodal point or empty signifier, where

> the multitude of 'floating signifiers' of proto-ideological elements is structured into a unified field through the intervention of a certain 'nodal point' (the Lacanian *point de capiton*) which 'quilts' them, stops their sliding and fixes their meaning. (Žižek 1989: 87)

As the discussion extends, however, it becomes clear that Žižek's answer goes beyond discourse into the materiality which sustains the empty signifier. If Laclau's schema works only at the 'level of meaning', then the full Lacanian analysis of ideology also requires the 'level of enjoyment' (Žižek 1989: 121). Enjoyment dominates meaning and the symbolic field, bending discourse to its perverse will: the paradoxes of enjoyment are perhaps the most original, intriguing and powerful insight of the Lacanian response to the discursive turn.

Jouissance, in all its paradoxical forms, is the central force of the human condition. It produces an excessive 'enjoyment' centred in the body and experienced via language, through a dialectic of excessive *jouissance* and the lack of the Real. For Lacanian psychoanalysis *jouissance* is the ultimate reply to the contingency suggested by forms of postmodernity and post-structuralism. If Lacan's analysis of the symbolic register has much in common with post-structuralism, such that Lacan has at times been mistakenly placed within this category, then *jouissance* allows Lacan's work to go beyond the confines of the symbolic order. This transgression has occurred because Lacan did not conceive of the cut of the signifier as a discursive act alone but, rather, one of symbolic castration: meaning is a bodily function.

Jouissance is a specifically Lacanian, as opposed to Freudian, concept and one that carries all the inherent brilliance and difficulties that stem from his work. Although most simply translated as enjoyment, *jouissance* is the paradoxical state of suffering/enjoyment that lies 'beyond the pleasure principle' (Evans 1996: 92). *Jouissance* goes beyond enjoyment or pleasure into a kind of troubling, excessive rapture that includes elements of transgression and suffering; *jouissance* is excessive because it serves no purpose, relating more to the death drive than any sense of 'biological instinct', evolutionary or otherwise (Levy-Stokes 2001: 101). As such, *jouissance*, like the Real, exists both beyond language and as an intimate part of language.

Jouissance is generated by the dialectic of language – of symbolic castration and the presence of absence – whereby the human being operates as a being of desire rather than of biological need. The human being, like any animal, is subject to a number of biological needs. Symbolic castration, the birth of the subject through their entry into the symbolic order, creates a division in the body between these needs and the signifier, which expresses the distorted instincts of the body as *jouissance* (Levy-Stokes 2001: 101). Castration means that desire becomes a biological property of the human animal, not one the infant is born with but, rather, one which impinges on the subject on account of its forced entry into language.

If *jouissance* is felt as an excess, it is generated by the lack generated in turn by the process of symbolic castration. For Lacan, lack is the prerequisite of the human condition, whereby language fundamentally alienates the subject from the body. This lack is not simply nothingness but has an ontological status *beyond* nothingness. Lack does not only imply negativity, but also excessive attempts to compensate for this negativity. For Lacan, lack has the same form as an empty set: an emptiness implying the possibility of fullness. Lack thus has the status of something missing, the 'presence of absence'.

Understanding Lacan's conception of lack is made more difficult by the inadequate translation of the French signifier '*manqué*' as used by Lacan. *Manquer* is translated as 'lack' in English because of the semantic inadequacy of the English verb 'miss' (Fink 1995: 52). Missing, more than lacking, implies both the lack of something and attempts to regain what is lost. These attempts (the 'missing' of the object) characterise the operation of desire, a 'lack of being' which generates a 'want to be' (Fink 1995: 103). For Ernst Bloch (1986), this dialectic exchange between lack and longing is evidence of the utopian demand at the heart of being.* Lack, Bloch suggests, cannot be articulated other than by imagining its fulfilment.

Jouissance is thus created through the process of returning to the body before symbolic castration. If a human being is defined by a dislocation from the body, this dislocation is felt as a longing to return: that longing is *jouissance*, whereby the body fuels a substitute satisfaction that both stages the possibility of the fullness of the body and produces an excessive enjoyment when this return fails to meet its mark.

In this regard, Bruce Fink (1995: 60) argues that there are two orders of *jouissance*, before (J_1) and after the letter (J_2). J_1 is the pure unmitigated *jouissance* that is thought to be sacrificed in the castrating entry into language: it is the subject's unmediated connection with their body. This original enjoyment is thought to be held by the Other, as if symbolic castration is a unique experience. It is for this reason, Žižek (1997: 64–5) suggests, that we become so resentful of the explicit enjoyment of our neighbour. The ultimate narrative of ideological fantasy is that castration has not occurred; language both produces the impossibility of moving outside itself and allows for the illusion that this is possible, that we can return to a time before castration.

This illusion is supported by attributing lack to an obstacle 'out

---

* Utopia, which is the focus of discussion in Chapter 7, can be read in two different manners. The utopian demand could refer to the 'perfect society', or in Laclau's terms, that society exists. This form of utopia would certainly be rejected by Lacan as an ethical or political position, although he would suggest that this form of utopia could be translated as *jouissance*. It would, however, remain equally impossible. The sense to which Bloch is referring, however, is a demand for the very impossibility of utopia; utopia as the very form of the suggestion that another mode of being is possible.

there' that is blocking the fullness of society. Politically, this position is often held by the immigrant; their very presence is held to be the antagonistic exception that prevents the full expression of nationality. Other such signifiers, such as 'Wall Street' or 'Jew', act as signifiers of lack and are identified as causes of the failure of J_1 *jouissance* and thus a source of *jouissance* in and of themselves – J_2.

Signifiers of lack or antagonisms are one element in the operation of J_2, which occurs when an object comes to substitute for the loss of J_1. The compensation is enacted through fantasy in the staging of impossible acts to regain this original *jouissance* (J_1 being impossible because the subject cannot return to a time before language). Such a failure sustains an unconscious instinct for a time without a sense that there is something missing from being. As J_1 is a creation of language, Žižek contends that there is no *jouissance* for the subject before J_2, surplus *jouissance*: if the surplus is removed from *jouissance*, it is *jouissance* itself which is lost (Žižek 1989: 52). For this reason Lacan suggested that lack must always be accompanied by excess; the lack of *jouissance* creates an excessive response. *Jouissance* is not a primordial and absolute enjoyment of the body, broken by language, culture and civilisation before being bastardised into compensatory forms. Rather, *jouissance* occurs only because of the failure of our bodies to obtain this imagined utopia through our forced choice into language and the reign of the signifier: it is nothing but this failure, sustained by an unconscious fantasy of unmediated bodily enjoyment.

Paradoxically then, *jouissance*, according to Adrian Johnston, is 'enjoyable only insofar as it doesn't get what it is ostensibly after' (2005: 239). The structure of language is such that *jouissance* (J_2) can be enjoyed only in its own failure, a failure that keeps alive the prospect of an enjoyment beyond that experienced through the structure of language; the only thing worse that the *ce n'est pas ça* of surplus *jouissance* is the prospect of meeting (surplus) *jouissance* in its bare naked form and, worst of all, knowing it. Such a horror turns the desire of 'that's not it' into the melancholic horror of 'that is all there is'. In this sense, Oscar Wilde's famous statement – there are two tragedies in life: not getting what you want and getting it – looks positively Lacanian.

In such a context, as Fink suggests, 'desire is an end in itself: it seeks only more desire, not fixation on a specific object' (1997: 26). Such is the emptiness of desire that the subject does not *really* want to obtain the object of their desire; instead what is desired is desire itself, a distance which is maintained by the construction of fantasy (Fink 1995: 90). It is the task of fantasy to maintain the dialectic between the two modes of *jouissance*, constructing the 'lure' that the semblance of *jouissance* in the symbolic order may lead to something greater. This impossibility is the central element of the role of fantasy in desire; fantasy supports the subject's desire, maintaining an appropriate distance from the object. This object is then retroactively posited as the cause of desire. The embodiment of this logic is the enigmatic *objet a*.

Objet a *and the Contingent Essentialism of Desire*

Objet a is the ultimate Lacanian answer to the stability of meaning and ideological formations. In *The Parallax View* (Žižek 2006b: 19), Žižek argues that *objet a* is 'the object of psychoanalysis . . . the core of the psychoanalytic experience'. Likewise, Richard Boothby (Boothby 2001: 242) considers *objet a* to be perhaps Lacan's greatest original contribution to psychoanalysis and certainly the most significant element of his work. We can consider *objet a* to be the embodiment of surplus *jouissance*, the 'coincidence of limit and excess, of lack and surplus . . . the left over which embodies the fundamental, constitutive lack' (Žižek 1989: 53; 2001: 149).

Objet a has a transitional status, split between the subject and the Other/object as both the object and the cause of desire. Moreover, *objet a* is integrated, yet not completely found, within each of the three Lacanian registers: the imaginary, the Real and the symbolic. Although often considered primarily as an imaginary object because of its status as the object of desire, primarily through Žižek's work *objet a* has been productively thought of as an element of the Real. Here *objet a* operates as the little remainder of the Real within the symbolic order, the unknowable x that forever eludes the symbolic and produces a multitude of symbolic responses through which the subject seeks to give it form. As such, *objet a* can be considered to be the residue of symbolisation, the last remainder of unity produced with the breakdown of *jouissance*. It is the positive 'waste' of symbolisation (Zupančič 2006b: 159).

Objet a takes the position of the missing element in being, the void at which the symbolic order remains perpetually riven. As such, via a fantasmatic relation, *objet a* connects the lack of the Real and the excess of *jouissance* by becoming both the object-cause – the gap that drives being – of desire and the object of desire. Here *objet a* becomes embodied in specific objects that signal both the limit point of the symbolic order and the possibility of its suture. The paradoxical logic of *objet a* is such that whilst an object may appear to be the cause of desire, that object is actually a largely arbitrary, unconscious, embodiment of the hidden cause of desire (Kay 2003: 166). An object, say a commodity item like a pair of shoes, may appear to be the cause of desire: 'I have to have those shoes, they are perfect for me because . . .' The illusion, however, is that this object is a substitute for the empty place of *objet a*, which causes the subject's desire. As such, desire has no object – only a cause, *objet a* (Fink 1995: 90–1). The manner in which *objet a* functions is thus dependent upon the manner in which lack is constructed in fantasy. This fantasmatic construction creates the illusion of consistency in the subject. For this consistency to operate, some object must be positivised so that it can stand in for the inherent lack that would otherwise threaten consciousness (Žižek 1997: 81). There is, however, always a gap between the cause and the object of desire, a gap which further prevents the satisfaction of that desire; the object can be obtained but when it is it ceases to be the object of desire. Instead desire continues on its metonymical chain.

Objet a allows Lacan to understand why meaning is not entirely contingent, even if there is no transcendental ultimate referent. *Jouissance* adds a material weight to the signifier; meaning does not simply drift from signifier to signifier but, rather, gets fixated upon certain nodal points. These points anchor the field of meaning, providing a certain consistency to the construction of shared social life. This conception of nodal points, however, is structurally identical to the dry analysis of Laclau's discourse theory. What lends power to Lacan's analysis is the ability to understand why these points hold a hidden power that operates beyond linguistic structure: *objet a*.

Through the logic of *objet a* certain signifier-objects become embodied with *jouissance*, a power which suggests the possibility of a traversal of symbolic castration and a return to the fullness of the body. This power allows certain signifiers to take not only a structural role in discourse but a determining function in the body. For this reason, radical change can only occur through a break with the ideological fantasy that structures political enjoyment. Thus, although Laclau's approach to hegemony reveals the manner in which political struggles can occur within a pre-established field (without taking into account the materiality of this battle), Žižek's psychoanalytic reading suggests that because of the grip of *jouissance* and the stability provided by the exclusion of exceptional points, radical change can only occur by 'traversing' ideological fantasy.

Fantasy, Ideology and Ideological Fantasy

Lacan argued that fantasy acts as a defence against symbolic castration and the lack in the Other, offering the prospect of reuniting the subject with *jouissance* through *objet a*. (Žižek 2006c: 40; Fink 1995: 60). Fantasy helps the subject maintain a manageable distance from the cause of desire (*objet a*), supporting desire but not getting burnt by the empty horror revealed by the substituted object. This fantasmatic construction creates the illusion of consistency in the subject. For this consistency to operate, some object must be positivised such that it can stand in for the inherent lack that would otherwise threaten consciousness (Žižek 1997: 81). This substitute can occur in either a positive or a negative manner, such as the antagonistic signifier previously identified as an example of J_2.

On the other hand there exist positive 'place-fillers', or empty signifiers, which suggest the possibility of full enjoyment. Barack Obama functioned as this signifier in the 2008 US presidential campaign, largely staying away from detailed policy issues and using signifiers such as 'Hope' and 'Change' which enabled a multitude of (often contradictory) signifiers to identify with his campaign. By contrast to the Laclauian empty signifier, however, *objet a* always carries with it an excess, a surplus *jouissance* that underlies the signifying chain.

Obama, for instance, became the signifier which suggested a fantasised return to the true (and great) fullness of America, a fullness and certainly greatness which is a historical fantasy.* Obama acted as the universal equivalent for anti-Bush-era politics, supplemented by an excessive enjoyment that saw some (largely African-Americans) crying in the street when he was elected. Conversely, this excess has a dark side. It is interesting to note that in 2009, once it had become apparent that Obama's presidency was not going to restore America – at least in a fantasmatic sense – an equally passionate reaction was experienced on the opposite side of the political spectrum. During town hall debates over health care reform, protestors were often

---

* The greatness of America is a fantasy no matter what our political position. Even if a nation was once somehow empirically the 'greatest' and has now fallen from grace, any attempt to return to that position remains a fantasy.

seen crying hysterically and yelling platitudes such as 'This is not my America!' Furthermore, impassioned attempts have been made to position Obama as an outsider, extenuating his apparent otherness through claims such as the 'birther' movement (which argues, despite all evidence, that Obama was born in Kenya, and which often insinuates that he is also a Muslim) or by labelling Obama a socialist, communist or Nazi. The core of these positions is not their factual basis, but the excess enjoyment attached to Obama as an outsider. If the fantasy of America is failing, then Obama's non-traditional heritage is implicitly positioned as the cause, one attached to an excessive enjoyment.

This positioning is not overt, but rather underlies the conservative critique of his politics, sneaking out at inopportune moments or through pundits who do not understand the 'rules' of ideology. The arch-conservative commentator Glenn Beck, for instance, accused Obama of having a 'deep-seated hatred for white people' and was later moved aside from his Fox News show under the cloud of an exodus of advertisers. This excess exists, but it cannot be explicitly acknowledged lest it disturb the official status of the fantasy.

Fantasy is ultimately a narrative about the deadlock of symbolic castration. Fantasy responds to castration and antagonism, explaining the lack of *jouissance*, teaching the subject to desire through language: because language is inherently intersubjective, so too is fantasy and desire. Fantasy is never singular but, rather, responds to the desires of others – the ultimate question of fantasy is *Che vuoi?* – What does the Other want from me? (Žižek 1989: 118). Indeed, the most powerful logic of fantasy is that the Other is responsible for my *jouissance*. That is, it is the Other who has stolen my *jouissance* – the *jouissance* owed to me exists in the Other (Žižek 1997: 7–44).

For this reason fantasy is always social – fantasy is always ideological fantasy – and politics itself is often a battle to defend fantasmatic enjoyment. Like fantasy, ideology is ultimately about the organisation of enjoyment into manageable and coherent forms, creating sense out of non-sense. By extending the Lacanian understanding of fantasy to ideology, moving from the clinical to social, Žižek turns the classical Leftist-Marxism understanding of ideology on its head.

The major difference between the Marxist and the Žižekian sense of ideology is that for Marx ideology consists of a partial representation (dominated by class power interests) of a total reality – the scientific laws of history are obscured by the ideas of those who own the means of production, as expressed through the superstructural mechanism of ideology. For Žižek, on the other hand (1989: 30–3), ideology entails a totalising attempt to represent partial social relations: against the inherent lack in language, ideological fantasy attempts to manufacture a coherent totality.

This critique leads to two significant consequences for Žižek's theory of Marxist politics. Firstly, knowledge of ideological illusion does not loosen the grip of ideology. Under the Marxist mode, ideology hid class exploitation from the working class. If the proletariat were able to understand their position and develop class consciousness, ideology would no longer hold. This is the symptomatic mode of ideology, whereby the presentation of inconsistency to ideology threatens to dislocate that ideology. By contrast, Žižek argues that ideology operates in a different mode today. Illusion does not lie in knowledge, but rather in belief. Ideology has become cynical: we may know that ideology makes no sense, that politicians are corrupt and that capitalism doesn't work, but we continue to act as if we don't. The everyday case of bottled water is a pertinent example of this cynicism at work. We all know that bottled water is no better than tap water, yet in developed areas we continue to purchase this product at increasing rates, all the while aware of our stupidity.

Nonetheless, the knot of ideological fantasy can still be untied, it just requires more sophisticated mechanisms than historical destiny and symbolic knowledge. As shall be developed in Chapter 6, Žižek's work provides a number of strategic opportunities for manipulating the presence of the Real – that point of dislocation that haunts ideology.

The second distinction between Žižek's Lacanian reading of ideology from its Marxist equivalent signals the major Lacanian critique of Marxian politics: the impossibility of *jouissance*. Žižek argues that Marx's utopian illusion was that universality – full and equivalent exchange – could occur without a symptom (1989: 23). Marx's mistake was to 'assume that the *object* of desire (the unconstrained expansion of productivity) would remain even when it was deprived of the *cause* that propels it (surplus value)' (Žižek 2000c: 21, original emphasis). This critique is exemplified in the homology Lacan identified between the logic of *jouissance* and the logic of surplus value. This homology has been extended by Žižek (2000c: 21) to produce a further critique of Marxian politics, one that has significant consequences for any politics derived from Žižek's work.

What Can Surplus Jouissance *Teach Us about Surplus Value?*

If Marx believed that by removing the contradiction within production – the private appropriation of surplus value – the productivity generated by surplus value would remain and could be utilised for the good of all, Lacan suggested that this is not the lesson of surplus *jouissance*. For Marx, the production of surplus value was the key to capitalist productivity and the expansion of capital through circulation that 'realises' that surplus value, turning it into profit: it is surplus value that is the goal (object) of capital. Although the worker is fully compensated for their labour power, the nature of labour as a commodity is that its use-value produces greater value than its own, a constitutive surplus which is appropriated by the owner of the means of production (Žižek 2006c: 57).

The structural homology between surplus value in capitalism and the surplus *jouissance* of the psyche can tell us much about the operation of capitalism. In both, the surplus is not an excess which is tagged onto the normal state of affairs. Instead, this surplus is the normal state, the cause which drives the excessive balance of the system. As with *objet a*, in surplus value there is produced what appears to be a waste, an unaccounted-for surplus, in the normal operation of the system (Zupančič 2006b: 162). Vitally, this surplus cannot be removed from the system to achieve a more balanced state: the imbalance is constitutive of the system itself. Thus the surplus value produced within capitalism cannot be tamed, nor integrated into a new mode of production. Instead, as Žižek suggests,

> the theoretical task, with immense practical-political consequences, is here: how are we to think the surplus that pertains to human productivity 'as such' outside its appropriation/distortion by the capitalist logic of surplus value as the mobile of social reproduction? (Žižek 2007a: 55)

This is a question, it seems, that Marxism is no longer equipped to handle. If Marxism has been unable to respond to the dilemmas presented by the discursive turn, it fares little better with the materialism of psychoanalysis, politically at least. What can be taken from the psychoanalytic response to the discursive turn is a deeper and more productive analysis of capitalism. If the deterministic essentialism of classical Marxism had proven unfeasible at best, the turn to language and culture removed any sense of economy, history and emancipationist drive that had held Marxist discourse together.

Lacanian psychoanalysis has not been able to restore the latter but through a reading of Marxism it has been able revive ideas of structure, universalism and materiality, albeit not in the classical mode. Although this rehabilitation of Marxism has allowed for a potentially stronger critique of capitalism, which shall be developed further in the following chapters of this book, it has not been able to develop a form of politics that might match the clarity and appeal of communism and the revolutionary subject.

If Žižek rejects the possibility of a Marxist communism through a reading of language and of *jouissance*, we must consider whether psychoanalysis is able to suggest any alternative relationship to *jouissance* and ideology that would both avoid the problems of Marxism and produce a viable alternative to communism. Within this question lies the central dilemma of Žižekian theory. The primary criticism of Žižek is that whilst he evokes a powerful form of ideological critique, his work is without any alternative vision of the future. As a consequence, Žižek's Marxism and critique of capitalism in the name of a renewed radical Leftist politics is nothing but posturing. It is to this critique that we turn in the following section, first considering psychoanalytic conceptions of a politics of *jouissance* before evaluating Žižek's response.

The Politics of Jouissance

Žižek's dismissal of Marxist theory signals *the* political difficulty with his construction of shared social life. Through this chapter I have come to argue that, despite the protests of postmodernists, the turn to language has not made politics entirely contingent. Instead, psychoanalytic theory suggests that social life remains in a general state of fixity based around the materiality of the language and ideology. In particular, the ideological organisation of *jouissance* means that cultural practices and political structures are difficult to dislodge. It is not simply a matter of rearticulating political meanings: at a certain point ideas hit a hard limit which remains remarkably stubborn.

It is the hard limit of *jouissance* that defines the psychoanalytic approach to politics. This approach is defined by an aversion to two factors thus far introduced: the ideological purity of the likes of classical Marxism and current forms of fundamentalism, and the passionless politics of both administrative Leftism and postmodernity. The first modality of politics is essentially an ideological fantasy of a return to *jouissance*, whereas the latter disregards enjoyment altogether.

Contemporary Leftism tends to overemphasise the fluidity of social life, failing to take into account the difficulty of shifting cultural structures infused with *jouissance*. The predominant form of contemporary Leftist politics, the administrative approach of the rights-based groups, ignores the role of enjoyment in political life, implicitly positing that rational argument will change political opinion. By contrast, conservatives, particularly in the United States, have no qualms about exploiting political passions, whether in matters of national identity or in seeking to redefine progressive programmes, such as health care and tax reform, as 'socialist' or 'class warfare'. This redefinition is not simply a matter of reasoned debate but, rather, a manipulation of the *jouissance* that underpins the fantasmatic narratives we hold.

It appears that the politics of the Left are stuck between these twin difficulties in responding to capitalism. Whilst seeking to avoid the ideological *jouissance* of past Leftist movements and contemporary consumerism, the psychoanalytic construction of social life outlined in this chapter suggests that any political intervention that is unable to take into account the role of enjoyment in politics is doomed to failure. It is not enough to call for change in political structures or to reveal the presence of contradiction, as if its human construction makes discourse infinitely malleable; instead, Žižekian theory insists upon confronting the materiality of language and politics.

In insisting on the role of *jouissance* in political discourse, however, it is unclear what kind of politics might emerge from psychoanalysis. Indeed, generating a political mode of psychoanalysis has proved difficult since Freud's initial reservations about the possibilities for the resolution of the contradicting desires of civilised order and human instinct. Arguing that ideological forms of 'the Good life' are nothing but the operation of the superego, Freud suggested that the pathological demands of the superego do not promote progressive forms of politics but, instead, suggest that morality places an excessive demand upon the body. Where Lacan himself worked to produce clinical interventions into these demands, attempting to enable the enjoyment that remains within the body after symbolic castration, subsequent readers of Lacan have attempted to translate this alternative reading of *jouissance* into political modes. Before turning to these readings, primarily embodied by Yannis Stavrakakis, I shall move through the Freudian beginning of political psychoanalysis and the politics of *jouissance*.

The Good as a Bodily Function

Vitally, both Freud and Lacan indexed the desire for an essential kernel of being to a moral demand upon the body. For Freud, essentialism arrived in the guise of the sovereign Good, otherwise known as civilised morality or the Law. Freud, primarily in *Civilization and Its Discontents*, begins with the premise that the body pays a high price for its insertion in civilisation. Consequently, Freud's psychoanalytic treatment sought to reduce the burden on the subject, through psychic realignment rather than political change, allowing it to receive some enjoyment from bodily instinct.

Freud was not so much concerned with the content of the Good as its formal imposition upon the body. For Freud, morality was a libidinally infused ideology that served to bind civilisation together against individual gratification. Like Marx, Freud's description of the structure of society and of the individual foreclosed upon the possibility of an abstract prescription of what should be. Yet Freud did not share Marx's hopeful reading of history and human endeavour. Instead, he asserted that the 'tendency to aggression is an original, autonomous disposition in man and . . . represents the greatest obstacle to civilisation' (2004: 74). As a consequence, Freud's primary political position was that civilisation represses and distorts the contrasting passions of human drive, represented as the battle between the drive towards life (Eros) and towards death (Thanatos).

Civilisation, through government and other forms of societal policing, then becomes a trade-off between individual gratification and collective security. This struggle is mediated by the ideals presented in the symbolic Other. That is, the subject itself needs no 'moral vocabulary' but, instead, is able to borrow from the resources provided by civilisation and ideological fantasy. If the subject, for instance, is thrust into circumstances in which bodily desire conflicts with the explicit requirements of civilised morality, the Other is able to step in to function as this morality. Let us take simple example in which an individual, knowing they 'should' eat healthily, acts on a desire to eat fast food. As I shall soon discuss, under the Lacanian reading of the superego, this transgression is a mode of *jouissance* itself. Conversely, the symbolic Other also provides resources to allow this action, as the subject is able to hold that if this action was so 'bad', then it would have been prohibited by the Other.

To rephrase this vital point, which will have extensive consequences for my subsequent exploration of the political potential of the Real, the Other not only imposes the symbolic law of civilised morality, but acts morally for the subject. In this way, whilst the subject is still interpellated by the interior imposition of symbolic norms, they are able to externalise responsibility to the Other and to the institutions that govern us. Essentially, the Other maintains the image of the good civilisation whilst we are able to go about fulfilling bodily desire. What upsets us most is not so much witnessing others work in their own self-interest – that is wholly accepted, particularly in capitalist society – but in the Other working in this interest.

An interesting example of 'the Other' acting for us comes from the recent rehabilitation of the McDonald's restaurant chain. Coming under increasing attack at the beginning of the twenty-first century as the embodiment of both 'Big Corporations' and the fast food industry, which was posited to be the cause of an increase in levels of Western obesity, McDonald's responded by introducing a new range of 'healthy' alternative foods. Recently, it was announced that McDonald's profits had been restored to pre-crisis levels – not, however, on the basis of increases in sales of these healthy alternatives. Instead, it seems that the existence of these alternatives has allowed the consumer to believe they are engaged in healthier eating practices, without actually having to eat the alternative products themselves. It is as if the Other is eating healthily for us. (Adams 2010).

Whilst the image presented by the struggle between the requirements of collective living and individual desire may suggest that constant external control is required, that libidinal anarchy is only held back by the explicit presence of external authority, Freud noted that this was not the case. Obedience does not require physical vigilance, only the internalisation of the possibility of violence into the body through the symbolic law as the subject takes on the ideological narratives supplied by the symbolic Other. The role of authority is taken on by the internalised expectations of the wider community, symbolised in law and experienced through societal forms of policing (Freud 2004: 78). It is as if, according to Freud, the body is a conquered town which is kept in check by a remaining force (2004: 77).

Freud called this internalised force the superego, that stern guardian whose vigilance never achieves satisfaction. If external authority can be satisfied by obedience, no such satisfaction is available via the superego (Freud 2004: 82). As Freud notes:

The more virtuous a person is, the sterner and more distrustful is his conscience, so that the very people who have attained the highest degree of saintliness are in the end the ones who accuse themselves of being the most sinful. (2004: 80).

For Freud, the superego, as the site of moral conscience or what Lacan would come to call the demand of the Other, was not at all progressive. It does not provide a gentle remainder of our responsibilities towards the Other, instead infusing the subject with a sense of guilt that fuels perversion and violence. Beyond the individual body, Freud was concerned with the collective expression of the repression of drive, suggesting that society puts too strong a demand upon the individual and experiences various negative consequences. Against his unease with moral consciousness in both individual and societal instantiations, Freud's clinical practice sought to establish a 'compromise' between the individual and the moral demands of society.

Alternatively, Lacan's reading of the Freudian superego and the associated demands of the Good holds to no such sense of balance. According to Lacan (1992: 6), the demands of the superego cannot be reduced to the requirements of civilised society, but are rather the effects of symbolic castration, his version of the Oedipus complex.* Lacan did not consider the Oedipus complex to be strictly an effect of the nuclear family structure. Instead, (symbolic) castration is an ahistorical trauma that is expressed in a temporal, historical, manner in terms of both the initial entry of the subject into the symbolic order and the repression and return of this trauma throughout the lifetime of the subject.

It is this kind of analysis that has led to psychoanalysis being accused of a Eurocentric ignorance of its own non-historical universalism, an accusation which must be wholly rejected as a misreading of the impetus of psychoanalysis. The trauma caused by the Oedipus complex is certainly ahistorical in itself, but it must be stressed that the complex itself does not occur (Lacan 1992: 308). The Oedipus complex (taken as symbolic castration and the subject's loss of *jouissance* upon their forced insertion into language) does not have a presence in itself – it cannot be the subject of positivist research – but, rather, is an absent trauma to which history (and subjectivity)

---

* If Freud referred to the Oedipal myth to explain the prohibition against incest, symbolic castration transfers this prohibition to *jouissance*.

is a response. Certainly the mechanism through which this collective dynamic is expressed may have altered – along with our methods of understanding it – but we can only endorse Freud's identification of this fundamental dialectic of the human condition.

The superego is ultimately a subjective reaction to the trauma of castration. In Lacan's rereading of Freud, the psychoanalytic understanding of morality and the superego has been extended, such that Lacan considered that the superego is not only the subject's 'moral' conscience but, more productively, an unconscious site of enjoyment. In the Lacanian conception, the superego is the obscene supplement to the symbolic law. Here Lacan's reference to the law is not limited to legislation but refers to the structures of civil society, whether moral norms or governmental structures. The symbolic law could otherwise be known as the 'Good', the moral standards of behaviour constructed and policed within society in order to make it coherent to itself. I have previously considered the symbolic order to be structured around empty signifiers which cohere the abstract (universal) imaginary field: ideological fantasy moving the symbolic law towards a transcendental sense of the Good. In this sense, Lacan ultimately came to conceive of the superego as the guilt that acts as a form of surplus *jouissance* supplementing the inadequacies of this order.

Nonetheless, as Žižek (2008: 89) suggests, for Lacan the superego 'has nothing to do with moral conscience as far as its most obligatory demands are concerned'. Instead, the superego demand is the point of ethical betrayal, urging the subject to ignore the cause of their desire and instead to suture the symbolic law. This demand is not a matter of the moral conscience filling out ambiguity in the law but, rather, an 'obscene' imperative to enjoy through the symbolic order. For this reason, Žižek comes to suggest that the law that is the object of psychoanalysis is the superego that emerges at the point of failure of that law (1994: 54). The superego is not the official ideology but, rather, the underlying relations of enjoyment which hold it in place. As such, this enjoyment is quite distinct from the order to which it is attached. The *jouissance* that stems from the superego – an enjoyment I have previously labelled J_2 – comes by way of a supplement to the 'official' order, such as the accusations against Obama noted earlier.

As a further illustration, if the explicit moral ideology of a community is anti-racist, both in its explicit laws and socially enforced norms – such that 'you are just a dirty racist' is a legitimate rebuke

– then the superego supplements this position as a transgressive undercurrent of racist jokes and unacknowledged racial boundaries. Indeed, Žižek (1994: 57) goes on to suggest that it is this undercurrent that provides the shared basis for community identification.

Colonel Kurtz in Francis Ford Coppola's *Apocalypse Now* exemplifies the superego supplement to an official ideology. Kurtz, a soldier in the elite unit, snaps after witnessing an act of brutality and begins operating independently of the army with a 'savagery' of which they disapprove. US Army generals state that he is 'clearly insane', whereas Kurtz explains to Willard, the agent sent to 'eliminate' him, that he now conceives of the act of brutality as genius, displaying the truth of warfare. The problem with Kurtz is that he displayed the underlying structure of army life too explicitly. In contrast to the official army doctrine of clean and fair war, Kurtz had come to see with 'clarity' the underlying truth of warfare. Where he was insane and had to be eliminated with 'extreme prejudice' was in demonstrating this point too literally.*

For Žižek, the enjoyment that stems from the superego provides the necessary support for the failure of the symbolic order. Conversely, this enjoyment cannot be displayed too openly like Kurtz did or Glenn Beck has, lest it disturb the law. Indeed, this kind of enjoyment can only really function as a transgression of the law itself – without the law it becomes psychotic. As has been noted previously, the failure of *jouissance* before the letter leads to attempts to find other forms that would provide a suture. Superego enjoyment is one of those forms – in attempting to fill out the symbolic order, the superego allows the subject an alternative sense of enjoyment. This enjoyment, however, is never enough, meaning that the more the subject experiences second-order *jouissance*, the more they require.

---

* Kurtz also illustrates the manner in which the trauma of the Real dislocates the subject and offers the possibility of radical change, when he recalls the horrific incident and its effect upon him: 'We went into a camp to inoculate some children. We left the camp after we had inoculated the children for polio, and this old man came running after us and he was crying. He couldn't see. We went back there, and they had come and hacked off every inoculated arm. There they were in a pile. A pile of little arms. And I remember . . . I . . . I . . . I cried, I wept like some grandmother. I wanted to tear my teeth out; I didn't know what I wanted to do! And I want to remember it. I never want to forget it . . . I never want to forget. And then I realised . . . like I was shot . . . like I was shot with a diamond . . . a diamond bullet right through my forehead. And I thought, my God . . . the genius of that! The genius! The will to do that! Perfect, genuine, complete, crystalline, pure.'

Indeed, this is the very structure of desire, as the inconsistencies within the symbolic law create desire in itself. Moreover – and here Lacanian theory links back to the morality of the Freudian superego – these failures lead to a sense of guilt within the subject.

Lacan suggests that the guilt imposed on the subject by the superego when the subject attempts to fulfil their primal loss is a secondary guilt. The true guilt of the subject occurs at the point of symbolic castration and the (forced) choice into language. That the superego presses more guilt upon the subject the more they attempt to suture this wound suggests that guilt is indeed misplaced.*

For this reason, psychoanalysis, in both its Freudian and its Lacanian variations, is strictly opposed to any sense of morality in an abstract sense. Freud did argue that the relaxation of moral prohibitions would be desirable for the health of the subject, but he did not believe that any sense of the Good could be invoked which would avoid the displacement of the superego. He postulated that guilt was the biggest problem facing civilised humanity: 'The price we pay for cultural progress is a loss of happiness, arising from a heightened sense of guilt'(Freud 2004: 91). Psychoanalytic practice refuses to add to this sense of guilt, instead seeking to reduce the burden felt by the subject in favour of an acceptance of that level of enjoyment still available to the subject.

In this context, psychoanalytic theory does not seek to postulate an alternative sense of the Good, arguing that any form is just another modality of *jouissance*. Nonetheless, those involved in attempting to articulate a psychoanalytic politics have certainly not withdrawn from this horizon. Instead, two themes have emerged. The first holds to the hope that an alternative relationship between ideology and enjoyment can be developed, one that avoids the sins produced under contemporary modes of fantasy and desire. The other side rejects this possibility, suggesting that psychoanalysis can only operate as a critique of enjoyment and ideology. If the former might be labelled the politics of *jouissance*, this alternative could be better considered the politics of the Real. We shall turn first to the former position, considering Yannis Stavrakakis's work in attempting to develop a politics

---

* Indeed, this is an argument not far from Freud's own reading. In his conclusion to *Civilization and Its Discontents*, Freud argued that not only may a variety of neurotic symptoms develop from the repression of drive but a sense of guilt may actually develop not from disobedience to the law but, rather, the prevention of satisfaction of the drives (Freud 2004: 96–7).

of *jouissance*, before examining the contours and consequences of the Lacanian Real in the following chapter.

Politics beyond Fantasy?

Psychoanalysis has largely been used as a reference point or a supplement to political ideology, rather than a direct contributor. Although psychoanalysis did enjoy a brief exposure as a hedonistic ideology in the latter half of the twentieth century – Herbert Marcuse's *Eros and Civilization* (1956), along with Gilles Deleuze and Félix Guattari's critical psychoanalytic study, *Anti-Oedipus* (1977), being the prime examples – it was Laclau's radical democracy that inspired the hegemonic reading of psychoanalytic politics.

Laclau, and most recently Stavrakakis, have drawn a direct parallel between the logic of democracy and that of psychoanalysis. Stavrakakis has taken this further, suggesting that Lacan's notion of feminine sexuation provides a form of *jouissance* or passionate attachment that mirrors the structure of radical democracy. Stavrakakis has sought to continue the radical democratic tradition, becoming the flag-bearer for the political institutionalisation of Lacanian psychoanalysis through the production of two influential texts; *Lacan and the Political* (1999) and *The Lacanian Left* (2007). The earlier text begins with the assertion that contemporary politics is a response to the decline in the symbolic efficiency of the big Other. Today, Stavrakakis contends, politics is split between various attempts to restore the utopian fantasmatic dimension of the Other and what he labels a 'politics of *aporia*'. The latter is an impotent form of politics without a motivating force, unwilling to reinstate the Other but unsure how to proceed (Stavrakakis 1999: 99).

In response, Stavrakakis asserts that the Left cannot resort to a 'politics of reoccupation' characterised by the fantasmatic hold of utopianism. Lacanian theory teaches that these fantasmatic attempts to restore the big Other can only be instituted upon the basis of the exclusion of an element that is then posited as the enemy: that which is preventing the (impossible) realisation of Utopia (Stavrakakis 1999: 107). The question, according to Stavrakakis, is how the Left can maintain democratic practice whilst maintaining affective political engagement.

Here Stavrakakis's work is a response to the kind of pessimism around psychoanalysis displayed by the likes of Sean Homer. According to Homer (1996: 109), psychoanalytic politics are impotent because they do not positively enter into the ideology of the Other. He suggests that although psychoanalysis may make for good theory, it does not allow for an effective mode of politics. If Lacan insisted that the big Other must be resisted, there are plenty of (ultimately more powerful) ideological positions willing to take up this space.

In reply, Stavrakakis argues that Homer assumes that fantasy and the status of the big Other are entirely universal. While acknowledging the importance of the question 'How can we have passion in politics without the Holocaust?' (Stavrakakis 1999: 111), Stavrakakis supports the 'possibility of a post-fantasmatic or less fantasmatic politics' that rejects the necessity of restoring the Other whilst engaging in affective politics (1999: 120). This form of politics is made possible by an application of a Lacanian approach that rejects the emphasis upon unity and harmony that has characterised liberal democracy in favour of a collective 'traversal of the fantasy of utopia' (Stavrakakis 1999: 122–7).

In this form of (radical) democracy, Lacanian ethics is utilised to perform an 'encircling of the Real' (Stavrakakis 1999: 130) best achieved by an identification with the *sinthome* – defined by Stavrakakis as that which must be excluded in order to constitute a universal totality – in order to make visible the point of lack which would otherwise be excluded. This 'ethics of the Real', which he attributes to Žižek (Stavrakakis 1999), needs to be institutionalised into the democratic order, allowing for a form of society in which democracy does not have an ontic presence, yet is able to produce a better and more free society (Stavrakakis 1999: 140). Nevertheless, in this first text Stavrakakis is unable to answer his two primary questions: How is a form of (democratic) enjoyment possible that does not require exclusion? And, how can this form of democracy be instituted?

At this stage in his theoretical development, Stavrakakis's work reads very much like Žižek's early texts (much of the conclusion to *Lacan and the Political* is attributed to Žižek). Nonetheless, as we shall see from our latter discussion of the politics of his work, Žižek does not believe that non-exclusive political structures can exist. It is this kind of positioning which leads the likes of Sharpe (2004: 248) to suggest that Žižek's demand to identify with the abject leads only to permanent critique. As this is precisely the limitation that Stavrakakis is seeking to avoid, it is almost in response to Žižek, as well as the continual problem of the feasibility of the democratic project, that *The Lacanian Left* begins.

In seeking to create a 'democratic ethos of the political' (2007: 254), for Stavrakakis, democracy is *the* political horizon, both in the sense that in its very structure it replicates the Lacanian rejection of the big Other, and because it allows for a greater degree of human freedom than any other political system. Furthermore, Laclau's radical democracy provides the ultimate democratic ethos because it allows for conflict and an acknowledgement of the lack in the Other: for Stavrakakis, it is the natural translation of Lacanian theory into politics. If the institutions of democracy – the empty place of power, the respect for conflicting conceptions of the polis – recreate the lack in the Other, what is required is a subjective ethos of democratic participation, one that celebrates lack and the unifying acceptance of disharmony (Stavrakakis 2007: 257). This is a democracy founded on an ethical acknowledgement of self-institution, one that comes to recognise its own lack of foundations.

Stavrakakis seeks, particularly in *The Lacanian Left*, to go beyond the institutionalisation of lack in favour of a democratic ethics of enjoyment. Rejecting Žižek's apparent conflation of radical democracy with the dry formalism of Habermas's deliberative democracy (a comparison Stavrakakis describes as 'astonishing' (2007: 277)), Stavrakakis seeks to find 'another *jouissance*, an ethos beyond the politics of fantasy . . . an *enjoyable democratic ethics of the political*' (2007: 268–9, original emphasis). This democratic enjoyment is the partial, or feminine, enjoyment which occurs after the subject has 'traversed the fantasy'.

This enjoyment strays away from the conventional notion of full *jouissance* that characterises Stavrakakis's reading of utopia. Instead, the other *jouissance* to which Stavrakakis refers is a feminine enjoyment available to the subject after they have traversed the fantasy. By traversing the fantasy, Stavrakakis contends that the democratic subject is able to come to terms with the antagonistic demands of the Other, an acceptance required for the restoration of the democratic project. If the goal of clinical analysis is for the analysand to acknowledge that the Other does not exist (and thus stop relying upon it for enjoyment), Stavrakakis's conception of a democratic ethic requires the same knowledge both in the subject and in the (democratic) structural practice which performs this knowledge for the subject.

Ultimately, for Stavrakakis, democratic enjoyment is an enjoyment of lack and its dialectical excess. Stavrakakis contends that this enjoyment can occur without the stabilising effects of the exception, conceived here as the Lacanian *objet a*, stating:

> The central task in psychoanalysis – and politics – is to detach the *objet a* from the signifier of lack in the Other to detach (anti-democratic and post-democratic) fantasy from the democratic institutions of lack, making possible the access to a partial enjoyment beyond fantasy. (2007: 280)

Here, Stavrakakis is attempting to follow Bruce Fink's argument in *Lacan to the Letter* (Fink 2004: 161), a rereading of Lacan's *Ecrits*. Stavrakakis (2007: 279) refers to Fink when he states: 'Only the sacrifice of the fantasmatic *objet petit a* can make this other *jouissance* attainable.' (Lacan used the terms '*objet a*' and '*objet petit a*' interchangeably.) The key to this statement rests upon the meaning of 'the fantasmatic *objet petit a*'. Two distinct readings remain open. Stavrakakis could be suggesting that *objet a* is a fantasmatic object; when one lets go of fantasy, *objet a*, as the object of desire, is no longer required. Alternatively, Stavrakakis could be referring to the fantasmatic, rather than Real, aspects of *objet a*, which allows for a more positive interpretation of Stavrakakis's conception.

The former reading of the status of *objet a* has been scornfully rebuked by Žižek. Rejecting the suggestion that society can operate without *objet a*, Žižek demands that a distinction be made between the statuses of *objet a* in desire and in drive – a distinction between *objet a* as the cause of desire and the object of desire (Žižek 2008: 327). Stavrakakis may be applauded in seeking to remove the illusionary utopian desire from politics, but one cannot remove the excesses of *objet a* altogether. Instead, even in the trans-fantasmatic realm of drive, *objet a* still dominates subjectivity. It is just that for Lacan the movement from desire to drive is a movement from the object as loss (and thus a desire to recapture it) to loss as an object itself.

Additionally, Žižek contends that a traversal of 'the fantasy' does not leave the subject without fantasy, as Stavrakakis advocates. By traversing the fantasy, the clinical subject alters their relationship to *objet a*. Both the object and the fundamental fantasy remain but the subject now identifies itself, rather than the object, as the cause of that fantasy (Žižek 1989: 65). In this sense *objet a* continues to exist but now only as a materialisation of the lack with which the subject must now identify. The identification with lack corresponds to an identification with the symptom and the realisation that it is only the symptom that gives any sense of consistency to the subject (Žižek 1989: 75).

Conversely, traversing the fantasy is not the ultimate road to *jouissance*. In traversing the fantasy, the subject does not obtain a 'post-fantasmatic' grasp of reality in which naked reality (and *jouissance*) itself appears. Then subject may have journeyed across the frontiers of their fantasmatic horizons but there is no escape from fantasy, only a key to its cause. The subject not only remains in the grips of *objet a* but is also more taken by the fantasy than ever.

Thus, to traverse the fantasy is not to confront reality and its antagonisms directly, as Stavrakakis's post-fantasmatic democratic ethos suggests. Rather, traversing the fantasy involves coming to terms with the co-ordinates of fantasy itself, to be caught up in it more than ever and to fully identify with one's subjective position in relation to it (Žižek 2008: 324–31). Fantasy is, so to speak, flattened: it exists but it no longer serves as a defence against the symptom. Losing the 'depth' that allowed the subject to enjoy the symptom, fantasy becomes two dimensional, no longer mediating against the exclusions which constituted its former boundaries.

Moreover, Stavrakakis seems to have been seduced by the power of the feminine. The feminine appears to have a strange mysterious quality within Lacan's work, largely because it provides an alternative to the masculine, despite Lacan providing limited detail on its potential shape. Indeed, as Žižek (1994: 151) notes, Lacan appears to hint that he will say more about the feminine when he ends *The Subversion of the Subject and the Dialectic of Desire* with 'I won't go any further here' (Lacan 2006: 700), suggesting there is more that can be said. However, he does not in fact extend further on the feminine, which has left the feminine with a mysterious alternative status, suggesting that an alternative form of subjectivity is available – one that would avoid the pitfalls of contemporary subjectivity and structure.

This conception of the feminine is, however, a major misreading of Lacan. For Lacan the feminine was indeed mysterious but only because of its very impossibility. If the feminine has an existence, it is as a supplement to the masculine enjoyment of the phallus (Levy-Stokes 2001: 105). The feminine is a structural clinical possibility – the subject can experience feminine *jouissance* but not without the phallus – but not an ideological one in any singular sense. This 'Other' *jouissance* is, as Fink (1995: 122) states, 'fundamentally incommensurate, unquantifiable, disproportionate, and indecent to "polite society"'. One cannot develop a political discourse of the feminine *jouissance* – this would be impossible in both the Lacanian and everyday sense of the term – and even if it was possible, there is nothing to suggest that this kind of enjoyment would have anything to say about democracy.

Following this critique, Žižek states that not only is his work a misreading of Lacan but 'Stavrakakis' political vision is vacuous' (2008: 331). Contending that Stavrakakis remains a 'Freudo-radical democrat' seeking to supplement a political theory with an ethics of enjoyment rather than developing a politics directly from Lacanian theory, Žižek argues that we should not be looking for a democratic ethos of enjoyment but, instead, considering why there is no passion invested in our current forms of democracy.

Žižek does not reject democracy outright – it is not that democracy is without value – but, rather, suggests that democracy is not the ultimate political horizon and holds no emancipationist potential at this stage of history. As Žižek states, radical democracy 'comes all too close to merely "radicalizing" this liberal democratic imaginary, while remaining within its horizon' (2000d: 325). Under capitalism, democracy is nothing more than an empty political supplement to capital: politics under capitalism is strictly post-politics, and it is on this point that Stavrakakis and Žižek are finally in agreement.

Nonetheless, Stavrakakis's position may still be in some degree compatible with Žižek's, if we take the alternative reading of his conception of *objet a*. Clearly, for Lacan *objet a* exists beyond fantasy. It is not only the object of desire but the cause of desire. If Stavrakakis comes to this reading – a fairly fundamental conception of Lacanian psychoanalysis – it could be that by 'the fantasmatic *objet a*', Stavrakakis has meant the fantasmatic element of *objet a*, not *objet a* as cause or a remainder of the Real. This is perhaps a little generous. Nonetheless, we must proceed from this point, taking Stavrakakis at his best. If we propose what Žižek deems to be the correct reading of the Lacanian *objet a*, does Stavrakakis's theory of radical democracy still hold?

In response this question, Žižek argues that Lacan's ethics of psychoanalysis simply cannot be institutionalised in any fashion: psychoanalysis cannot become an ideological form of politics, nor does it suggest any mode of political justice. What must be taken from Lacan's work is not so much the content of his analysis but, rather, the form of his dialectical approach. Here, the focus is exposing that upon which being rests yet cannot be acknowledged. It is this formal process of analysis – finding the point of exclusion, symptoms or cause of desire, which dissolve through analysis – that can be transposed across contexts and beyond the limits of clinical practice.

Žižek's interpretation of Lacanian psychoanalysis is certainly a valuable philosophical contribution to an understanding of our shared social life. Against the contingency of language yet within the boundaries of the discursive turn, Žižek reasserts the material solidity of ideology whilst rejecting any utopian ambitions in the name of *jouissance*. As I shall expound in the work that follows, this theory is particularly valuable in explaining the seductive functioning of capitalism, notably in relation to desire, consumerism and *objet a*.

Conversely, it is not immediately clear why, in rejecting Marxian notions of communism, as well as ideological forms of politics based upon the Good or democracy, Žižek's politics are such a valuable response to global capitalism. In order to understand this value, I will now turn to the other side of psychoanalysis, developing Žižek's theory of the Real and considering the practice of Lacanian ethics, before extending these conclusions to produce a critique of capitalism and a Žižekian reading of political strategy in the chapters that follow.

4

Universality and the Trauma of the Real

Thus far I have presented social life as a resilient matrix of ideological enjoyment. If the discursive turn had emphasised the death of objectivity and the fluidity of shared social life, the psychoanalytic rejoinder has been the materiality of language and the fixity of being. The fundamental premise of psychoanalysis, however, is that change can, and does, occur. More than this, particularly in its Lacanian mode, psychoanalytic theory is founded on the notion that change can potentially occur on a radical scale in a way that could not possibly be understood within the previous order.

It is here that the value of Žižekian theory lies. If I have hitherto rejected the desirability of any institutional or ideological mode of politics inspired by Lacanian psychoanalysis, this does not mean that psychoanalysis is divorced from the political. Instead, Žižekian theory offers a reading of the potential instability that exists within any ideological foundation. Moreover, Žižek's conception of this volatility, one that relies upon the trauma of the Real and the operation of exclusion and universality, can be utilised as a critique of capitalism. Based upon the kind of dialectical operation on which the Lacanian ethics of psychoanalysis were formulated, this critique does not identify the content of an alternative future but, rather, exposes the points of instability that can generate this future.

Although the range of Lacan's clinical interventions did not extend beyond the individual, Žižek's interpretation of this approach has extended his analysis to the political sphere. Here, whilst Žižekian theory constructs a materialist reading of social life as anchored by the ideological organisation of *jouissance*, the possibility still exists for radical change that breaks up this matrix of fantasmatic enjoyment. The Lacanian basis for radical change lies in the Real, the third register of the Lacanian triad that also includes the imaginary and symbolic.

Lacan's early work largely focused upon the imaginary and the mirror phase of development before moving on to focus upon the intricacy of the symbolic order. It was only the late Lacan that began to consider the dark complexities of the Real. It is, however, upon this period of Lacan's work that Žižekian theory is based: for most of Žižek's readers, the late Lacan *is* Lacan.

By placing the Real at the centre of analysis, Žižekian theory is primarily focused on the possibilities for change through the trauma and anxiety imposed by the presence of the Real. As we shall see, however, the politics associated with the Real are complex and controversial. Because the Real cannot be directly represented, and is instead felt only in its effects, these politics are not directly determined but instead involve an interpretation of concrete circumstances.

Initially, this chapter presents the other side of psychoanalysis to that offered in Chapter 3. If I had suggested that postmodernity and the likes of Ernesto Laclau's discourse theory gave too much power to the fluidity and contingency of language, such that life was infinitely malleable, the Žižekian response emphasised the materiality and 'stuckness' of politics. As a consequence, whilst there is an ebb and flow to political life as ideological horizons move around, changing chains of nodal points, this fluidity only masks the essential stability of ideological fantasy. Indeed, what appear as decisive moments of change often act to preserve the status quo and our most intense moments of activity often work in service of the system itself.

The trauma and anxiety of the Real provide a radical rejoinder to the stability of this dynamic. To understand the Real and the political possibilities that stem from it, in this chapter I will begin by developing a Lacanian account of the Real, making a vital distinction between its different modalities. This understanding will be extended through a Žižekian/Hegelian reading of universality that seeks to integrate the operation of concrete universality, exceptionality and the Real.

Concrete universality occurs at the split between that which is excluded from the abstract universal horizon or the hegemonic ideological fantasy that structures the political terrain, and this horizon itself. If Laclau emphasised the political salience of the empty place of political equivalency, for Žižek the question is what must be excluded to establish this hegemonic terrain. This split signifies the moment of truth within any given discourse: that point which is truly universal. Vitally for the debate in this chapter and the book as a whole, this split within the universal acts as a point of trauma or disruption within ideology: the Real. In order to remain coherent, ideology must keep at a distance that which it excludes, primarily through the reproduction of this exclusion in a more palatable form.

Thus, any mode of politics seeking to break from the grip of an ideo-logical system must tarry with the Real – an engagement that defines the Žižekian response to capitalism. Before turning to this position, I will first consider Žižek's construction of the Real.

Lacking the Real

The Real is one of the three Lacanian registers – the other two being the symbolic and the imaginary – which come together as rings in a Borromean knot. Within Lacan's lifetime, it was the symbolic and the imaginary that dominated Lacanian theory: the imaginary was informed through the 'Mirror stage' of the early Lacan and the sym-bolic through Lacan's focus on semiotics, the signifier and the uncon-scious. The Real came to the fore only in Lacan's latter work and has been increasingly prevalent in readings of Lacan inspired by Žižek.

The Real can be most broadly defined as both that which resists symbolisation and the very distorting effect which prevents access to that resistance: both the presence of lack and that excess provoked by attempts to ameliorate the effects of absence. The Real cannot be understood outside language, yet exists only as the point at which language itself fails. The Real is, in essence, that point which reveals the impossibility of language ever existing as an objective entity.

If I have thus far presented language as an incomplete, negative substance within which meaning is chased from signifier to signifier, this constitution also drives itself towards unity and coherence. The lesson of symbolic castration and *jouissance* is that whilst the process of human being is one of seeking lost unity and grasping sense from non-sense, it is also one of the death drive that means that this desperate ambition is always defined by an excess that never seems enough.

Excess, however, is only one side of the story of symbolic castra-tion and the madhouse of language. The other half of this dialectic is the Real, trauma and anxiety. Opening up to the points at which language fails is a traumatic experience: these points also constitute the failure of ideology and of meaning. Where *jouissance* massages the flow of meaning and understanding as we chase desire from one element to the next, the appearance of the Real has us searching for the next point to hang on to as the supportive illusions of fantasy are momentarily punctuated. The flows of *jouissance* are akin to surfing a wave: one is never in control but not yet out of control, going with the flow yet moving within it. Being struck by the Real is more like being cast amongst cliff-side rocks: at once drowning and being battered, our only wish is to get a grip on a solid rock, no matter how jagged. We see this process in the after-effects of a trauma or disaster where the focus is on finding meaning in the situation, of reconstituting the common sense. Those who cannot, whose universe has been so shifted that 'nothing makes sense', are those that suffer the most.

The Real is not, however, a linear or singular concept. Instead, according to Terry Eagleton (2009: 141), the Real is 'an enigmatic concept, as well as . . . an analogous one, working at several different levels simultaneously'. It is because of this simultaneous operation – one more akin to music than to science* – that the Real is such a difficult term to grasp. The Real does not persist in and of itself: the effect of the Real plays out within a variety of different discursive positions such that one can only speak of the Real in the singular in terms of an abstract form.

In regard to its instantiation in language, we can identify a variety of modalities of the Real. Indeed, this signals the operation of the Real – a singular impossibility which produces a plurality of responses. We can refer to it in terms of desire or drive, in the operation of fantasy and *objet a*, or in the antagonistic points of exclusion which sustain a discourse. Indeed, as I shall discuss in detail in Chapter 5, Žižek suggests that the operation of global capitalism can be considered a modality of the (symbolic) Real.

Žižek introduces this enlarged notion of the Real, involving a symbolic Real, in the foreword to the second edition of *For They Know Not What They Do* (Žižek 2002: xi–xii). This distinction came as a response to Žižek's own criticism of his first book, *The Sublime Object of Ideology* (1989), against which he claims he endorsed a 'quasi-transcendental reading of Lacan' and the Real. That is, Žižek argues that his reading of Lacan implicitly constructed the Real as a point of failure with the consequence that ethics involves the acceptance of failure and finitude. Instead, Žižek insists upon the Real as not only symbolic failure but as a positive point of excess, enabled within the symbolic and imaginary realms, such that the Lacanian triad of 'Real–Imaginary–Symbolic' is reproduced within itself. That is, we can have an imaginary form of the Real as well as a symbolic form of the imaginary.

Certainly the Real is not reality in itself, some pure unadulterated access to materiality or biology that shines through where language

* I am indebted to Wendy Bolitho for this point.

fails. This is the Real of those with absolute faith in the scientific method who believe that underneath their increasingly complex methods of measurement lie solid and material truths called the laws of nature. That may be so, but the key insight from the discursive turn is that none of this is meaningful to humanity until it is constructed within language: the subject does not have access to the material except through language. That we have to resort to a scientific *method* signals the linguistic nature of materiality. Even the most material of reactions – say, unwittingly placing one's hand upon a hot stove and crying out in pain – is one of language. The material reaction may be the initial movement, a burning that would not vary from hamster to human, but it is only meaningful through language. Language does not change the occurrence of the event, but it is only through language that the event can be said to occur at all.

What is important to the Lacanian is not this original material reaction but, rather, how our understanding of this reaction in the reality created by language is punctuated by failure, which we have identified as the Real. We then have three ontological layers. There is what might be known as the pre-ontology of materiality, where events and reactions occur unknown to humanity even though they may affect humanity – radiation emitted by communication towers might be an example here. Then there is the ontic level of reality and the realm of appearance created in language and cohered by *jouissance*. This level is punctuated with the third level of ontology, the Real, a non-ontic black hole in the field of representation.

Similarly, and akin to his construction of *jouissance*, Bruce Fink suggests the Real can be considered as two modalities, the Real 'before the letter' (R_1) and the Real that is 'after the letter' (R_2). R_1 is the signifier given to that beyond language, an illusionary time and space generated by signification itself such that R_1 appears to be without absence. It is only R_2 that cuts up R_1 through the generation of 'reality' in the symbolic order. These cuts occur because the symbolic realm cannot fully grasp what is beyond its limits, creating a gap between reality and the Real. In essence R_1 exists only as an absence but this absence is given a name and thus an existence; without the operation of naming in the symbolic, R_1 would only be felt as an absence: that of pure materiality (Fink 1995: 24–5). The Real before the letter is thus an original trauma, the fantasmatic point of symbolic castration that turns the pleasures of animal into the torturous being of man. It is a phenomenon best described by Eagleton (2009: 143–4) when he states:

We can grasp this alien phenomenon only by constructing it backwards, so to speak, from its effects – from how it acts as a drag on our discourse, as astronomers can sometimes identify a celestial body only because of its warping effect on the space around it . . . This void is the precondition for the order's effective functioning but can never fully be represented there.

Conversely, because absence can be felt only through the failure of presence, the Real cannot simply be considered external to symbolisation in the form of either R_1 or R_2. The Real is not just what is excluded from the symbolic but, rather, it has what Lacan termed an 'extimate' relationship with the symbolic order, being both within and outside the symbolic at the same time. Thus, although the Real resists symbolisation, it is not alien to the symbolic.

The gap between reality and the Real is strictly internal to reality – there is no reality without the Real. This is the case for R_1 because it establishes the very limits of symbolisation but also for R_2. R_2 operates as the factor that distorts symbolisation from within, it is the disavowed 'X' that warps symbolisation in a manner in which we cannot be aware at the time of 'understanding'. Thus, the Real is not simply a time or space before/outside language (this would be R_1), it is also the cuts within the symbolic order – that which cannot be symbolised from within a certain ideological constellation. What may be Real to me may not be to you; what is unsymbolisable within one matrix is not within another. Debate over the possible absence of a transcendental God may have a Real effect on a pious churchgoer – so that they feel anxious and destabilised by such a thought, often reacting defensively – yet be a mundane signification for an atheist. This point has significant consequences for the practice of psychoanalytic politics.

The Real between Discourses

The discursive field exists as chains of differentially connected signifiers such that the meaning of one is established by reference to another, establishing a logical connection in which signifiers form combinations that make sense only by reference to the remainder of the ideological chain. In this conception, the discursive system exists as overlapping chains that often clash at antagonistic points at which meaning is disputed. This is not to suggest that discursive chains are always incommensurable but, rather, that terms cannot be simply transposed whilst maintaining the same meaning: certain chains of

reasoning make sense only by reference to the exigencies of the signifying chain. In this sense the Real is still, as Lacan (2006: 388) stated,
the 'domain of whatever subsists outside symbolisation', yet parts of
this domain can be symbolised in an alternative discourse and remain
absent in another.

An example of this kind of parallel linguistic logic can be illustrated in the biological world. In January 2010, the American physi-
cist Paul Davies argued that alien life may have co-existed with what
has become human life since the beginning of the latter (Associated
Press, 2010). Davies suggested that there was no necessary reason
for all life on Earth to have evolved from a single origin. Instead,
an 'alien' form of life could have developed concurrently but was
unable to evolve past a certain point. Thus alien life might well exist,
Davies argued, amongst currently unexplored forms of bacteria. In
this case, multiple chains of life might be present on the planet, each
with its own biological logic that prevents a connection between
them. Moreover, each chain would have different logical impossibilities such that what is impossible within one form of life, say sexual
reproduction, is part of the structure of another.

Likewise, language is always cohered in chains and patterns, filled
with clichés and dominated by metaphors that produce a fantasmatic
unity of understanding between speakers: one of the most obvious
bonding points of a community or culture is their shared construction of language. Because these chains overlap, there are constant
points of conjecture – say, over the meaning of freedom across the
political spectrum or between cultures – antagonistic points that
Fink would label R_2. Political discourse within the United Kingdom
and United States, for instance, whilst containing many of the same
terms within the same language, remains subtly distinct. As a result,
terms cannot simply be transposed – 'freedom' or 'fairness' do not
mean the same thing across both discourses – because the chains of
meaning that fill each signifier are not the same. Moreover, the exclusions and points of impossibility within each discursive environment
are subtly different. What might be 'impossible' to say within the
United States – perhaps a presidential candidate admitting that he
or she does not believe in God – might not even register in a British
general election campaign.*

We must be careful here not to get caught up in the abstrac-

* A reverse example might be a rejection of the monarchy, which remains politically
impossible within the United Kingdom.

tion necessary to make this point. It is not as if discourses are self-contained branches, never merging into each other and easily identified, like strands in a bowl of spaghetti. The point, however, remains: language is not infinitely differential but, rather, is cohered into certain patterns through ideology via the imaginary – patterns which allow for some conceptual chains but not others. Thus, whilst the Real as R_1 is operational as the original trauma which produces discourse itself, within individual discourses unique patterns and impossibilities emerge which we have identified as a different modality of the Real – R_2.* Indeed, Lacan suggests a similar logic in his concept of the four discourses – that of the hysteric, the master, the university and the analyst – each of which identifies a different logic of intersubjectivity.

Žižek suggests a comparable operation to the parallel-universe approach to discourse analysis in his notion of the 'parallax view' – the apparent displacement of an object caused by a shift in the position of the observer. For Žižek, the philosophical twist is that

> the observed difference is not simply 'subjective', due to the fact that the same object which exists 'out there' is seen from two different stances, or points of view. It is rather that, as Hegel would have put it, subject and object are inherently 'mediated', so that an epistemological shift in the subject's point of view always reflects an 'ontological' shift in the object itself. (Žižek 2006b: 17)

The parallax view then produces a 'multiplicity of symbolic perspectives' (Žižek 2006b: 18) around an 'unfathomable X' – a pure difference that is an object in and of itself. A parallax produces what Kant called a 'transcendental illusion', the illusion that there exists a point of mediation between two discourses. This mediatory point exists only as the presence of absence, the Real. Vitally, however, the Real becomes an object itself – the parallax Real. This modality of the Real is the gap which occurs in the parallax shift from one perspective to another. This gap might exist, for instance, between an American conservative politician and a Marxist in discussion over freedom: the chains of meaning that each is using to fill the signifier 'freedom' are entirely incommensurable. Such a disjuncture produces the effect of the Real. Again, the Real here is both that point to which access is not possible and the obstacle itself which prevents

---

* Fink (1995: 16–19), following a model given by Lacan, gives an excellent example of this logic in the coding of a coin-toss game.

this access (Žižek 2006b: 26). Žižek goes on to state that the parallax Real brings with it a revision of the standard Lacanian notion of the Real as that which always returns to its place (Lacan 2006: 17). Rather, the parallax accounts for the multiple appearances of the Real itself – the fact that the operation of the Real can occur at entirely different points within discursive chains because each chain reacts differently to its inherent failure.

The parallax Real is then itself a second-order variation of the Real: it is not the trauma of symbolic castration but, rather, the impossibilities inherent in attempts to symbolise the absence born of castration. The Real within language is felt through its absent presence – the primordial example being the Freudian slip, whereby the limitations of a particular discursive structure are revealed only through the performative failure of that structure – as well as through actually occurring elements that are incommensurable within an internal logic of a discourse, yet can be symbolised from another perspective. The key example of this process comes from the exceptional elements that each discursive perspective must exclude to establish itself as a set. Every ideological formation has an exceptional blind-spot that simply cannot be included within the set if that set is to maintain its consistency. It is to these exceptions (and exclusions) that we now turn.

The Presence of the Real: On the Condition of Exceptionality

As I have noted, Lacanian theory suggests that the symbolic order is faced with dual pressures: a quest for the imaginary coherence of the body and the dislocatory effect of the Real. Language can never be objective – it can never be a closed system but, rather, always requires the presence of another signifier – but it is also always in the process of seeking objective closure, a process that Lacan associated with the body and the trauma of symbolic castration. The only way to achieve a fragile, ideological, objectivity is by way of an exception to the discursive formation. This exception provides a fragile sense of unity by offering a sense of what the discourse is not: the exception provides an outside that defines the boundaries of discourse.

The notion of exception often causes confusion within the psychoanalytic field of politics. Much of this confusion comes from the conflation of different modes of exceptionality into one. This assumption stems from Lacan's theory of sexuation: the manner in which men and women are structured differently in relation to castration and the lack of *jouissance*. Sexual differentiation has nothing to do with biological essence (Žižek 1994: 155) but is rather a structural position in regard to the cut of the signifier: it is entirely plausible to have subjects with female genitalia identifying with the masculine position.* From this distinction between the masculine and the feminine Lacan argued that 'there is no sexual relationship'. This does not mean that sexual intercourse does not occur but, rather, there is no logical relationship between masculine and feminine positions. Not only do they represent different structural responses to castration but these responses themselves are not together compatible. As a consequence of the failure of the sexual relationship, Lacan identified sexual difference as *the* antagonism by which both sexuality and sociality are riven; sexual difference is the primary modality of the Real as all forms of discourse are a response to the wound of sexual difference.

Sexual difference can also be conceived of as a logical problem in relation to objectivity and exceptionality in language. The Other is lacking because it cannot complete itself – it cannot name itself within its own set. For there to be an inside there must be an exterior that designates the presence of the inside, otherwise what is internal ceases to be exclusive. By naming the inside that name then becomes part of the set and another exterior signifier is required to constitute the set. Thus, the complete Other, the complete set of signifiers, cannot exist – there must be at least one exceptional signifier that names the set, thus exceeding the horizon of that set.

Fink (1995: 29–30) uses Bertrand Russell's example of the paradox of the catalogues of all catalogues which do not include themselves as entries to explain this point. If the catalogue does not include itself within the catalogue, then the list is incomplete – it has an exception, itself. If, however, the catalogue does include itself, then it should not be included within that category. Such a paradox is the key to Lacan's understanding of the masculine and feminine; from there to exist a masculine set (a set in which all are included), an exception to that set must exist in order to define the presence of a set. By contrast, the feminine set includes its own exception but loses the ability to define itself, becoming an infinite series.

These positions are not just logical possibilities but, rather,

---

* Although, as Kay (2003) notes, the link between biological sex and sexuation is a difficult issue in Žižek's work. It is not immediately clear why biological men tend to be subjected to the masculine position.

responses to symbolic castration; they suggest a different relation both to the phallus* and to *jouissance*. For Lacan, the masculine is altogether subject to symbolic castration and the phallus: man is subject to the *jouissance* of the phallus, otherwise known as symbolic *jouissance*. Man can be wholly submitted to symbolic castration only by the presence of an exception that is not submitted to these conditions. According to Lacan, that exception had the status of Freud's primordial father in *Totem and Taboo* (1913), the father that has not been subject to castration and was thus able to control and enjoy women fully.

Nonetheless, the naming of the set which must necessarily exceed the set is only one of the forms of exceptionality. The other is the universal exception, otherwise known as the point of concrete universality. This form of exceptionality is the form predominately used by Žižek and is the key to his theory of universality, by which he uses Hegel to read Lacan.

Žižek, Hegel and Universality

In *The Ticklish Subject* (Žižek 1999: 100–1) Žižek suggests – and rejects – three separate positions on universality. The first is the standard neutral and positivised universal, indifferent to its particular content; that which is universal applies to all possible circumstances. This conception of universality relies upon a singular and essential foundation and has largely been the subject of critique from the discursive turn, suggesting that an objective and universal Truth is impossible in a world mediated by language.

Nonetheless, it is the image of universality assumed by those seduced by the scientific method, the possibility of positive knowledge and the white man's burden. This positivist universal assumes that knowledge can be entirely objective, provided that it is subjected to the correct checks and balances. This position should not be immediately dismissed. As part of the Enlightenment, the scientific method has produced a great many advances, even if it has been subject to the odd embarrassing reversal.

---

* Lacan broke with Freud in identifying the phallus not with the penis but with the signifier. Again, however, there is a major ambiguity in psychoanalysis around the link between the symbolic phallus and the biological penis, the pertinent question being why the biological penis comes to represent the symbolic phallus – the link appears more than 'radically contingent'.

The political interpretation of this method has proved less problematic. Two versions can be identified, corresponding roughly to the early and later forms of modernity. The first broad ideology endorsed a naturalistic universal perspective in which objective truths emerged from the nature of our being. That man was considered superior to woman was simply an inequality granted by God and defined by our bodies. Likewise, racial inequality and poverty were simply a matter of evolutionary development. Whilst this is a broad caricature that possibly has more in common with pre-modern forms than the pure modernity of the Enlightenment, the difficulty of political universalism remains evident: there is no universal position from which to determine these truths.

This difficulty is acknowledged more within forms of later modernity which, whilst acknowledging the value of universalism, have paid greater heed to the problem of objectivity. Taking a reflexive stance, late modernity has tended towards the axiomatic universality of human-rights discourse and democracy, whereby the universal is considered to be fluid and constructed. There are, of course, a number of points of dispute here, whether in regard to the false contingency of democracy or the illusion of human rights as the face of global capitalism. Nonetheless, there is definitely value in asserting certain values – say the universal right to food – despite a lack of ultimate foundation. There is little political value in spiralling into the contingency of postmodern relativity in the face of politically generated injustice. Yet this form of universalism, like any other, must exclude in order to cohere itself. The problem, therefore, is not so much that there is a universal, but that current forms of universalism within capitalism are insufficient.

This critique leads us to Žižek's second form of universality: universality as an illusion generated by power relations. Here the universal is neither true nor neutral, but rather a particular reflection of the existing hegemony. Typically, this version is marked by a Marxist conception of ideology, whereby the universal is a partiality, hiding the true, universal totality of social relations. This form of universality is not postmodern; theorists of a postmodern bent tend to assert that the only possible form of universality is an illusion. By contrast, this 'Marxist' form of universality introduces a split between an illusionary universal and a true underlying universal.

Finally, Žižek offers the universal as contingent yet always already hegemonised by particular content. This is the version proposed by Laclau in which universality occurs when a signifier is abstracted to the point where it represents nothing but itself: an empty signifier. This universal itself is empty, but is always filled by particular elements in a hegemonic battle to hold the place of the universal equivalent for society. These particular elements establish a 'chain of equivalence' that fills out the abstract universal horizon so that it coheres our understanding of shared social life.

Thus, Laclau's work on hegemony suggests that the universal occurs only through its abstraction from a chain of particular signifiers. This 'abstract universal' provides the hegemonic imaginary horizons – the signifiers and images that support any concept of shared social life – that people use to guide their actions, such as the concepts of individual freedom or human rights. This universal imaginary stands in for the lack that constitutes the social domain. The abstract universal is normally based around an empty signifier, or an *objet a*, which in Lacanian terms provides a suture for that primal lack and, because of the sense of fullness that it gives, supplies the subject with *jouissance*.

Indeed, it is *jouissance* that provides the key to all these modes of universality: *jouissance* provides the desire for coherence and unity offered by a cohesive idea of shared social life. We see this most clearly in the resentment and excessive enjoyment that is generated when universal cultural customs are broken: tourists holding up workers on their daily commute, immigrants (or just outsiders distinguished by the colour of their skin or tone of their voice) who are too loud, too smelly, too *excessive*, on the bus or in your neighbourhood. To borrow a Žižekianism, *is this not* the truth of universality – the unseemly diffusion of resentment that occurs when common-sense ideology is threatened by the excessive Other?

Returning to the example of freedom, liberal democratic discourses may be structured around the empty signifier 'freedom', which can be taken to mean any number of things. The content of these meanings is not important, unless you happen to be caught under the ideological grasp of one or more of them. In that case the freedom of avoiding the male gaze through a full-body burqa or being bombed into submission in the name of 'freedom' may be of some consequence. In terms of our theoretical argumentation, however, what is important is the ideological form that allows 'freedom' to stand in for the presence of absence and structure the field of liberal democracy. In turn, the abstract universal extends this horizon as an ideological formation, taking on further signifiers in a Laclauian logic of equivalence. The condensation of particular elements around a central imaginary horizon through the logic of equivalence offers the prospect of a return to fullness and *jouissance*.

Such a process occurred during the 2008 US presidential elections, where Barack Obama attempted to mobilise support under the empty signifier 'change',* for example 'Change we can believe in' or 'Barack Obama is the leader who will bring the change our country needs'. The strength of this strategy was that change meant nothing in itself, save an opposition to the establishment Republican Party – it tapped into an undercurrent of dissatisfaction with the status quo. Moreover, it allowed for different political formations to identify with the signifier, whilst setting up a frontier against Republican candidate John McCain's appeals to leadership and experience, 'Country First'.

Žižek, however, rejects all three of these versions of universality. That said, he holds that there is some value in Laclau's work, particularly in the assertion that the universal is a necessary, yet impossible, object. Despite this apparently radical conclusion, Žižek argues that Laclau is not radical enough – he leaves in place the exclusion which allows for universality in the first place. For Žižek, the question of universality is not 'Which particular content hegemonises the empty universal?' but, rather, 'Which specific content has to be excluded so that the very *empty form* of universality emerges as the "battlefield" for hegemony?' (Žižek 2000a: 110). As such, Žižek contends that rather than a split between the universal and the particular (causing the universal to be impossible) the universal itself is split between its empty abstraction and the concrete remainder, otherwise known as the universal exception.

Žižek's understanding of universality is exemplified in a defining chapter in his first major text, *The Sublime Object of Ideology* (Žižek 1989: 11–53), where Žižek suggests that Marx 'invented' the Lacanian symptom by

---

* Early in his campaign, Obama utilised 'Hope' as this empty universal signifier. Although Hope remained prominent throughout the campaign, it largely gave way to 'Change'. This move was most likely enacted in order to avoid splitting the energy of the campaign. Conversely, this example shows that such signifiers are not strictly empty but, rather, carry with them a long history of associations – what Laclau calls a chain of equivalence. The switch from the aspirations of hope to the more mainstream change is not simply a contingent move between equal signifiers but signalled a change in political strategy. Nonetheless, this does not change the fact that – once in place – each 'empty' signifier can be articulated by any number of discourses.

detecting a certain fissure, an asymmetry, a certain 'pathological' imbalance which belies the universalism of the bourgeois 'rights and duties'. This imbalance, far from announcing the 'imperfect realisation' of these universal principles – that is, an insufficiency to be abolished by further development – functions as their constitutive moment: the 'symptom' is, strictly speaking, a particular element which subverts its own universal foundation, a species subverting its own genius. (Žižek 1989: 20)

Here, Žižek is specifically referring to Marx's understanding of freedom. If liberal capitalism is based around an empty signifier of freedom, which becomes universalised through an abstract hegemonic horizon, then this notion is subverted by the freedom to sell one's labour on the market. Although this freedom is a vital element of liberal capitalism, the very act subverts that freedom – in selling one's labour power, the worker loses their freedom (Žižek 1989: 21). It is this freedom to sell labour power which is the universal exception to the abstract universality of bourgeois freedom.

Further to this, the same symptomatic element exists in relation to the production of surplus value. Žižek argues that once labour becomes a commodity – that is, for sale on the market – 'equivalent exchange becomes its own negation' (Žižek 1989: 22). Although the worker is fully paid for their labour (according to the market), the very form of surplus value is one of exploitation. The worker is exploited not because they are underpaid but because of the position in which they exist – having to sell their labour as a commodity.

Here then we have an abstract universal notion of freedom. It is one which is subverted by a concrete element that is simultaneously part of the set and beyond that set. It is this element that Žižek labels the universal exception which produces concrete universality. The universal exception is thus the cut of the universal whereby one of these particulars asserts itself as universal by its very exclusion from the abstract universal. The universal thus encounters itself in the form of its opposite within itself. Universality proper thus becomes a struggle between the particular elements involved in a battle for hegemony and the singular element which belies this horizon (Žižek 1991: 33–6).

As such, Žižek states:

With regard to the opposition between abstract and concrete universality, this means that the only way towards a truly 'concrete' universality leads through the full assertion of abstract negativity by means of which the universal negates its own particular content: despite misleading appearances, it is the 'mute universality' of the particular content which is the predominant form of abstract universality. In other words, the only way for a universality to become concrete is to stop being a neutral-abstract medium of its particular content, and to include itself among its particular subspecies. (Žižek 1999: 92)

Concrete universality thus not only signals the presence of an exception to a (false) abstract universalism but 'persists in the very irreducible tension, non-coincidence, between these different levels' (Žižek 2006b: 31). One should not distinguish between abstract and concrete universality but consider universality as the place of this split, not so much the exception itself but both the exception and the plurality of responses which occur in response to it – this is universality proper, universality as struggle (Žižek 2006b: 34).

Thus, in Žižek's reading of universality, difference occurs not between the neutral, mediating universal and its particular elements but, rather, between the universal and its own exception. This difference is experienced as an absence that can be understood as the presence of the Real. It is by bringing this absence into the symbolic order, not in a manner in which it can be pacified by understanding but, rather, in direct contrast to the official horizon of understanding that a proper critique of universality can occur – by revealing the exceptions upon which the 'false' universality is founded (Žižek 2000a: 102). Thus, the Hegelian triad of the universal, particular and singular (exception) is expanded in its Lacanian reading – a fourth element exists in the very gap between the universal and its particular, the Real (Žižek 1991: 43–8; 1999: 79).

Politically, the central value of this particular identification of the exception is that the exception operates as a modality of the Real, yet can be symbolically identified. That is, this mode of the Real exists not only as an anxiety-provoking absence but also a mobilisable political element. If we consider concrete universality to reveal the place of a constitutive exception – an element of the set that is excluded from that set – then we see that the exception takes a material form and yet does not have a presence on the abstract horizon: its intrusion produces a dislocation. Thus the Real can have an existence, or at least a non-existence in Lacanian parlance, outside the discursive construction of a certain narrative. Concrete universality threatens the horizon from which it is excluded and also constitutes the point of the distortion which prevents its own appearance.

To reiterate this vital point, if (abstract) universality occurs as a reaction to symbolic castration, attempting to belie the lack at the heart of the human condition in the name of *jouissance*, this process produces exceptions that signal the position of true universality: the particular elements that remain consistent throughout every articulation of the discourse. The presence of such an exception is felt as a gap between the abstract universal imaginary – the political common sense – and its inability to fully universalise itself because of the necessary exclusion. This produces the effects of the Real: effects without an apparent cause. Nonetheless, the Real *qua* concrete universality does have a presence, it is just outside the hegemonic ideology.

In terms of my previous example in which I identified the freedom to sell labour as the exceptional element of freedom, not only does this dislocating element exist in form – we can identify a formal necessity within the wage-labour system to have an element incommensurable with its ideological narrative that cannot be acknowledged within this narrative – but the political operation of this structure produces actually existing exceptions that are excluded from the ideological fantasies that structure global capitalism. It is these points of exclusion which provide the strongest tension within ideology.

As will be expanded on in the following chapter, we see those excluded from wage-labour in the new forms of the lumpenproletariat that lie beyond the wage-labour system yet constitute its existence. That is, in order for wage-labour to exist as a form of freedom where one can sell labour on a market, then has to be a surplus of non-workers who, in their willingness to take the place of the worker-as-commodity, coerce the sale of this labour. Because this excess cannot be included within our ideological understanding of the processes of employment within capitalism – if they were the worker would no longer be considered free to sell their labour – it both coheres ideology by providing an exterior boundary and threatens its functioning. This excluded surplus exists as an exception to the operation of capitalism and more pertinently the ideological narratives of freedom and justice around which capital functions. In this case the lumpenproletariat is not universal itself – the universalism of capital lies in the gap between its abstract and concrete instantiations – but it reveals the concrete existence of a point that cannot be included, or properly acknowledged, within the abstracted horizon of understanding. In doing so, it acts as a modality of the Real within capitalism.

Because of this threat, whereby the injustice of wage-labour cannot be included (in fact it does not even make 'sense' within the discursive chains that make up global capitalism), wage-labour and its concrete embodiment within the slums of the developing world act as a point of Real tension within capitalism, always threatening to explode onto the surface. Indeed, the whole purpose of cultural forms of Marxism has been to investigate how the superstructure, the realm of ideological fantasy and *jouissance*, prevents this explosion. The aim of psychoanalysis and this interpretation of Žižekian theory is to see how these forces might be unleashed.

Importantly in this regard, an antagonistic point can be resignified within an alternative discourse where it does not act as a point of trauma or a threat, often being represented in a more palpable form or positioned as an exterior threat to ideology The economic immigrant, for instance, is not constructed as a tragic figure cursed by the forces of capitalism that maintain Western wealth but, rather, a threat to *our* jobs and *our* way of life. By contrast, within most forms of Marxist discourse, the economic immigrant suffers from the fickle flows of global capitalism.

As such, a vital opportunity exists whereby the Real is not simply an unrepresentable absence. If the Real cannot be named within an ideology (the naming of the Real makes it representable and instantly a part of reality) it can exist in a symbolic form outside that ideology. Here, the manifest presence of the Real offers the possibility of evoking the Real foundations of an ideological order. I shall develop further upon this in the chapters that follow, in which I outline both the presence of excluded labour within capitalism and the subsequent political strategies that emerge from this position.

For now, however, it is enough to acknowledge that Žižek's reading of the Real offers a distinct rejoinder to the image of shared social life as entirely intractable. Instead, Žižekian theory suggests that ideology is always threatened by what it must exclude: the Real and the exceptional exclusions to universality. By evoking the Real, I have argued that psychoanalytic discourse suggests that change is not only possible, but possible on a radical scale whereby the very presence of the Real is likely to cause a level of anxiety and trauma that reconfigures ideological organisation entirely.

Where this reading leaves political engagement, however, is again unclear. I had begun this text by suggesting that Žižek's work provides a particularly effective response to global capitalism. The value of that approach is most likely not immediately apparent from our debate so far, particularly for more critical readers of Žižek.

Instead, a number of loose ends have emerged. One in particular appears especially pressing. I have oft remarked that the major critique of Žižek's work is that it offers nothing but the critique of ideology. Caught up in the violence and cynicism of psychoanalytic theory, Žižek is unable to formulate either a vision for the future or the basis for the practice of politics beyond capitalism.

Consider the issue of universalism. Whilst dismissing various forms of universality as illusionary, Žižek does not reject the need to live under a universal horizon: his emphasis is simply on the cost of this horizon and in particular the structure of that cost under global capitalism. Indeed, Žižek often insists upon the importance of acknowledging the dirty aspects of power, the necessary inequality and exclusions that arise.

Whilst Žižek does produce an alternative reading of universality, it is not one that provides the basis for an alternative society. Instead, Žižekian theory offers a practice aimed at invoking the disavowed foundations of the existing universal order. This practice is akin to the dialectical operation of Lacanian ethics, which sought not to institute a new image of the subject but, rather, to disrupt a subject's pathological aspects by evoking its repressed elements. It is this operation, more than any political imaginary, which informs the practice of Žižekian politics.

Žižekian Politics

Žižek's location within the Left – as both saviour and disappointment – has meant that his work is the subject of much frustration, speculation and adulation, and he is sought out as a mysterious messiah, a misguided conservative or a confused pluralist. Žižek is both none and all of these things, depending on our construction of his work. He does not offer a concrete alternative vision of a more just society, nor could such a vision stem from psychoanalysis. In this respect, Žižek is misplaced as a redeemer of the Marxist tradition, nor does he offer much guidance for the kind of Leftist politics that wishes to proceed 'one step at a time'. What Žižekian theory does offer, however, is a reading of shared social life that effectively identifies both the mechanisms of its stability and the potentially fraying edges.

Žižek has utilised this dialectical analysis to critique an infinite range of subjects, from theology to cinema and communism. Despite the apparent plurality, however, these positions can be considered to be fundamentally a response to a singular ontological commitment in the Lacanian Real. This commitment defines Žižekian politics, which do not produce a singular political vision but, rather, a series of strategic political manipulations of the Real according to structural interpretation of concrete circumstances. Conversely, these strategies are based upon a singular perspective – the Real and Marxism – with reference to ontology and politics respectively.

Moreover, Žižek has begun to identify these approaches with a single signifier: class struggle as a modality of the Real and the 'communist hypothesis' as the political horizon. As shall be developed in the following chapters, however, neither of these points provides any positive sense of coherence. Žižek's understanding, however, of concrete universality and of class struggle does aid the rethinking of some of the issues of Marxism after the discursive turn. In particular, it speaks to the question of how to renew Marxist political practice at this point of history, given the theoretical failure of scientific Marxism and the revolutionary subject, as well as the meta-hegemonic dominance of capitalism.

Žižek's reading of Marxism through Lacan and Hegel allows for a return to materiality and the question of economy. Conversely, Žižek has decisively argued that the failure of Marxist politics and communism results from an inability to consider the impossible dialectic of lack and excess that is the basis of the psychoanalytic intervention. Yet, I have contended that psychoanalysis alone is unable to provide the resources for a feasible alternative modality of shared social life, particularly in terms of the materiality of our economic reproduction. What psychoanalysis does suggest is a dialectical approach for understanding shared social life and deconstructing ideological formations.

This interpretation of Žižek's work becomes a strategic one: how to mobilise his theoretical work on universality, class struggle and the Real against the contradictions and deprivations of the global economy in the twenty-first century in a manner which provides hope of a better future. It is to this point that I shall now turn in the next section of this book. Here, having constructed the problems facing Marxism after the signifier and the Lacanian reading of politics, I will construct a Žižekian response – and beyond – to these dilemmas.

This response proceeds in three stages. The first consists of a reading of Žižek's work on the economy. This move is necessary because so much of the criticism of Žižek's politics is based upon either a lack of understanding of his reading of capitalism and the ontic status of the economy, or a blatant disavowal of the consequences of this move. Much of the positioning of Žižek as 'good theory, poor politics' is based on a refusal to acknowledge how his 'theoretical' construction of capital and global capitalism cannot be divided from his politics.

In particular, Žižek's use of class struggle and capitalism as a modality of the Real suggests crucial limitations in the range of political action available in response to the meta-hegemony of global capitalism. It is in light of these limitations, along with those established in this chapter in relation to Lacanian politics, that I will begin to construct a Žižekian political approach to politics in general and global capitalism specifically. The task in the next chapter, however, is to consider Žižek's (Marxist) construction of the economy. This move has three points, taking into account the meta-hegemonic dominance of capitalism, Žižek's reliance upon class struggle, and the political alternatives that have emerged in relation to class struggle.

5

Žižek's Capitalism: What Can Sexual Difference Tell Us about New Forms of Apartheid?

Žižek holds a symptomatic position within Leftist politics: his work grapples with the very difficulties of representation that have contributed to the downfall of classical Leftist politics – namely that there is no ultimate foundation from which politics can be guaranteed – yet he maintains that the Left must not abandon the political terrain either by giving way to these dilemmas or by losing sight of materiality and of the economy. If the foundations of Žižekian theory suggest that his work would be quite comfortably included within Cultural Studies curriculums, Žižek's radical provocative political imperatives have caused considerable consternation. Where Žižek variously argues for a return to the radical dimensions of the Marxist critique of political economy and the revolutionary overthrow of global capitalism, he certainly does not outline a master plan for these objectives.

In this regard, whilst I have argued that Žižek is able to produce a form of political analysis based upon a Lacanian reading of the dialectic between lack and excess, he has (willingly) been unable to renew Marxist politics in their classical form – one which holds to the inevitability of history and communism. This is not to suggest that Žižek's (Lacanian) form of politics elides a Marxist reading. The fundamental position taken in this book is that Žižekian theory can be used to produce a disruptive critique of capitalism and restore the primacy of Marxist analysis. In opposition to Geoff Boucher and Matthew Sharpe's (2010: 225) contention that 'for Žižek, despite his professed Marxism, there are no dialectical contradictions at the very heart of capitalism, as Marx thought', I suggest that Žižek's theory of capitalism and rehabilitation of Marxism rests upon the identification of these contradictions and the mechanisms preventing their eruption.

Žižek's construction of capitalism allows for a thorough understanding of the continued flourishing of capitalism against its apparent contradictions. We have reached a pivotal moment in human history and the cyclical development of capitalism. Capitalism is facing a number of increasingly apparent crises of its own making. Not only is worldwide poverty proving troublingly stubborn, but inequality is on the rise within developed and developing nations. The global ecological crisis continues to develop unabated, as policy-makers prepare to respond to the fallout whilst politicians continue to pay lip service to reducing admissions. Not only has the global economy failed to recover from the financial crash of 2008, respond-ing neither to stimulation nor to austerity, but compromises made in the name of fiscal stability have revealed the powerlessness of democratic processes in their current form.

Yet, even in these times of financial crisis and political unrest, capitalism remains the unquestionable political horizon such that its continued operation is self-fulfilling: political ideas are understood to be working only by way of their practical reception by the agents of capital. Whilst we might be entering into the phase of what could be labelled 'end-capitalism' (see Cremin 2011), not only is there no alternative, but the structural demands of capital remain as dominant as ever.

Moreover, without the venerable traditions of Marxism to fall back on, the Left has struggled to understand the continued success of global capitalism and muster a critique that holds the possibility of breaking with capitalism. As noted thus far in this text, too many forms of Leftist politics refuse to engage with capitalism, implicitly holding it as an unassailable horizon known only as 'the economy'. These forms, the now-forgotten 'Third Way' chief amongst them, have focused upon the politics of the redistribution of surplus, rather than how this surplus was produced. As this surplus has apparently run out, the mainstream Left has been bereft of ideas. Fortunately, this has led to the fledgling development of popular resistance to cap-italism, although at the time of writing it is too soon to tell what will come of these movements. At this stage, it appears that we remain blind to the consequences of our betrothal to capital. Many forms of environmental concern, for example, demand wholesale changes in the way we live and produce without considering the economic struc-tures maintaining this lifestyle, or the consequences of the required changes in economic activity.

In this regard Žižek suggests that whilst capitalism's contradic-tions have inevitably come to the surface, global capitalism has become so dominant that it operates as a symbolic mode of the

Lacanian Real. Here all resistance to capitalism is always already countered by the system itself. Extending this understanding by using a Lacanian schema to rehabilitate the Marxist idea of the base–superstructure model, we can identity two dimensions to the success of global capitalism.

On an imaginary-ideological level, the contemporary subject is encouraged to enjoy capitalism through a superego injunctive to consume. Beyond consumption, this imaginary enjoyment is supplemented by ideologies that soften the contradictions of capitalism, predominately through the apparent justice of the democratic model and through a celebration of multi-culturalism that is limited to the commodification of identity. Alternatively, the rise of capitalism in China and the Middle East suggests that the supposed link between capital and democracy is nothing but an ideological illusion.

Working within this ideology is the symbolic operation of capitalism, in regard to both its structural stabilising mechanisms and the actual circuit of capitalism. Each of these factors makes capitalism entirely self-reinforcing. Not only is resistance countered within capitalism such that the system functions by profiting from its apparent contradictions, but the dominance of the circuit of capital is such that finance capital – the circuit in its pure form – holds to ransom all other forms of political endeavour. That is, the dominance of financial markets is such that it dictates the fate of all political movements, as is becoming painfully evident in the wake of the continuing fallout from the 2008 financial crisis.

Capitalism, however, is not unbreakable. Instead, as both Marx and Žižek have suggested, capital produces the germs of its own demise. Where certain readings of Marxism have suggested that the contradictions in the mode of production led to inevitable political consequences, the rethinking of this analysis within Western Marxism placed more emphasis upon political and cultural factors. Where much of this rethinking has relied upon psychoanalysis to provide a theory of ideology and subjectivity, Žižek focuses upon the punctuation of ideology by the Real and a return to political economy. For Žižek, political action against capitalism must stem from a return to the economic base of social life. This economic base, however, is not envisioned in any way like the vulgar forms of Marxist economism. Instead, Žižek locates this base as class struggle, which he positions as a mode of the Lacanian Real.

Whilst some critics (see Sharpe 2004: 12, 209) have suggested that Žižek explains the flourishing of capitalism too well, preventing any

possibility for its defeat and leaving him to make hysterical statements about the need for radical action, Žižek's identification of
class struggle as a modality of the Real leaves open the possibility for
negating capitalism in a manner that is unable to be countered by the
system, what Glyn Daly (2010: 15) calls the 'subversion of subversion'. By translating Marx's economic base into the Lacanian Real
qua class struggle, Žižekian theory is able to avoid the determinism
that plagued Marx's original model, yet retain the economic critique
of capitalism. Moreover, Žižek is able to return to *political* economy
by suggesting that the indeterminacy of class struggle means that the
economy is always already political.

Conversely, Žižek's construction of class struggle is particularly
difficult as he argues that it occurs at the point at which representation fails, eliding any attempt to positively signify this struggle.
Against this reluctance to develop upon the Marxist foundations
of class struggle, in this chapter I come to argue that by reading
this modality of the Real through Žižek's Hegelian notion of
universality and exceptionality, a strong critique of capitalism
becomes evident. This critique is based upon an identification of
new modes of what Žižek has called 'new forms of apartheid' and
we shall term the lumpenproletariat, in the masses of urban slums
which are becoming increasingly prevalent across the planet. These
non-workers are not the classical Marxist proletariat, but those
outside the wage-labour structure, working what Michael Denning
(2010) labels a 'wageless life' in the informal sector. As such they
operate as an exception to the ideological fantasies that structure
capitalism, producing a Real tension that threatens to disrupt these
fantasmatic binds.

In maintaining the functioning of the wage-labour system and
increasingly threatening the Western world through migration, these
groupings offer the prospect of the determinate negation of global
capitalism without restoring the inevitability of the revolutionary
subject. The question – to be addressed in the following chapter – is
how to mobilise this exclusion from capitalism. Initially, however, I
shall consider the validity of reinvoking Marx's base–superstructure
analogy through a Lacanian schema.

Lacan, Superstructure and Base

In Chapter 2 I noted that the determinism evident in vulgar Marxist
forms of economism, such as the infamous base–superstructure

model, had been largely set aside by the discursive turn. Developed primarily in his preface to A *Contribution to the Critique of Political Economy*, Marx argued that the relations and forces of production (combining to become the mode of production) constitute the real foundation of society, upon which a political, cultural and legal superstructure develops.

A number of issues have stemmed from that deterministic analogy. It is primarily cited as an example of vulgar materialism and economism, whereby Marx is deemed to argue that the manner in which we materially reproduce our society *determines* the very stuff of our consciousness. For any position that takes language to mediate any access to this materiality, this determinism is both false and dangerous. Politically, this model is said to lead to false forms of economism where only economic action and class struggle can bring about real change: ideological struggle is thought to be illusionary, a side-show to effective class struggle. Instead, the role of cultural and ideological critique was only to reveal the true structure of economic life to the working class, who could then take on their destiny as the revolutionary subject.

In its raw form, it would appear that any theory that draws upon psychoanalysis should have no truck with such an outdated position. Yet, through a thorough Lacanian rereading, I argue that Žižek posits a very similar theory of capitalism. Of course, this Žižekian model of capitalism relies much more upon Lacan – in particular Lacanian notions of causality – than Marx. Here, in place of the material base and cultural superstructure, we can invoke the Lacanian registers of the symbolic, the imaginary and the Real to understand the grip of capitalism and the possibilities for untying the ideological knot under which we currently labour.

The model remains productive because it expresses the basic operation under which the Real base of society is not only economic, but is also a point of contradiction within contemporary hegemonic modes of ideological fantasy. In doing so the model suggests the possibility for a Žižekian rereading of the relationship between the economic and the political within capitalism by reworking the dialectical intimacy between the symbolic-imaginary substructure and the economic Real. Here Žižek suggests that ideology is fundamentally a response to class struggle, which itself punctuates the symbolic-ideological framework of capitalism. This does not mean that all ideology is class ideology, as if it were simply a reflection of the ruling form of property relations. Instead, class struggle must be read in a particularly Žižekian way, such that – as a modality of the Real – class acts as an absence within the symbolic order. This absence produces a need for ideology and surplus *jouissance*, but is not directly determined by class struggle.

As a consequence, in order to evoke the Real foundations of capitalism and disturb its operation, the ideological responses to these foundations must be disrupted. Moreover, whilst acknowledging the value of enjoyment within capitalism, we must come to understand the strength of the symbolic structure that underlies capitalism. This symbolic structure entails the 'circuit of capital' that formed part of Marx's original base. This circuit, particularly in its raw form as finance capital, includes the self-revolutionary feedback systems that allow capitalism to thrive by reconstituting its own contradictions as opportunities for profit and expansion. Let us begin to unpack this vital contribution, one that outlines the value of Žižek's work for Leftist political theory and in terms of rehabilitating a Marxist response to global capitalism, by expanding upon Žižek's construction of the symbolic-imaginary matrix of capitalism.

Capitalism: Enjoy!

The contradictions of capitalism are becoming increasingly hard to ignore. The global financial crisis of 2008 emphasised our powerlessness against the movements of capital and the desires and follies of its privileged agents. Inequality is rising strongly amongst Western and developing nations whose governments appear ever more impotent to act against these developments lest they offend the flows of international capital. Despite the fantasies of international agencies, global poverty is proving notably obdurate and climate change continues unabated, such that it has become an acknowledged aspect of political life: the debate is no longer how to prevent climate change, but how to respond to its effects.

Despite all this, capitalism appears as much of a vampire now as it did to Marx. We can identify two primary reasons for the continual expansion and flourishing of capitalism. Firstly, capitalism continues to operate as a self-revolutionary force: what appears to be an obstacle to the free flow of production is re-established as an opportunity for profit. This expansion of the market-place has also meant that counter-cultural threats to the status quo become a source for profit and have left potential revolutionaries with no alternative: the 2011 British riots, like those in France a few years earlier, were marked by a political agnosticism bereft of any point of political identification (Žižek 2011).

More than these systematic elements, however, capitalism continues to flourish because it allows for and incites enjoyment. Capitalism operates best as a discourse of desire under a consumerist ideological fantasy that suggests the accumulation of commodities is the answer to our inherent alienation. Indeed, if there was any message to the London riots, it was one of consumer desire. The rioters were not alienated by commodity fetishism but, rather, because they had been excluded from this fetishism.

The celebration of consumer identity has come as a new phase in capitalism through which, Žižek suggests, superego enjoyment has become the prevalent form of contemporary *jouissance*. This is not the superego of the Freudian moral conscience but, instead, the excessive Lacanian demand to enjoy. Where it was once considered that enjoyment must be prohibited to prevent the worker rising up and demanding a more satisfying life, the enjoyment of consumerism lures the subject into capitalism. Enjoyment is no longer prohibited by moral norms* but, rather, explicitly demanded and administered largely through the consumption of commodities.

The enjoyment society is characterised by the structuring of desire through the commodity form (Stavrakakis 2007: 232). Commodities act as the embodiment of *objet a*, offering the prospect of full enjoyment. The failure of a commodity to achieve the promise of this fantasy is taken to be a sign of the failure of a singular act of consumption, and desire is deferred to the next purchase, the next object that offers the possibility of full enjoyment. Enjoyment is forever postponed but this deferral is the epitome of desire and *jouissance* itself. Such is the logic of advertising. Effective advertising constructs a fantasmatic scenario around the commodity such that the commodity itself does not suggest a certain lifestyle, but the image of the lifestyle itself suggests the commodity (Stavrakakis 2000a).

In regard to the role of consumer ideology under capitalism, Žižek describes Coca-Cola as the perfect embodiment of *objet a* and the ultimate capitalist merchandise, deeply embedded in the logic of the superego and surplus *jouissance*. In Coke, we have a drink removed of all the objectively necessary properties of a satisfying drink: it

---

* This move can be read both spatially, as totalitarian regimes have given way to capitalism and Western values, and temporally, as a development within the now globally dominant Western society.

provides no nutritional benefit – it certainly does not quench thirst – or provide the 'satisfied calm' of an alcoholic beverage. Instead, all that is left is the mysterious 'X', the surplus over enjoyment that is characteristic of the commodity. Žižek thus argues that Diet Coke is the final step in this process – the commodification of nothing itself – since the caffeine that gives Coke its distinctive taste has been removed and 'we drink the nothingness itself, the pure semblance of a property that is in effect merely an envelope of a void' (Žižek 2000c: 23).

The Coke marketing team have perhaps taken this critique as a challenge. They certainly seem to have been reading Žižek's books;* witness the recent launch of Coke Zero – quite literally nothing in a can. Coke's marketers further revealed their understanding of Lacanian theory with the marketing campaign that accompanied Coke Zero. This campaign portrayed Coke Zero as an element of perfection as its malignant elements have been removed; the advertising slogans were culturally specific variations of 'Why can't all the good things in life come without downsides' or 'Ridding the world of the negative consequences that limit us all'. Ultimately, perhaps Coca-Cola and Marx have more in common than one might think, both attempting utopia by retaining the object without the obstacle that propels the cause.

Conversely, Daly (2009: 290) argues that the enjoyment of consumption should not be reduced to 'materialistic superficiality'. Rather, the increasing influence of 'ethical' consumption has come to supplement the interaction between superego guilt and enjoyment: not only does the commodity itself not fill the gap, but it is also never good enough for the liberal conscience – the paper is never recycled enough, fair-trade coffee does not quite pay the farmer a fair price or the bottled water does not donate to the correct charity.

Capitalism, therefore, does not restrict the freedom of the individual to chase and cultivate their desires. Instead, all forms of desire and identity are elicited, so long as they are profitable. Points of cultural identification become points of consumption and sites of profitability. From fitness to fetishism, every desire can be included within capitalism, but never satisfied. Dissatisfaction with a consumptive life (a dissatisfaction that is the catalyst for consumer desire fuelled by the fantasy provided by advertising and media identity),

---

* Previous marketing campaigns – 'Enjoy!' and 'Coke is *it*' – suggest that this is the case.

however, is supplemented by wider ideological fantasies about the structure of life under capitalism.

THE DEFENCE OF IDEOLOGICAL CAUSES

Contrary to the likes of Mark Devenney (2007: 46), who have argued that if Žižek seeks to disrupt the fantasmatic basis of capitalism, he must outline the structure of capitalist ideological fantasy, ideology within capitalism tends to be divorced from the direct interests of capital. If Marx had suggested that ideology within capitalism reflected the ideas of the ruling elite, subsequent cultural interpretations have suggested that the correlation is not so straightforward. Certainly, ideological fantasy within capitalism does support the interests of capital, but this support tends not to be articulated in relation to capital. Moreover, it is difficult to articulate a singular sense of ideological fantasy in support of capital. Instead, ideology should be seen as a plurality of responses to the singularity of contradiction within capital, rather than a singular identity of capital itself.

There are certainly a number of fantasmatic versions of capitalism that exist, but the dominance of capitalism is such that these are rarely disseminated outside business schools or economic think-tanks. We might be able to identify the predominant economic theories that justify the operation of capitalism, and these theories are certainly ideological. Conversely, their presence does not tend to be hegemonic within capitalism: not that they are challenged, but that justifications for capitalism tend not to focus on the circuit of capital itself. If capitalism can be said to have a hegemonic ideological presence in the twenty-first century, it is in the disavowal of its own presence, through its representation as the universal 'economy', rather than as a particular mode of production. Ideologies concerning economic management do exist, but they are often apolitical struggles revolving around the management of the economy, not its very status, structured around signifiers such as 'Growth' and 'Progress' that suggest a common Good rather than a plutocratic system.

Thus, whilst there may be ideologies of capitalism, they tend not to be the ideologies that 'protect' the interest of capital itself. To traverse these fantasises is certainly necessary in moving past capitalism – we must conduce capitalism to stop believing in itself – but it is not politically effective to target these mechanisms. Instead, we must consider those ideological forms that support the operation of capital. Thus, whilst progress and growth are economic signifiers ultimately caught up in the circuit of capital, within Western societies they are framed by the discourses of democracy and liberalism.

Democratic ideology suggests that all citizens within nominally democratic states have the opportunity to participate in the management of the state. Of course, this fantasy elides the limitations of democratic participation: not only the obvious limitations on representation caused by voter apathy and the dictatorship of the majority, such that many elected governments have the official support of around a quarter of the population, but that the key economic elements involved in the material reproduction of society are outside democratic control. And yet, the democratic fantasy continues. The strongest rebuke to the 'Occupy' movement that arose in 2011 has been that the activists should utilise the democratic political process, that if the people really believed in their cause – if they were really the 99 per cent – then their political party would be elected to power (*Economist* 2011). Such a position reveals both the overwhelming fantasy of democratic participation and the limitations of democracy itself. Moreover, it suggests that democracy is the ultimate ideology of capitalism: an ideology that is seen to be beyond ideology.

Thus liberal democracy provides the primary sense of justice within Western societies. Some schools of thought have deemed there to be an affinity between democracy and capitalism, suggesting that the rule of capital naturally extends political and economic freedoms. Certainly, democratic ideology is strongly hegemonic within Western forms of capitalism. Democratic ideology, and the multi-culturalism that often supplements it, both help to promote the image of capitalism as a just social order and to soften the blows of the profit motive. The kind of environmental management laws that the agents of capital love to deride may not be capable of provoking global emancipation, but they do provide a useful buffer against capital, helping the subject to identify their way of life as committed to a sense of justice.

Ultimately, democracy presents a fantasmatic faith in the potential for justice within capitalism. Democracy, the control of the people, is officially thought to provide equal opportunity for each to have their say in the running of the state. There is no need for those opposed to capitalism to march or protest, because democratic mechanisms are in place to cover their demands – if these demands are truly representative of the public. What this position elides is that the global economy and the actions of capital are outside the control of individual states and democratic mechanisms. This is the overt message of the Occupy movement, which emerged late in 2011: that the global economy is arranged in such a way that only the elite benefit, and there are no mechanisms to mediate against this, as politics has become entirely corporatised.

The obviously Left-liberal response to this dilemma is social-democratic reform. Yes, democracy no longer fits the form of the contemporary economy and so new processes must be developed in order to re-establish the legitimacy of Western democracy. On the other hand, Žižek (2011b) suggests that democracy here acts as the final fantasy of the capitalist subject. By having faith in democracy, we fall short of taking radical action against capitalism. Instead, liberal democratic measures become the unquestionable Good in the debate, with the protestors provoking considerations of how we could get capital to conform to these processes. In this sense, Žižek suggests that if the Occupy movement is to have any success in shifting our understanding of capitalism and producing political action, it must traverse the democratic fantasy that holds the idea that change can come from within the system itself.

Ultimately, what these ideologies allow is the maintenance of the fantasy of the Good Other. That is, if under capitalism social interactions tend to be structured around self-interest, it is still postulated that the sum-total of this self-interest is the common Good. For this reason, we can still maintain an image of ourselves as good, civilised animals who are not responsible for the evident injustices of our world. Whilst a direct encounter with a symptom of the contradictions of capitalism – say a homeless beggar – may provoke superego guilt/enjoyment, on a larger scale responsibility can be redirected to governing institutions. In turn, the ideologies that cohere the symbolic Other seek to mediate against the Real effect of these contradictions through signifiers such as 'Progress' and 'Democracy'.

Nonetheless, despite the appeals of the likes of Stavrakakis and Laclau, democracy offers little hope for those who suffer from the articulation of capital. Often used ahead of capitalism as a description of our mode of politics, democracy signals the individualistic ideal of formal equality before the law such that all citizens are free to succeed or fail on their own merits and efforts. This ideology, of course, does not take into account the structural inequalities of capitalism such that wealth is simply a reflection of ability rather than an injustice: an owner should be celebrated for the wealth they create, rather than degraded for the vulnerabilities they exploit. Instead democracy offers a narrative of political empowerment that can justify these inequalities. Interestingly, the fall of communism did not bring with it a celebration of capitalism, except from those in a position to buy up public assets and accumulate incredible private wealth. Instead, eastern Europeans rejoiced at the prospect of democracy.

The substitution of democracy for capitalism as the overt Western ideology suggests that the former appears more palatable to the global polis. Whilst economic, and specifically capitalist, ideologies may exist within the West, they tend to grip the hearts and minds of only those who most benefit from capital. The middle classes go to war for democracy and freedom, even if they are sent in the interests of capitalism.

Conversely, recent events, specifically the rise of capitalism in China and areas within the Middle East, have suggested that capitalism and democracy are not an inseparable couplet. Authoritarian values, even in extreme forms, are perfectly compatible with capitalism, so long as the economy continues to grow and those lucky enough to fuel this growth are able to continue to consume. Indeed, as capitalism becomes more overtly unjust this may be the model for the future, as governments seek to maintain political order in the face of vast and intolerable inequalities. In particular, the threat of more widespread migration to the West may accelerate the move towards authoritarian capitalism.

What is important here is not so much the content of the ideology that dominates society under capitalism, but that ideological fantasies operate to cohere the operation of capitalism and mediate against the contradictions of capital. These ideologies do not specifically respond to the content of class struggle, as Marx would have had it, but rather the trauma of the Real, of which class struggle is one mode.

Moreover, there is no natural ideology that stems from capital to form capitalism, rather ideology helps to sooth the wounds of the polis caused by the contradictions in the articulation of capital. Indeed, we should stress that the reactionary ideologies that supplement capitalism are potentially infinite, in so far as they do not affect the flows of capital. Everything from strong nationalism to ultra-liberalism is compatible with capitalism. If capitalism is complemented by permissive ideologies which allow for diversification and greater commodification, the contradictions of capitalism are also supplemented by authoritarian ideologies that allow for more fixed points of identification. Indeed, they may co-exist within Leftist elements focusing on more manageable aspects of capitalism. One of

Žižek's central points of critique of contemporary Leftist politics is that, by depoliticising the economy, these forms of politics often act only to smooth the wounds of capital, effectively making the job of neo-liberals easier. The message here appears to be: neo-liberals can run the economy and liberals will soften the dissent (Cremin, 2011). If the alternative is to remove dissent altogether, it is difficult to argue with the practicality of this approach.

The point here is not to map out all forms of ideology within contemporary capitalism, simply to suggest that ideology is a reaction to the contradictions of capitalism whilst not determined or conditioned by these contradictions, even if they are a response. Whether that ideology is authoritarian or liberal does not particularly matter for the analysis of the structure of capitalism, although it may be of great importance for those who labour within it. What is important is that ideological fantasy, which we have defined earlier as the organisation of enjoyment and 'common sense', coheres our sense of social life and politics under capitalism.

These ideological fantasies, along with the pervasive enjoyment of the commodity (consumerism itself being an ideological fantasy) and self-revolutionising symbolic structure of capitalism, constitute the imaginary element of the superstructural basis of capitalism. Where Marx considered this superstructure to be conditioned by the economic base, and thus consisting of a certain fluidity, the Žižekian model of capitalism insists upon the relative fixity of the superstructure. This fixity stems from the enjoyment that infuses language and ideology, along with the feedback mechanisms that maintain the structure of capitalism. It is for this reason that capitalism can be considered a mode of the symbolic Real, a point to which I now turn, extending the superstructural aspect of capitalism by adding a symbolic-structural element to the imaginary-ideological operation of capitalism.

Capitalism as the Symbolic Real

Žižek argues that capitalism is not an object like any other: capital is not just one element in the field of hegemony, but has rather hegemonised the place of hegemony itself. As he states:

> In so far as we conceive of the politico-ideological resignification in terms of the struggle for hegemony, today's Real which sets the limit to resignification is Capital: the smooth functioning of Capital is that which remains

the same, that which 'always returns to its place', in the unconstrained struggle for hegemony. (Žižek 2000b: 223)

For this reason, Žižek holds that the only possibility of invoking radical change within capitalism is the internal rupture of capital itself – there is no outside that could force a cleavage within capital. This claim, along with the associated notion of capitalism as a modality of the Real, has been the source of much consternation from his critics. The primary accusation is that by constructing capitalism in such a manner, Žižek leaves room only for the Lacanian act as a mode of radical politics. Laclau, for example, states:

According to Žižek, capitalism is the Real of present-day societies for it is that which always returns. Now he knows as well as I do what the Lacanian Real is; so he should also be aware that capitalism cannot be the Lacanian Real. The Lacanian Real is that which resists symbolisation and shows itself only through its disruptive effects. But capitalism as a set of institutions, practices, and so on can operate only in so far as it is part of the symbolic order. And if, on top of that one thinks – as Žižek does – that capitalism is a self-generated framework proceeding out of an elementary conceptual matrix, it has to be conceptually fully graspable and, as a result, a symbolic totality without holes . . . In that case, capitalism as such is dislocated by the Real, and it is open to contingent hegemonic retotalisations. *Ergo*, it cannot be the *fundamentum inconcussum*, the framework within which hegemonic struggles take place, because – as a totality – it is itself only the result of partial hegemonic stabilisations. (Laclau 2000a: 291)

Whilst Laclau is correct in identifying that capitalism is part of the symbolic order, he ultimately misses the subtlety in Žižek's argument. Žižek is not suggesting that capitalism is the Real in a strict Lacanian sense of that which cannot be represented. Instead, Žižek expands upon the Real to suggest that capitalism is a mode of what he labels the 'symbolic Real', the symbolic background that operates as the hard limit in the battle for hegemony.

An initial analysis may suggest that Žižek is engaging a rhetorical device through which to make a point about the status of capital: capital has become *the* political-hegemonic force of our time, the point to which everything returns without becoming a specific modality of the Lacanian Real. Nonetheless, as is always the case with Žižek, there is truth in appearance. Žižek is not simply using 'capital as Real' for shock value. Rather, this assertion suggests a deeper point to which he returns in his later work.

Žižek does indeed argue that global capital has become the determining factor in contemporary world affairs. It has done so, however, with a twist. Capitalism is not dominant in the totalitarian sense of exhausting all opposition, although both violence and systematic megalomania lie – disavowed, rather than dominant – at the heart of the beast. Rather, capitalism, taken as a whole, is a modality of the *symbolic* Real because it is the both the point to which all symbolisation returns and a limit point to political expression. It is, as Mark Fisher (2009: 2) suggests by reference to both Žižek and Fredric Jameson, easier to imagine the end of the world than the end of capitalism.

Žižek's definition of capital as a symbolic form of the Real stems from his distinction (in the foreword to the second edition of *For They Know Not What They Do*, written in 2002) between the triadic modalities of the Real (the Real also having imaginary and symbolic dimensions). Of most interest to this argument is the symbolic Real, which Žižek describes as 'the Real as consistency'. Here capitalism is the consistent background against which shared social life operates, even if capitalism is inconsistent in itself (Žižek 2002: xii).

Žižek's development of capital as the Real has been a relatively sedate and contemporary occurrence. It was not until 1999 in *The Ticklish Subject* that he began to speak of global capitalism and the Real in the same terms, stating (in reference to global climate change and the El Niño effect): 'This catastrophe thus gives body to the Real of our time: the thrust of Capital which ruthlessly disregards and destroys particular life-worlds, threatening the very survival of humanity' (Žižek 1999: 4). Here, though, Žižek is using the Real in a more conventional Lacanian sense: as a traumatic point within the symbolic field, rather than as the unsymbolisable logic of consistency in a symbolic field.

Žižek's initial conceptualisation of capital as the symbolic Real arose through his three-way collaboration with Laclau and Judith Butler, *Contingency, Hegemony and Universality* (2000). Here Žižek considers capital as the background against which all symbolisations must relate, a 'limit to resignification' (2000b: 223). Furthermore, he goes on to describe capital as 'structuring in advance the very terrain on which the multitudes of particular elements fight for hegemony' (Žižek 2000d: 320). He is clear, however, to make a distinction between the economy/capital as an essentialist limit to signification and hegemonic struggle, and capital as the positive condition that creates a symbolic background against which hegemonic struggle occurs (Žižek 2000d: 319).

This last point is vital. It is not that capital prevents the production of non-capitalist discourse but, rather, that these discourses occur in an environment (which remains politically implicit, unless provoked) that restricts the parameters within which they can operate. It is in this way that capitalism is a modality of the Real: as a non-explicit limit. It can appear that an outside to capital exists, as not all relations are capitalist relations. Nor is every articulation of capitalism somehow pure, unadulterated by other concerns. Capitalism in China is very different from capitalism in Sweden or capitalism in the United States. Nonetheless, the interests and influence of capital remain the same in a global sense. In this manner we can consider capital to be structured like one of its iconic manifestations, the shopping mall.

The mall allows all apparent freedoms and is experienced as a site of consumptive enjoyment. One is free to move around and experiences no apparent repression, except in acting against the interests of the mall. What the mall has achieved is the subsumption of public space: the historical village centre, with all its associated public space and room for dissent, is now contained within the mall itself. One can be free within the mall – and within capitalism – only by following the rules and internalising the structures of the mall. Yet, beneath the benevolence of the mall and the doctrines of capitalism lies a more openly coercive sense of power, in terms of both symbolic restraint and an undercurrent of violence.

Ultimately, the success of capitalism lies in its ability to combine resistance and subversion into the ideological dialectics of power: what appears to be a counter-cultural or subversive movement is always a possible opportunity for profit, whether it is the Green, Pink or Punk dollar. Moreover, if the likes of Greenpeace provide the most visible point of resistance today, it is a form of subversion that only serves to make capitalism more sustainable. These movements, amongst which we can incorporate various forms of progressive action, including unions and 'rights' groups, act only as a 'conscience' – with all its superego connotations – upon capitalism, ultimately smoothing the wheels to prevent political unrest (Cremin 2011; Daly 2009: 291; Hawken 1997; Žižek 2006d: 238).

FINANCE CAPITAL AS A SELF-FULFILLING PROPHECY

That capitalism has become a self-revolutionary truth is nowhere more evident than in the tumultuous dominance of financial capital.

Finance capital is the most 'raw' form of the circuit of capital, working to its base formula, as capital is used to buy commodities to earn more capital, without any need to refer to the use-value of those commodities.

Financial capital, although always operative in some form throughout the modern era, established its dominance in the 1970s, which saw the advent of two vital and interlinked trends: overproduction and the decoupling of the dollar from the gold standard. The crisis of overproduction, combined with the oil shocks early in the decade, led to a mass of surplus looking for an investment home. Whilst much of this surplus was redirected into newly established Third World markets and increased market differentiation with the West, the core of the problem remained. The solution was the development of the financial industry, whereby 'excess' currency was able to be put into circulation and expanded without any physical reference (Jameson 1996; Wade 2007; 2008).

The key to this move was Richard Nixon's breaking of the US dollar from the gold standard (Hardt & Negri 2000: 26). The move to floating currencies was followed, at various speeds, by the majority of governments, allowing for the trading of currencies themselves, rather than through physical trade. The trading of currencies for profit, whether nominally attached to commodities or not, has become the basis of the international financial industry, trading itself reaching an estimated US$4 trillion per day in 2010 (Bank for International Settlements 2010).

This move was of massive historical significance: along with the development of the financial industry, the dropping of the gold standard removed the guarantee of the 'general equivalency' of money. Instead, in a definitively postmodern (or feminine) manoeuvre, money no longer exists, there are only currencies.* Such a move is part of a historical development from money being an element of value itself, to being supported by an item of supposed value (the gold standard), to its current state as a purely virtual occurrence given a presence only because we believe in the value of its presence.

Indeed, physical commodities are no longer the primary basis of much trade. Certainly the growth in physical trade, production and

---

* Interestingly, in a Laclauian dynamic, although money itself does not exist, this does not mean that the international trading market exists as a series of particular currencies alone. Instead, one currency – the US dollar – has come to take the place of money, acting as a hegemonic general equivalent.

consumption continues, as the materiality of our ecological crisis reveals. Nonetheless, increasingly commodities are traded simply as placeholders for currencies – livestock might be bought in euros only to be traded when the value of that currency rises – particularly through mathematical 'derivatives' trading, through which value is 'derived' via various instruments of finance trade. This trading has established a certain distance from the 'real' economy, such that the material operation of the economy in the sense of fulfilling the 'needs and wants' of consumers no longer occurs. Latent ideological fantasies about the expansion of capital in the name of meaningful material progress drift away and the circulation of money becomes an end in itself, detached from consumptive use-value and the well-being of producers.

Instead the real economy – in the sense of value and influence – lies in the financial centres of the Western world, where value rises and falls based upon the second-order expectations of those who control financial products developed only for monetary gain. The financial crisis that first became apparent in 2008 saw these self-destructive tendencies in action as the credit 'bubble' burst, most of all because people lost their faith in money and reaffirmed the uncertainty in risk. To a certain degree actors came to realise that money does not exist and withdrew from the virtuality of the system, moving investment back to gold in particular. Indeed, one of the initial tasks of the Obama administration in handing over unthinkable amounts of US currency to its financial institutions was to restore confidence in the value of money.*

It is with financial capital that we see the truly 'Real' nature of capital as all other values are submitted to the decentralised whim of financial trading. The price of food commodities can happily be pushed up by financial speculation without any regard for their ultimate use-value. Moreover, arms-dealers can thrive in environments such as the 2011 'Arab Spring', where British companies were selling arms to both corrupt regimes and rebels alike, irrespective of official

---

* One of the more interesting elements of the financial crisis was the confusion amongst the general public as to the contraction of the economy – the paradigmatic question here being 'Where did all the money go?' as if someone had to have 'the money', that it could not simply be lost. The (comedic) illusion here is not that we tragically had money and then lost it but that the money never existed in the first place. It seems, however, that most investors were without a philosophical sense of humour.

government policy (Drury 2011). Ultimately, the success of political policy is measured by its reception on financial markets, which provides a degree of accountability beyond the demands of the 'people'. Sadly, under 21st-century capitalism it is the financial elite that is providing the answers to the questions this elite itself is setting.

The identification of capitalism as a form of the Real has significant consequences for political action. Firstly, it suggests that capitalism can have no 'outside' from which to establish an alternative position with any traction against capitalism. Just as in the mall analogy, an alternative or outside position can only exist so long as it is not a threat to the existence of capitalism.

Furthermore, any radical political approach that attempts to gain traction within capitalism hits a limit at capital itself. This is the fundamental limitation of the democratic approach of Laclau and Stavrakakis, or the deconstructionist ethics of the likes of William Connolly (2002; 2008) and Simon Critchley (2007b). These theorists are regular critics of Žižek, accusing him of political impotency. They suggest that Žižek's work holds no political value because he refuses to partake in political 'activity' within capitalism. Connolly and Critchley, for example, each argue that we should 'chip away' at the capitalist structure, making whatever possible progressive political adjustments within the system. Ultimately they are social democrats, appealing for greater tolerance and environmental standards. What these theorists fail to understand are the limits to action posed by capitalism.

These limitations are most clearly evident in responses to climate change. It is clear that the most overt cause of ecological degradation is the scale of economic activity, whether in terms of the use of resources, carbon emissions or species extinction caused by the spread of human activity into new environments. Therefore, to effectively respond to the problem, the global economy must be reduced in size. Yes, technological efficiencies are necessary and of great advantage, but they are no match for the expansion of the economy, particularly in the face of a rapidly expanding global population. Ultimately, capitalism operates as a system that requires constant expansion through the development of new markets and new consumers, to the detriment of everything that comes into its path (Kovel 2007: 38–47; Marx & Engels 2004: 7).

This is a conclusion that cannot be properly acknowledged within the ideologies that dominate capitalism, whether conservative, progressive or otherwise. Whilst many environmentalists argue for a reduction in consumption, promoting events such as Buy Nothing Day, they miss the fundamental logic of capitalism – that it must continue to expand. Ultimately, any reduction in consumption must adversely affect those who produce, those for whom what is required is a radical growth in economic activity to lift them out of poverty. This contradiction within capitalism – that climate change is caused by the scale of economic activity, yet to alleviate global poverty the economy must rapidly expand – signals the limits of its appeal for true Leftists. To allow the poor to develop systems through which to feed themselves at a level that satisfies human dignity and flourishing, yet save our global ecology from collapse, it is clear that capitalism must be forced from the planet.

Capital will not go quietly, nor can it be gently persuaded into the grave. Chipping away at the system will not work: instead, any true action against capital in the name of those it does not serve must by definition by radical. If the superstructural form of capitalism appears to suggest that it is an unbreakable matrix of enjoyment and self-revolutionary feedback systems, it is not without weakness. Instead, Žižek has come to identify class struggle as a Real point of antagonism that permeates every aspect of capitalism. The identification of this emergent void within capital opens the possibility for radical political action.

Class Struggle and the Universality of the Lumpenproletariat

For Žižek, class struggle is the Real antagonism that constitutes the base of capitalism and provides a constant obstacle to its development. As with his writings on capitalism and Marxism, Žižek's development of class begins at a relatively late stage in his work. Class is first mentioned almost as an aside in *The Sublime Object of Ideology*, where he declares (in reference to the Real):

> In this way we might reread even the classic notion of 'class struggle': it is not the last signifier giving meaning to all social phenomena ('all social processes are in the final analysis expressions of the class struggle'), but – quite the contrary – a certain limit, a pure negativity, a traumatic limit which prevents totalization of the social-ideological field. (Žižek 1989: 164)

In his next major text, *For They Know Not What They Do* (1991), Žižek explicitly outlines not only the Lacanian status of class struggle but begins to link this reference to the Marxist tradition. Although positing class struggle as *the* totalising moment in society, Žižek rejects the classical Marxist notion of class as a positive guarantee for social life. That is, class is not the anchoring point against which all other social positions can be determined. Instead class struggle acts as the totalising antagonism that prevents the final occurrence of society. In this sense class struggle is a modality of the Real; it is both the antagonistic point to which direct access is not available and the factor preventing this access. Class struggle is not only the failure of each symbolisation, but also operates so as to 'conceal and "patch up" the rift of class struggle' (Žižek 2002: 100).

Class struggle is comparable to Lacan's understanding of the failure of the sexual relationship: just as for Lacanian theory there is no sexual relationship, Žižek suggests that there is no class relationship (Žižek 2006b: 82). Žižek argues that class struggle structures political economy by way of its failure, much as Lacan identified sexual difference as *the* antagonism by which both sexuality and sociality are riven. If for Lacan sexual difference is the primary modality of the Real, as all forms of discourse are a response to the wound of sexual difference, Žižek suggests that class plays this role in the economy, which, through capitalism, has come to dominate all forms of social life. Subjectivity may be defined by sexual difference, but ideological fantasy is always a response to the trauma of class struggle.

In order to further illustrate this relationship, it is helpful to return to an exemplar regularly posited by Žižek and cited in the introduction to this book; that of Claude Lévi-Strauss's example from a tribal village. As a reminder, Lévi-Strauss asked a group of villagers to illustrate a representation of the ground layout of their village. Some of the villagers drew a village divided by a linear split, others as divided into a central circle and an outer circle. Žižek takes Lévi-Strauss to be suggesting that we should neither take a relativist reading of this split – each representation being a valid construction of really – nor seek an empirical truth (say by finding a satellite image of the village) but, rather, try to understand the disavowed antagonism which is causing this division in representation.

For Žižek, that antagonism is class struggle. He suggests that class struggle is the unrepresentable distorting point which is the (absent) cause within society: 'class struggle as antagonism is, as it were, its own obstacle, that which forever prevents its own expression into clear symbolic or positive terms' (Žižek 2004: 100).

It is through class struggle that Žižek attempts to bridge the gap between politics and economy that has dominated Western Marxism.

The discursive turn emphasised the end of economic determinism and the logic of historical materialism, suggesting that at the least the economic position of the working class did not necessarily correspond to a form of politics. If much of Western Marxism has been an attempt to bridge that gap, often losing sight of the economy altogether, Žižek suggests that class reveals that the economy has always already been political: the indeterminacy created by class struggle means that the mode of production is always a political construction (Žižek 2006b: 55). For Žižek, this explains why Marx's analysis of class struggle always breaks from the economic back into the political: the latter is the true source of class struggle (Žižek 2006a: 566).

Conversely, when Žižek begins to consider class struggle himself, rather than in a discussion of Marx's reading of the concept, he does not establish any link to the economy. Indeed it would be generous to Žižek to suggest that he even implies that class struggle has any Marxist genealogy. Not only does his rereading have little to do with empirical changes in class structures, but he makes no reference to the endless debates around class, class struggle and essentialism within Marxist discourse. It is left to the reader to simply infer that class struggle *qua* the Real remains an economic concept.

This apparent disconnect between Žižek's application of class struggle and its Marxist tradition bears witness to a significant difficulty in his Lacanian reading of Marxist political economy. Žižek posits that class struggle is the negativity around which all attempts at positivity are a response. In effect, if class struggle is a modality of the Real, it cannot be represented – class becomes literally impossible, another name for the non-existence of society that precedes any actually existing class groupings, which are themselves only a reaction to the impossibility of class struggle (Žižek 2010: 198).The difficulty with this reading is that as there is no meta-language in which to discuss class, it cannot be the subject of any positive research, which Žižek suggests explains Marx's curious failure to include it within his *Capital* (Žižek 2006b: 82; 2010: 201–2).*

The difficulty, well identified by Žižek's incredulous critics, is that in translating class struggle as a mode of the Real, Žižek avoids an encounter with the empirical problems that had plagued the concept and practice of class struggle, replacing them with Lacanian doxa

---

* Interestingly, Marx had originally planned a book on wage-labour as part of six-volume set that would form his 'economics'. See Lebowitz (2003) for further discussion on this matter.

without any regard for the exigencies of political economy. Whilst it is clear that Žižek wants to position class at the forefront of Leftist and anti-capitalist politics, it is not exactly clear what this would mean for either political practice or Marxism itself.

Devenney, for instance, contends that Žižek's account of both class and capitalism is inadequate because of this apparent refusal to elaborate upon the discontinuity between Žižek's class and the Marxist tradition. Suggesting that Žižek's argument is 'extraordinary', with the only purpose that it 'allows Žižek to wear Marxist labels' (Devenney 2007: 54), Devenney roundly dismisses Žižek's contention that an element (specifically class) can come to structure the social through its absence. For Devenney, this is a statement entirely without 'evidence' (2007: 54).

In reply, Žižek is equally critical of Devenney, in particular his 'faked ignorance' at the possible structuring role of an element which, whilst being present symbolically – we can write the word 'class' – is absent at the level of the imaginary, in so far as we cannot imagine the presence of something that is absent: a full class relationship (Žižek 2007b: 212). For Žižek, and other readers of Lacan, the effect of absence (in the form of the Real) does not equate to an absence of effect. A phenomenon can form an absence within ideology, yet it is this absence that propels ideology itself. Such is the nature of the Lacanian Real: although it 'does not exist' within the positive contours of reality it produces a range of effects that identifies its presence. Moreover, whilst these effects can be represented symbolically – we can discuss the political effects of an encounter with the Real – the absence of the Real cannot be the imaginary basis for ideology in itself.

To be fair to Devenney, the problem is not so much that Žižek mobilises the Lacanian Real as a mode of causality in response to Marxist essentialism but, instead, that he mobilises it in the name of class struggle. Because of this Žižek appears ill equipped to respond to the problems that have plagued Marxian notions of class (Eagleton 2011; Hall 1977; Hunt 1977a; Lebowitz 2003; Wood 2004).

Indeed, it is unclear if Žižek's class struggle is even an economic category, let alone what it has to say about post-industrialism or structural adjustment programmes. The most pertinent line of critique of Žižek's position, one taken by both Laclau and Devenney, is that it doesn't say anything about the operation of real-world capitalism. Class struggle as a mode of the Real is an ahistorical concept: it is not specific to capitalism but cuts across all possible modalities of the economy. And yet, following the likes of Zygmunt Bauman (2004), David Harvey (2008) and Mike Davis (2007), Žižek has become increasingly compelled by the presence of large surplus populations in developing urban areas.

It is indeed this point which Žižek identifies as *the* antagonism threatening global capitalism today. Contrary to his apparent production of capitalism as an monstrous juggernaut, Žižek argues that four points of antagonism currently threaten capitalism: the possibility of ecological collapse, the contradictions between immaterial labour,* intellectual property and private property, the development of new scientific technologies which are changing the nature of life in its barest form and the new forms of political exclusion (Žižek 2008: 420–5).

Under this construction it is the latter element that defines the group: the other three contradictions have been able to be included within the limits of capitalism. Environmentalism, despite the apparent radical possibility of a chaotic breach of nature, has become sustainable development. The contradictions of private property have become a legal challenge and bio-genetics has developed into an ethical, or even scientific, struggle. For Žižek these three elements are part of the battle for the commons. Here Žižek (2008: 428) follows Michael Hardt and Antonio Negri in suggesting that the commons – particularly in the postmodern articulation of the commons in immaterial labour and knowledge – are increasingly being enclosed and privatised. In relation to these specific antagonisms, environmentalism equates to the commons of external nature, intellectual property to the commons of culture and bio-technology to the commons of internal nature. Whilst this enclosure and exploitation of what is common to all evokes the necessary use of communism, it is only the fourth symptom, that of exclusion, which adds the dimension of universality in that it is the element which constitutes the construction of capital.

In evoking the exclusion of the lumpenproletariat from capital as the primacy contradiction, Žižek could be said to be both engaging in traditional class critique and breaking with Marx in identifying the 'universal class' not as the working-class proletariat but, rather,

---

* Žižek's original formulation of these antagonisms, within *In Defense of Lost Causes* (2008: 422), was named 'the inadequacy of private property', but in *Living in the End Times* (2010: x) this was expanded to include other imbalances such as battles over raw materials.

those outside waged life. Yet, he does not link this positioning back to his own work on class struggle. Despite suggesting that class struggle never directly appears, Žižek does make regular references to class formations. Matthew Sharpe (2004: 202–5) argues that this is a hesitation within Žižek's work, contending that his identification of class formations contradicts his reference to class struggle *qua* Real. Here, Sharpe suggests that Žižek becomes entwined in the impossible game that haunts contemporary Marxism: the identification and necessary enlargement of conceptions of the working class. If Žižek is to speak of class as an empirically locatable phenomenon, then a more detailed analysis of class structure is required. Sharpe comes to argue that today such a description has become impossible and it is for this reason that Žižek can only refer to class without expanding upon it.

Indeed, Žižek does make fairly regular references to changes in class structures which, in Sharpe's terms, can appear 'ad hoc' or 'journalistic'. Sharpe (2004: 197), for instance, cites Žižek's distinction between the 'symbolic' class of Western professionals, the middle class of Western manual labour and the excluded class, which Žižek links to the symbolic, the imaginary and the Real respectively (Žižek 2000d: 323). There is a certain logic to Sharpe's critique; such an analysis does not engage with the difficult history of class structure, nor does it appear to have a strong empirical backing. Conversely, the mapping of class structure is not Žižek's central point in this passage; rather it is the subsequent reference – a reference Sharpe ignores – to the manner in which class antagonism is the underlying factor beneath all these political forms of identity.

Thus, the difficult question of the relationship between class struggle and class structure remains. We must consider how Žižek can posit what appears to be an empirical reading of the structure of class under 21st-century global capitalism without linking this interpretation with his reading of class struggle *qua* the Real.

It appears that Žižek is holding to two separate theories of class. If class struggle itself is the antagonism underlying social life – what we might determine to be the economic base of shared social life – and therefore prior to the existence of the social groupings defined as economic classes, these classes nonetheless exist as a positive reaction to the impossibility of a determinate class relationship. The problem is that whilst Žižek's reworking of class struggle *qua* the Real allows for a redevelopment of the base–superstructure model, it does not tell us anything about how class operates in contemporary capitalism. Although we can take from Žižek's work that class struggle is the underlying antagonism in all forms of economy, in order to develop a productive critique of capitalism, we must begin to consider how this impossibility plays out within global capitalism. To do so, however, requires that we re-engage with the difficulties of identifying the positive structure of class struggle.

SYMBOLISING CLASS BEYOND THE IMAGINARY

Although class is often taken to be one of the core elements of Marx's work, it is a concept which he did not fully develop, particularly in regard to wage-labour or the operation of the working class (Lebowitz 2003). Whilst, as Stuart Hall (1977: 15) notes, class struggle could be said to be at the core of everything Marx did, in *Capital* he continually postponed a conception of class and it remained incomplete. Tellingly, Marx had more to say about class struggle in his more political work, specifically *The Communist Manifesto* (1848), where he asserted that the history of the world is the history of class struggle and that within capitalism this battle is characterised by the battle between those who own the means of production and those forced to sell their labour. Moreover, if the circuit of capital is infinite, Marx suggested that it was only the working class that offered an exit from this infinite reproduction (see Lebowitz 2003: 14).

In identifying the working class as the grave-diggers of capital, much of the politics of Marxism has focused on delineating the co-ordinates of the 'two great classes directly facing each other' (Marx & Engels 2004: 4). Yet, as both Marxism and capitalism have developed, it has become increasingly clear that the finite economic groupings posited by Marx are no longer sufficient. As a consequence, a significant rethinking of class has occurred, often moving away from the determinism of property relations to cultural identification. This has led to the kind of position suggested by Laclau (2000b: 201–5), whereby cultural identifications with class positions are becoming increasingly irrelevant.

Against this dismissal of class, those interested in rethinking Marxism within a discursive context have sought to restore the primacy of class as an economic category. Several theorists working within the umbrella of the Association for Economic and Social Analysis, largely publishing through the *Rethinking Marxism* journal, have attempted to reformulate the essentialist history of class, suggesting, in line with Louis Althusser's work on overdetermination, that class be reconsidered as a set of processes – understood as the 'processes of producing, appropriating and distributing surplus labour' (Graham & Amariglio 2006: 200). This rethinking has not been a uniform process, with several variants emerging, often inspired by Lacanian or deconstructive approaches.

One of the most productive of these approaches stems from the work of Ceren Özselçuk and Yahya Madra. Like Žižek, Özselçuk and Madra (2007: 92) argue that class struggle is '[the] foundational, constitutive lack as the absent cause, the foundational antagonism, the constitutive impossibility, around which sociality is constructed'. Although sharing the same ontological commitment – that there is no class relationship – Özselçuk and Madra diverge strongly from Žižek in their epistemological interpretation of this commitment.

Most saliently, they have not shied away from symbolising the structure of class struggle. Whilst Žižek has (implicitly at least) rejected a definition of the structure of class antagonism, Özselçuk and Madra base their work around a deconstruction of class struggle. They state that concrete class structures do exist, but any attempts to find a 'normal' or transcendental class relationship will necessary fail. Özselçuk and Madra argue that Žižek's refusal to delineate the cause of class relations, rather than its effects, results in an inability to see past specifically *capitalist* class relations.

By contrast Özselçuk and Madra argue that class formations 'are fantasmatic and libidinally animated formations, structured around an impossibility that stains all attempts to institute a stable and harmonious organisation of production, appropriation and distribution of surplus labour' (2007: 78). If class struggle is impossible, then this impossibility occurs within ideological formations that attempt to seal the wound of their foundation. Žižek, no doubt, would suggest that any position taken on class struggle can only be ideological: one cannot get outside class struggle to speak about class struggle. Whilst Žižek suggests that class struggle occurs in the imaginary only to the extent of staging the presence of absence, Özselçuk and Madra argue that by identifying both the symbolic formula of the impossible class relationship as well as the manner in which it is subjectively embodied as a form of fantasy, a new, non-exclusive class formation is possible.

Whilst the value of Özselçuk and Madra's work is limited by these attempts to produce a feminine politics of class struggle, in much the same way that Stavrakakis evoked a feminine notion of democracy (see Chapter 3 for a critique of this position), they do establish two basic steps that greatly assist in developing a Žižekian theory of class struggle within capitalism. Firstly, the basic economic parameters of class processes are outlined. These parameters – production, distribution and appropriation of surplus – do not evoke any sense of essentialism or economism beyond asserting that class is an economic category. In developing the minimum symbolic co-ordinates of class structure, Özselçuk and Madra are able to establish class struggle as part of the economy without positing the imaginary fullness that prevents Žižek's development of the concept.

Thus, following Özselçuk and Madra, whilst class relationships are impossible, they are nonetheless structured around the production, distribution and appropriation of surplus – class is thus understood as the politics of the mode of production, a process rather than a position. These politics, however, remain as a wound within the symbolic order. Class itself may define the mode of production, but it doesn't evoke a positive presence in regard to determinate groupings.

Furthermore, Özselçuk and Madra suggest that whilst class struggle is the antagonism against which society is founded, this does not mean that class relationships do not occur. By specifically defining class relationships as fantasmatically defined entities, Özselçuk and Madra are able to close the gap between Žižek's conception of class struggle as a mode of the Real and the occurrence of class struggle within capitalism. This point is vital. Moving beyond Özselçuk and Madra's reading, by utilising Žižek's notion of concrete universality we are in a position to consider possibilities for subverting the limitless reproduction of the circuit of capital through an identification of those excluded from class struggle in order to produce a fantasmatic class relationship.

Here, Žižek's two notions of class – class struggle and the exclusion of the lumpenproletariat – can be unified by his reading of universality. The split operation of the universal reveals the effect of the Real upon society. In order to expel the violent effects of the Real upon symbolisation and the body – remembering that the Real itself is nothing but a reaction to the body entering symbolisation – an imaginary coherence is attempted to be produced through the installation of an abstract universal horizon, based upon an empty signifier/*objet a* and competing 'chains of equivalence'. This horizon attempts to construct an objective sense of social life, but only through the exclusion of an exceptional element – it is this exclusion that allows for the abstract constitution of a universal set. Žižek, through Hegel, identifies this exceptional exclusion that constitutes the universal imaginary as concrete universality. His point is not that concrete universality is the true point of universality – although it opens up the path towards Truth – but rather that the site of universality proper is the gap between the abstract and concrete functions of the universal. This gap can be identified as a modality of the Real, at least within the ideologies that structure capitalism and prevent the acknowledgement of any injustice that exists at its core.

In relation to class struggle, this construction of the operation of universality suggests that class struggle operates as the universal gap in symbolisation, but it nonetheless occurs: every instantiation of the economy produces an abstract conception of this gap – one that attempts to elide its presence – and a concrete remainder of its exclusion. Here we can return to Žižek's (1989: 21–3) suggestion that it was Marx who invented the symptom, whereby he detected an imbalance in workings of labour that spoke to the universality of the system. Whilst labour is formally free to sell itself as a commodity on the market, this freedom is in fact coerced by labour's vulnerability to capital. The worker is forced to sell their labour on the market as a commodity, both because they are unable to reproduce themselves independently of capital and because of an oversupply of workers: if one individual worker does not sell their labour, there is always another to take their place.

Class struggle is, therefore, a modality of the Real. If we refer, however, to the 'parallel' construction of the Real suggested in Chapter 4, in which what might be an example of the Real within a discourse can be ideologically represented within another, then an alternative construction of class struggle becomes available. The expression of class struggle is always a reaction to the formal impossibility of itself, yet it nonetheless occurs: class struggle is both the formal impossibility of political economy and attempts to elide this impossibility by creating fantasmatic class relationships.

Within capitalism the remainder of the failure of the class relationship lies in the excesses of labour that plagues the planet. These excesses are beyond the 205 million officially unemployed, lying more in the almost 40 per cent of the global population outside official employment as the world economy increasingly struggles to integrate growth in working-age populations (International Labour Organization 2011). Although popular ideology attempts to disavow the presence and status of this surplus of labour, through the analysis presented in this text we are in a position to assert its volatile presence.

Such an identification allows for a more productive understanding of exclusion, and the effect of the Real, within capitalism. By suggesting that the exclusion of this grouping is the evidence of class struggle in capitalism, we are no longer seeking to provide the ideal politics of class struggle – such a relationship is impossible – but, rather, a way of invoking this impossibility at the heart of capitalism. The lesson to be learned here is that class struggle is not simply a matter, as in traditional Marxist communism, of the exploited working class overthrowing their capitalist masters in order to achieve their promised destiny. This is a mistake made by a number of Žižek's critics, when they accuse him of wanting to return to a politics of the 'dictatorship of the proletariat' (Laclau 2000b: 206; Sharpe & Boucher 2010: 186–93).

Moreover, Žižek's understanding of class struggle is not strictly limited to the battle between classes for the benefits of production. Instead, class struggle relates to the disavowed and distorting effects of the Real within social life: we literally struggle with the impossibility of class justice. Nonetheless, these two positions are not entirely divorced. History does not require the proletariat to cast off their shackles. Yet it is their exceptional status that provides the central friction with capital, a friction I have identified as a modality of the Real.

If these are class relations within 21st-century capitalism, they are not divorced from Marx's original conception. There are two significant differences, however. The first is how class struggle is conceived; the second is the empirical content of workers within global capitalism today. In regard to the first point, if Žižek has argued that class relationships do not exist, I have insisted, following Özselçuk and Madra, that the class relationship still occurs, yet fails. That is, all modes of production necessarily produce a form of class struggle, it is just that this struggle is never complete. Instead, to produce an ideological image of itself, some element of class struggle must be excluded.

By conceiving of class struggle as a mode of universality, we see that the excluded element, or, more accurately, the gap between the exclusion and the point of its exclusion, is a modality of the Real and one that threatens to disrupt ideology. If ideologies within capitalism come to orientate themselves around notions of freedom, order or even consumption, they are unable to recognise the constitutive exception around which they are based: the existence of a surplus of labour that constitutes the presence of capitalism and the wage-labour system. It is this exclusion which signals the Truth of capitalism, an ever-present Truth that threatens to break through the ideological bonds of capitalism. The question is how this might occur. To understand this, we must turn to the second significant difference from Marx's original conception: the place of the universal class.

UNIVERSAL CLASS IN THE TWENTY-FIRST CENTURY

Marx did not see any particular virtue in the working class, or in working itself (Eagleton 2011: 164). Nor did he conceive of the working class as the most needy or suffering group in society. Instead, for Marx the working class holds a vital economic position in being the producers of surplus without appropriating that surplus. Furthermore, a vital distinction occurs between the working class and the proletariat. Where the working class holds a strictly economic position, for Marx, the position of the proletariat is one of engaged political subjectivity (Žižek 2006a: 564).

This political split also speaks to Marx's dismissal of the revolutionary power of the lumpenproletariat, literally the 'rabble' proletariat, whom he once described as 'the dangerous class, the social scum' (Marx & Engels 2004: 17). As Žižek suggests, in contrast to Laclau, the distinction between these two groups is not between an objectified grouping and its excess, but two separate forms of excess (Žižek 2006a: 564). Here, the lumpenproletariat is separated from the proletariat by its subjective position: rather than producing the threat to the social body that its discarded status would suggest, Marx argued that the lumpenproletariat is a freer-floating element more suited to reactionary movements.

For Laclau, Marx's dismissal of the possible universality of the lumpenproletariat displays the limitations of his economic determinism – the lumpenproletariat held no political potential for Marx because they did not pose a threat to the economic order. By contrast, Laclau, particularly in his populist mode, insists on the political character of this group and its possible integration into the politics of populism as an 'absolute outside' that threatens the coherence of ideological identifications (Laclau 2005: 144–51).

At times, Žižek appears to share Laclau's contention that the lumpenproletariat are politically excluded, by contrast to the economic exclusion of the proletariat. Attempting to identify a 'crucial' difference between the 21st-century lumpenproletariat and the traditional Marxist proletariat, Žižek suggests that the latter group are defined by their economic exploitation, whereas the lumpenproletariat are characterised by their non-integration into the political order. They are outside state power, the Agambenian *Homo sacer* who, whilst being physically alive, has no positive legal status (Žižek 2008: 425).

Nonetheless, at the same time, Žižek asks, 'What if the new proletarian position is that of the inhabitants of slums in the new megapolises?' Suggesting that these developments are the crucial geopolitical event of our time, Žižek argues that these non-workers are not a 'redundant surplus' but are rather a 'necessary product of the innermost logic of global capitalism' (Žižek 2008: 424). Here Žižek shares the same conception as Eagleton when he states, in regard to Marx's conception of the working class:

> Because it is both necessary to and excluded by the capitalist system, this 'class which is not a class' is a kind of riddle or conundrum. In a quite literal sense, it creates the social order – it is on its silent, persistent labour that the mighty edifice is reared – yet it can find no real representation within that order, no full recognition of its humanity. It is both functional and dispossessed, specific and universal, an integral part of civil society, yet a kind of nothing. (Eagleton 2011: 166)

What can we make of this apparent disjuncture? What Žižek appears to miss is that whilst the lumpenproletariat are outside the protection of the state and civil society – often by the explicit desire of the state in the creation of 'free' economic zones where the established laws of the state do not apply in order to encourage multi-national investment – they are intimately integrated into the flows of *global* capital. The lumpenproletariat migrate as cheap, often indentured, labour in rapidly developing zones of the world. These flows are particularly prominent in China, where poor and uneducated populations outside the benefits of the economic boom travel to the more celebrated cities. The erection of Dubai and Abu Dhabi has been based on quasi-slave conditions in which workers' passports are seized and wages slashed.

These are the populations of urban slums, now estimated to total 827.6 million in 2010 (UN-Habitat 2011), who toil for the benefit of capitalism. More precisely, it is those excluded from this toil, those who lead what Michael Denning (2010) calls a 'wageless life', who are utterly invisible yet essential for capitalism. It is they who enforce the discipline required to keep subsistence workers in the factories and in the farms on the most minimal of wages and the most despicable of conditions. These non-workers, surplus to the direct requirements of capital, enable the continual functioning of capitalism. These people are not so much workers as informal capitalists. Where the worker is forced to sell their labour as they do not own the means to produce, the urban lumpenproletariat is unable to sell their labour – for economic or political reasons – so is often forced to become an informal trader, buying gormless consumer products to hawk to tourists.

Most of all, however, the lumpenproletariat are integrated into global capitalism as a way of regulating the price of labour (Žižek 2010: 209). Capital and its agents stalk the globe seeking cheaper and more 'free' sources of production. For the capitalist wage-labour system to operate, an excess of workers must exist so that they can be coerced to sell their bodies for this labour. As has been seen in previous historical examples – the colonisation of Australia, for example, in which the ready availability of land made it difficult to establish a labour force during the early years of settlement (Pappe 1951; Marx 2007: 839–40) – without the compulsion to work for the profit of others, the wage-labour system does not function efficiently. What provides this compulsion is an excess supply of workers such that a worker who refuses to accept work at market prices is easily replaced by another.

To some degree, this operation is subverted by the existence of minimum-wage and welfare laws in Western nations, so that not only do wage prices not drop to the market price determined by supply, but the unemployed are afforded some protection.* The displacement of large elements of production – whether manufacturing 'sweatshops' or cash-crop farms – to the developing world, often attracted by the absence of these conditions and the massive surplus of labour, produces a different result. Not only do wage prices often fall to subsistence levels, but those in the position of excess to the labour force suffer extreme material deprivation. The necessary consequence of the capitalist wage-system which produces Western wealth and an increasing culture of consumption is the death of those 'extimately' placed within the system.

---

* The unemployed who are deemed legally worthy, that is. The way around these 'stifling' limitations on the labour market is often to employ illegal migrants who stand outside the law, allowing for a purer mode of exploitation. A similar structure exists in the creation of 'economic free zones' in developing countries, where many aspect of labour protection are suspended.

This tragedy is not a contingent aberration – it is not a matter of extending Western protections (many of which were demanded in *The Communist Manifesto*) to the developing world – but is rather caused by a structural oversupply of workers located in large part within the massive growth of urban slums in the developing world, which has occurred over the past half-century. Moreover, it is also caused by the structural requirement within capital for only a minority to own the means of production. I have suggested that the lumpenproletariat are extimately located within global capitalism in the sense that they are necessary for the functioning of capitalism yet not ideologically included with capital. That is, for capital's apologists and the official managers and measurers of the system – whether the United Nations, the IMF or the World Bank – the problem is that the poor are not included within capitalism. For development theorists and apologists for capitalism, such as the American economist Jeffrey Sachs, special adviser to Ban Ki-Moon on the United Nations Millennium Development Goals project, the movement of capital from post-industrial economies to the sweatshops of the Third World is a positive move, allowing for an extension of the 'development ladder' to those who have not yet experienced the benefits of capital (Sachs 2005).

By contrast, Marx called the existence of an excess of labour the 'reserve army of labour', the presence of the unemployed who act as an anchor to the demands of the working class (Marx 1999: 350–62). In this way, the lumpenproletariat are essential for the continued functioning of capital, not only in terms of maintaining the vulnerability of the proletariat but if there is any possibility of the global economy remaining compatible with earthly ecological limits, these non-workers cannot be allowed to develop – at least whilst there exist the über-wealthy who dominate the flows of capitalism.

Capital is a system that requires a continual revolutionising of its own conditions to produce future growth. Although increases in efficiency resulting from improved technology, or a willingness to tackle the effects of consumption upon the environment are of benefit, they are an inadequate response to the continued growth of the world economy. Indeed, as this growth is compounded by the predicted increase in the global population to 9.3 billion by 2050 (United Nations Department of Economic and Social Affairs 2011), it is evident that the level of planetary economic activity is going to rise well above the earth's carrying capacity. What is required is a global reduction in consumption. As noted, calls for a reduction in consumption in the 'post-industrial' economy are a strong element of the mainstream green movement. What this position elides, however, is that such reductions in consumption will necessarily result in a fall in employment for those most in need: the Third or developing world. For this reason, a widespread rise in material standards of living for the poorest citizens of the planet is not ecologically possible – within the current mode of production – as it is clear that capitalism is incompatible with both equality of consumption and the sustainable reproduction of global ecological systems (Kovel 2007).

The lumpenproletariat are thus a vital part of global capitalism, yet they play no part in its ideological construction of itself, whether in the enjoyment of consumption, the justice of democracy or the good of the nation. They can be regarded as the universal exception, the point of concrete universality within capitalism and class struggle. To recount this point, if class struggle is impossible and acts as a modality of the Real, class relationships nonetheless occur: class struggle is the foundational wound around which the mode of production is constructed. It is ideological fantasy that attempts to regulate this wound, to create sense out of the contingent power struggle around production, distribution and appropriation of the economic goods that allow for our reproduction. Yet this ideology, this abstract universal sense of ourselves, requires an exclusion in order to maintain its narrative. The lumpenproletariat are this exception and it is for this reason that they hold a revolutionary status within capital. Where the proletariat now have an established place within capitalism, propping up middle-class consumer desires, the lumpenproletariat still act as the excess, both maintaining the functioning of capitalism and taking the brunt of its horrific cost. If Marx (1999: 362) stated that, 'Accumulation of wealth at one pole is, therefore, at the same time accumulation of misery, agony, toil slavery, ignorance, brutality, mental degradation, at the opposite pole', then the lumpenproletariat is the location of that misery. It is not so much that Marx got it wrong in locating revolutionary potential in the proletariat rather than the reserve army, but that historical global conditions are such that the location of the place of exclusion has altered.

For this reason an expanded Žižekian theory of class struggle returns full circle to the more classical Marxian approach whereby it is only the universal class, rather than any other grouping, that can bring about the dissolution of capital. This universal class not only signals the Truth of capitalism – that horror and misery are at the heart of the functioning of capitalism – but its weakness. This vulnerability occurs not only because capitalism could not continue without the presence of a reserve army, but because this horror lies at odds with the ideologies that cohere capitalism. Although there is no distinct hegemonic ideology of capitalism, the fantasies that persist within it emphasise either harmless consumer enjoyment and expression, or the justice of formal equality and progress whereby our symbolic institutions manage collective life in the name of the Good. That these institutions – primarily global markets – succeed only on the basis of others' suffering remains a point of distinct trauma: an element of the Real.

However, this analysis does not simply lead into a form of politics. Instead, the true value of Žižek's work lies in the strategic manipulation of the element of trauma within the concrete circumstances of contemporary capitalism.

Determinate Negation and Global Capitalism

In this book, I have thus far rejected any essentialism which stems from a predestined chosen revolutionary group. Nonetheless, a different kind of approach, stemming from Žižek's reading of both Lacan and Marx, suggests that the most productive form of anti-capitalism today is associated with the existence of this excluded group that I have constructed as the lumpenproletariat. This potential comes not from the group itself, nor any alternative economic construction that might attempt to include this group but, rather, a strategic manipulation of the tension that exists between the ideological narratives of the global West and the necessary exclusions from this conception of shared social life – that the wage-labour system operates only on the basis of a surplus of labour which cannot be acknowledged within Western civilisation itself. To restate this in base terms, the tension within capitalism lies in the disavowed Truth that capitalism is constructed in such a manner that for the living standards of Western civilisation to continue unfettered, an excess of workers must remain outside the wage-labour system, and as a consequence of this status, the quality and length of their lives are significantly reduced.

The revolutionary potential here lies in the intrusion of this disavowed element of our civilisation into the ideological narrative of the West, whether in relation to justice, equality, freedom or some other high-minded abstract ideal, to potentially cause a revolutionary dislocation in the structure of that narrative. This disruption has the potential to open up space for alternative modes of political action.

How these responses occur, as well as generating a dislocation in the first place, is the battle of politics.

Although Žižek does identify the Lacanian structure of class struggle, he makes only an implicit reference to the history of Marxism. This is not a lapse in his scholarship; rather, he does it because of an ontological commitment to the Real status of class struggle. Nonetheless, as I noted in Chapter 4, reading the Real through Žižek's concept of (concrete) universality allows for an identification of the point of exclusion in relation to class struggle, an identification that potentially allows for a disruption of ideology.

This is a vital point, and shall be a central focus point in the final two chapters. These chapters concentrate upon formulating a Žižekian-inspired politics in response to the contradictions of global capitalism. Thus far I have rejected both classical Marxist politics and the production of alternative forms of shared social life based upon Lacanian psychoanalysis. Moreover, this chapter has illustrated Žižek's construction of the ontic structure of capitalism, one that limits the range of political action available. My Žižekian political response begins from this point, expanding upon this reading of class struggle to identify those strategic opportunities for political action that stem from Žižek's work, including the utopian demand of the 'communist hypothesis'.

6

Žižek's Realpolitics

In this book, I have thus far established four firm premises: that Žižek's work should fundamentally be conceived as a response to capitalism; that a psychoanalytically inspired politics cannot posit an alternative form of 'the Good life' but, rather, a temporary rearrangement of the relationship between the Real and ideological fantasy; that global capitalism acts as a self-revolutionary system that integrates and exhausts all opposition; and that capital is nonetheless plagued by the 'extimate' exclusion of the lumpenproletariat through class struggle. It is this exclusion that ultimately threatens global capitalism and provides the fulcrum for a Žižekian response to capitalism. Conversely, there is no 'natural' link between the existence of this antagonism and political practice. Instead, any mode of politics must be strategic, taking into account concrete circumstances and in the relationship between the Real and its symbolic-imaginary minders. Having considered the structure of these circumstances within capitalism, in this chapter I will discuss the strategic alternatives for political practice that emerge from Žižekian theory and I will reflect upon the productivity of these alternatives in regard to the contradictions of capital embodied by the lumpenproletariat *qua* the Real.

By rejecting the possibility of a collective and institutionalised normativity stemming from a Lacanian conception of shared social life, I can now offer an alternative Lacanian approach to politics. Chapters 3 and 4 established that Žižek's construction of political life does not lead to a reductive or institutionalised approach, instead suggesting the development of a range of strategic possibilities based around the Lacanian notion of the Real. These strategic positions should be read not as chronological developments – as in Matthew Sharpe and Geoff Boucher's (2010) argument that Žižek's theory takes a radical (and incorrect) turn around 1997 – but as contextual attempts to rearticulate the destructive effects of the Real.

As constructed in the previous chapter, our time in history is such that we cannot simply posit alternative modes of being and hope that they will flourish. The strength of capitalism means that there is no outside space immune to its reach. Any point of otherness, whether resistant to capital or not, is drawn into the logic of capitalism. As a result, alternative understandings or practices only 'make sense' or 'work' if they fit in with the operation of capitalism.

This historical positioning of capital produces a rather bleak picture of 21st-century politics – at least for those who are on the sharp end of Western progress. Nonetheless, although history appears 'stuck' in the self-revolutionising flows of capital, I have been able to nominate a central fault line: the exclusion of a portion of the polis from the benefits of capital that is nonetheless necessary for the continued functioning of capital. By understanding this excess of labour as both the central contradiction of capitalism as well as a modality of the Real, new possibilities for disturbing the operation of capital are revealed.

Conversely, identifying the disruptive presence of an excess of labour does not naturally evoke either an alternative form of social life, one in which this surplus is dissolved, or a predestined political response. Although the identification of this point of exclusion as a potentially revolutionary site evokes images of the rise, and subsequent dictatorship, of the proletariat, Žižek's work strongly rejects such a (Marxist) reading of historical progress. This is a point that appears to be misunderstood by his critics (Sharpe & Boucher 2010: 186–93). Whilst Žižek does evoke the infamous term 'dictatorship of the proletariat', his reference has moved beyond the control of the state and the institutionalisation of different forms of governance.

Instead, I will suggest a reading of Žižek that evokes a strategic form of politics based on an expansion of the Lacanian theory of the Real discussed in Chapter 4. This dialectical understanding allows for multiple forms of political intervention relative to the positioning of the Real within an ideological framework. Here politics becomes a politics of disruption and re-examination: exactly what is required in the all-encompassing face of global capitalism. In this regard this chapter makes reference to three distinct yet intertwined interventions that feature through Žižek's work: the act, subtractive politics, and the practice of concrete universality.*

---

* Although each of these strategies features prominently throughout his work, Žižek has not identified these positions as strategic alternatives. It is difficult, and somewhat undesirable, to attach an objective coherence to each of these strategies. Rather they are similar processes which relate back to the singular operation of the Real within ideology as identified throughout this book; they are processes more than objects.

It is through these strategies that I shall respond to the issue that this chapter ultimately addresses: how to translate Žižek's work into a political response to the disavowed foundations of global capitalism. In response to this specific question, this chapter suggests that whilst 'the act' formulates the basic Žižekian political strategy by opposing activity to revolutionary action, it remains too 'crazy' to be considered an effective political formulation. It is unable to resolve not only the limitations of psychoanalysis as a political force, but also the difficulties of responding to the reign of global capitalism.

More productively, the subtlety of subtractive politics suggests that the grand reformation of the act can occur through minimal political action. Here Žižek has argued that in a 'post-ideological' age of cynicism, withdrawing from the ideological framework through which capitalism is understood is the most effective form of politics. In this chapter, however, I argue that the practice of concrete universality – a form of politics which involves the active juxtaposition of an ideology with its exception – alone holds this potential on account of its use of the tension between the suffering of the lumpenproletariat and Western ideological fantasies.

This position is not the final word on Žižekian politics, however. Recently, Žižek has also begun to make reference to Alain Badiou's notion of the communist hypothesis, a reference that invokes the presence of utopian theory and Fredric Jameson. Through this reference I return to the question of normativity, Marxism and the future significance of Žižekian politics. For now, though, my task is to consider how the most common Žižekian strategies might operate as interventions into global capitalism.

Strategic Politics of the Real

Žižek's work does not provide a psychoanalytic conception of the ideal form of shared social life. If his early work, following the likes

The danger here lies in reifying Žižek's position to a form of methodologism through which each political strategy becomes a separate object. The intent in labelling these positions is to identify different possibilities in approaching the Real rather than pacifying the Real as a form of presence. Indeed, the manner in which each strategy attempts to avoid such a pacification is a key focus of each construction. Whilst these strong divisions would not occur in the messy practice of street level politics – it is only the level of abstraction required by philosophical inquiry that creates these problems – there is significant value in the subtler delineation of the distinctions between these approaches, each of which produces differing responses to capitalism.

of Ernesto Laclau, focused upon the possibilities for a more radical form of democracy inspired by Lacan, a more powerful current has subsequently come to the fore. Here Žižek has become what I termed in the Introduction a comedic philosopher of the Real, a political philosopher whose interest lies in the form in which the Real appears within discursive structures. This interest is inherently political: it entails an understanding of what is excluded from a discourse to induce its internal coherence and the kind of political practice that would break these binds of enjoyment. As Levi Bryant suggests:

> Rather than looking to Žižek's various texts for a theory of practice or what we should do, we should instead read these texts themselves as a form of practice. That is, we should not ask whether Žižek's interpretations are true or false but should instead ask what these interpretations do. (2007: 22)

If Žižek's politics are best understood as both a strategic politics of the Real and a response to global capitalism, as discussed in the previous chapter, we can regard the exclusion of a non-labouring polis from formal employment to be an element of the Real within the circuit of capital. The Real is not only an absence but becomes embodied in an actually occurring element that holds an extimate position within the symbolic-imaginary order. Attempts to suture this impossibility are rife throughout the ideological defences that act to cohere the operation of capital.

If we consider ideological formations to be structured in order to minimalise this absence and the resulting production of an exception, then Žižek's political approach entails various attempts to consider how that fantasmatic coherence can be disturbed. In disturbing the fantasmatic formations that hold together global capitalism, it is envisaged that gaps will appear permitting the occurrence of action that would be otherwise impossible within the current operation of global capitalism. The most prominent of these strategies is Žižek's political construction of the Lacanian act.

THE ACT

The (Lacanian) act is the paradigmatic and most controversial element of Žižek's political strategy. Standing as the universal procedure of Žižek's political practice, all other modalities of his politics stem from the basic division Žižek identifies between the act and activity. By contrast to everyday activity, an act makes a radical break from common sense: its basic form is action that reformulates a systematic logic such that it retroactively produces its own conditions of possibility. The act comes from an unthinkable and impossible place within a discourse, appearing as a moment of madness that cannot be accounted for within conventional reason. As such, in terms of a Lacanian schema, an act occurs when the excluded presence of the Real bursts into a symbolic-imaginary framework, changing the way it is constructed. If this framework had previously repressed the 'unthinkable' presence of the Real, such an evocation rips up the previous established logic of 'reality' and produces a desperate grasping for fantasmatic security. An act might occur at a personal level, for instance, when previously repressed sexual desires are suddenly expressed in an unplanned outburst, 'I love you!', such that the relationship can never be the same again.

A true act occurs without any objective guarantee, appearing as a moment of madness at the time of its occurrence. As such, it is quite divorced from predominant Leftist political narratives such as Laclau's battle for hegemony, the inevitability of historical materialism or managerial Leftism. By contrast, an act – in so much as one can begin to describe the collective shape it might take – comes with a sudden seizing of the moment and as such is associated more with revolutionary terror than policy planning and political strategy.

The act is thus radically opposed to the kind of 'politics as usual' approach that dominates late modernity and maintains the dominance of global capitalism. Here, often by particular reference to the economic problems this book responds to, Žižek notes a prohibition on radical politics. Writing on the general rejection of Lenin as a political philosopher, he states: 'The moment we show a minimal sign of engaging in political projects which aim seriously to challenge the existing order, the answer is immediately "Benevolent as it is, this will inevitably end in a new Gulag!"' (Lenin 2002: 168). This is a typical ideological response to global development issues: do not engage in radical politics; although they appear necessary to produce change, they will only end in genocide or capital flight.

Instead, responses to the contradictions of capitalism are the political equivalent of biting our finger nails: they provide a semblance of action in the face of anxiety. Changing our homepage to Google Black may not change the world, but at least we are doing *something*. What we are doing, really, is keeping the anxiety of the Real at bay by participating in fantasmatic narratives of gradual change. On a larger scale, a range of 'activist' Leftist political movements have moved away from debating with capitalism specifically, instead discussing its (ethical) management, whether in terms of human rights organisations such as Amnesty International, animal rights bodies of the likes of PETA or environmental groupings such as Greenpeace. These groups certainly address legitimate concerns and perform admirable work, but they produce a limited politics framed by the inherent notion that a radical Leftist universalist politics could only reproduce the horrors of the twentieth century. Whilst they highlight some of the contradictions of capitalism, these contradictions are not linked to capitalism itself, but are instead viewed in isolation (see Cremin 2011).

Žižek heartily rejects this approach and instead insists that we must trace economic symptoms back to the very logic of the mode of production, suggesting the necessity of a radical break from the logic of capital. It is this demand for a radical break from ideological fantasy, one at the heart of the Lacanian clinical procedure, which is perhaps the productive element of Žižek's political interventions: they urge us to reject the ideological co-ordinates through which an issue is understood. Moreover, an act entails not simply a rejection of ideological logic, in the way one might politely decline seasoning with a meal, but a violent break based upon sudden action that casts aside all previous considerations. Because capital has become a self-revolutionary and referential structure, swallowing up any threat to its existence, such revolutionary action appears to be a productive possibility for those opposed to its reign.

Yet the Žižekian act has been the subject of severe critique, with critics suggesting that Žižek's rejection of notions such as human rights (Žižek 2005a) in the name of the act cannot be divorced from those apologists for capitalism who do the same (Robinson & Tormey: 2005). The act comes to stand for the general difficulty of translating psychoanalysis from a clinical treatment to a collective politics, particularly as it appears to reject both a normative vision and strategic reflection. If the act is a moment of madness from outside conventional morality, can it be considered political at all?

Certainly, Žižek's references to the act do not focus on its practicality. Instead it appears to have a miraculous foreign element: acts 'just happen' (Žižek 1999: 375). It is this theological element of the act that provokes the strongest criticism. Critics have focused upon the 'crazy' (in the sense of being without justification) aspect of the act, unable to conceive of it as a considered strategic intervention (see Boucher & Sharpe 2010: 181–2). Žižek's examples of the act, particularly in his earlier work, do not help here. Shooting one's own family, as in the example Žižek gives in *The Fragile Absolute* (2000c: 149–50) of Keyser Soeze in the movie *The Usual Suspects*, provides little inspiration for responding to capitalism. Neither can we seek political inspiration from Mary Kay, the teacher convicted of raping her thirteen-year-old pupil. Žižek describes her as taking an 'authentic subjective stance' – the authentic *act* of being in love (1999: 385–6, original emphasis).

In this regard, Žižek often argues that the act is not intentional – there is no subjective or ideological control – but the subject must nonetheless take responsibility for a truly ethical act, positing themselves as the cause of the act:

> The paradox of the act thus lies in the fact that although it is not 'intentional' in the usual sense of the term of consciously willing it, it is nevertheless accepted as something for which its agent is fully responsible – 'I cannot do otherwise, yet I am none the less fully free in doing it' . . . The paradox is thus that, in an authentic act, the highest freedom coincides with the utmost passivity, with a reduction to a lifeless automaton who blindly performs its gestures. (Žižek 1999: 376)

The key point for Žižek's act is that it has a subject but no agent; 'the agent is *not* "on the level of its act" . . . he himself is unpleasantly surprised by the "crazy thing he has just done", and unable to come to terms with it' (Žižek 1999: 376, original emphasis). As such, Žižek deems Kay to be an ethical subject because she remains faithful to her desire. What he ignores is the cause of Kay's desire: is she acting pathologically through her unwavering fetishistic attachment to her young lover, or is she 'refusing to give way to the cause of her desire' at the expense of everything else? In either case, Kay's faith to her cause provides little political inspiration and indeed contradicts Žižek's original point – such blind faith is more likely to suggest ideological activity, not the act.

Given the lack of intentionality and control inherent in the act, we must ask whether it could be performed in the name of a particular political horizon. At best, Žižek suggests a reformulation of the coordinates of the situation based upon a momentary suspension of the symbolic logic such that new opportunities for action become available. On this basis, both Soeze and Kay have acted in a manner which has no justification within its given structure. Here, we must agree that such an action does reconstitute the situation, yet not only is it difficult to translate this action from the subjective to the collective, but it appears to strongly push aside any aspect of political consideration, reducing Žižek's politics to the kind of empty formalism that his critics love to address.

Furthermore the act suggests a kind of avant-garde faith that the new will be inevitably better than the present: there is no indication of what might follow this radical act of destitution, except an assumption of difference. The act, like all the strategic positions to be discussed in this chapter, is ethical in a Lacanian sense – it provides an opportunity to reconstitute politics and subjectivity – but this ethics is the ethics of a moment, not of political formations and especially not of an ideological form of the Good. When we speak of global capitalism, there may be some value to be held here, but as a form of politics it is not difficult to see why Žižek* often looks to a form of (materialist) theology to supplement his approach. Moreover, because the act cannot be referenced to any sense of Good – the act is strictly in excess of the Good and the Law – it is difficult, if not constitutively impossible, to distinguish the act from evil (Eagleton 2009: 282).

In addition to this normative lack, another of the central reproaches against the act, and Žižek in general, is the apparent blindness to strategic opportunities for action outside total revolutionary transformation. This critique speaks directly to that announced earlier; if I have sought to construct Žižek's work as one of a collection of political strategies, how can the act be considered to be strategic, or indeed political?

Much of the difficulty stems from the translation of the act from the subject to object. One of the hegemonic criticisms of the use of psychoanalysis in political discourse is that it transposes categories used for the analysis of the psyche onto society, treating the collective as if it was an individual (Sharpe & Boucher 2010: 112–36). Whilst many of these positions do not take into account the role of language in bridging this gap, it does appeal particularly apt regarding the act. If near-total transformation can occur in an individual body through the traversal of a fundamental fantasy, this is possible because the fantasy was fundamental to that entity. Circumstances are rarely as clear cut in complex societies.

Taken strictly from a Lacanian reading of the clinical process of the subject 'traversing the fantasy' and coming to a new relationship within their enjoyment, it is difficult, if not impossible, to consider

---

* And Alain Badiou, in his related notion of the event.

what a (collective) political act might look like. Not only are the exigencies of the body difficult to reconcile with those of the interactions of bodies, but an ethics which takes its guidance from the Real struggles to make a distinction as to differing forms of shared social life. Waging war or saving the poor could be equally justified, the former more easily than the latter. One can imagine political leaders engaging in an act which has substantial political consequences, but collective action has too many bodies involved to truly fit a clinical category of the act. That is, if the act just happens, collective action requires too much communication, too much strategy to be without (an) agent(s).

Let us a take a recent political event, what might be considered a political act in the sense that it came without justification, without any support from the symbolic order: the 2011 London riots. Stemming from the suspicious shooting of Mark Duggan by police in the deprived Tottenham area of north London, disenfranchised youths set off on several nights of rioting throughout the city, disorder that spread to the cities of Manchester and Birmingham. This violence might be regarded as an act conducted by the lumpenproletariat: those outside the political order engaging in action that appears as madness from within that order. Rather than simply accepting their place in the society and performing the kind of activity expected of them, the rioters moved directly to action that the Conservative Prime Minister, David Cameron, labelled 'pure criminality'. Moreover, this action displayed the potential for political action as social media, as in the Arab Spring, aided decentralised mass communication outside official channels.

Yet these rioters did not engage in a true act for two reasons. Firstly, their actions did not break with the ideological fantasy in which they were held; rather, they sought to be properly included within this realm. They did not reject the consumerism and class relations that imprison them, but sought to enter into these relations by engaging in some light-fingered consumerism themselves. In this sense it was not an act, but acting out, what Lacan called the *passage à l'acte*.

Moreover, the extended duration of the events displays the difficulty of a true political act. The initial action, and some isolated moments, may have had the structure of an act, but through communication and excessive media discourse much of the Real element disappeared in the name of strategic calculation on both sides. An element of the Real lingered, of course, as the meaning of the riots remained unclear and the community continued to be unsettled, but what begun spontaneously was now engrained in *jouissance*. A break had occurred, one that allowed for a momentary rejigging of understanding, but after that it was politics as usual.

Certainly, hegemonic ideologies and ideas can fail when they are unable to account for occurrences of the impossible, but competing positions are always ready to take the place of lost enjoyment. If our faith in the market is shattered by the collapse in property prices, this does not mean capitalism itself collapses but that competing explanations begin a hegemonic battle to fill the void: the crisis of capital is due to bankers, greed or governments. The task of political strategy is to perform the process of determinate negation such that these remnants of ideology no longer hold. The Lacanian act does not have the tools for this trade.

Furthermore, as Žižek (2011a) contends, the rioters can hardly be thought to be posing an economic challenge to the political order. Whilst they were almost universally poor, they are more akin to the rabble that Marx envisaged as the lumpenproletariat than the universal class of capitalist class struggle that I have suggested here. Instead, the hopelessness of the rioters cause, their inability to articulate solidarity through anything but the narrative of consumerism, displays the true dominance of capitalism.

What then is the value of the act in relation to capitalism? Žižekian politics are not directed towards the kind of political reforms which are so often immensely beneficial to so many people. We cannot deny that the expansion of health and education provision in many areas, along with policies which promote greater equality amongst social groupings, should be celebrated. This, however, is not the direction of Žižek's work, which instead argues that a radical break must be made within capitalism. Those who argue that Žižek's use of the act is needlessly radical ignore his patient construction of the ontic contours of capitalist political economy and his increasingly explicit demands to move beyond capitalism. As such, our consideration is whether the act, as one of the political modes which emerges within Žižek's work, is capable of producing such a break.

Against his critics, Žižek keenly insists that the act is not simply a performance of total madness – although it may appear to have this form at its time – but, rather, retrospectively creates its own conditions of possibility such that what is of upmost political importance is the day after. The imposition of the Real, which is by definition alien to symbolic coherence and understanding, is only ever a momentary break. After this disruption, disregarding how it has been generated, politics concerns the reintegration of elements to achieve ideological coherence and to make sense of the catastrophic break. As such, most acts appear disruptive only at the moment of occurrence, before they are inscribed in the symbolic order.

Moreover, Žižek claims that a genuine act is distinguishable from mere frenetic activity. We can attribute two reasons for this distinction. Firstly, the good terror of the French Revolution and the bad terror of Nazi Germany can be distinguished by a purely formal reference to the structure of fantasy and the symptom. For Žižek, a true act occurs at the point of symptomal torsion, so that the underlying fantasmatic structure of either the subject or the ideology is radically disturbed. As such, the September 11 attacks were not an act because they did not invoke a suspension of fantasy, of either the attackers or the attacked, but cemented existing relations (Žižek 2003).

Secondly, revolutions do not just happen; they are made through strategic intervention. Although rapid political change often comes as a shock to many, the fall of the Berlin Wall and the 2011 revolts in the Middle East being prime examples, they are not spontaneous miracles for those involved in their instigation. This point brings us to the vital distinction between a clinical and political act, one not made by Žižek, who does not distinguish between those occasions on which he is discussing what Lacan meant by the act and those when the discussion turns to how this notion might be translated into political action.

If we translate Lacan's notion outside the clinic to political life, particularly to that constructed in Chapter 4, whereby political discourses can exist in a parallel manner such that reality can be quite literally split, a different (strategic) potential arises. Here, an act can occur within a collective when an ideology is ignorant of its point of exclusion or repression: in this case we can have intensive planning and intentionality to produce a political act which breaks with ideological fantasy. Moreover, this act could have a wholesale notion of the Good – a Marxist narrative, in this case – even in the form of an ideological fantasy. A procedure of this kind could only occur in conditions of extreme repression where an uprising appears as a violent outburst of the Real, bursting open symbolic co-ordinates that were not prepared for such an intrusion.

What is required is a subtler version of the act. It appears that critics of Žižek, and perhaps even Žižek himself, imagine the act to be a total transformation on a universal level – no wonder they reject it. In this regard, acts occur every day when something that was both unthinkable and outside our imagination changes our fantasy of a coherent reality. As crazy as the act seems, it is a vital (and always political) engagement with a world in which politics entails making existing processes more efficient. If our demand is for a widespread change, however, then a different mode of political action is required. The act provides the basic formula for that mode.

As a strategic practice, the politics of the act suggest the kind of sudden action which comes with an uprising that is unthinkable within the current common sense. Such an uprising could not come from a group with a position in the 'official order' but, rather, from a point of repression, forcing open a hole within the symbolic fabric from below. We saw, in different shapes and forms, a number of such unexpected uprisings across the Arab world during 2011. These movements have succeeded in transforming their society to varying degrees, depending on both the depth of the wound punctuated through political life and the scope of state violence rained down upon them. Such examples of the unexpected provide evidence that Žižek's politics of the act – bastardised as they have been here – are a viable form of political intervention.

By contrast, it is extremely doubtful that such a transformation could occur on an international level within 21st-century global capitalism. The politics of the act take us back to a time of a strict Marxist revolutionary narrative, except without the support of either history or political calculation. Although there is no predestined relationship between the act and the lumpenproletariat, as the symptomal point within global capitalism, they appear to be the most likely point of transformation. It is not, however, a point of revolutionary calculation: there is nothing scientific about the revolutionary narrative. Instead, an act would occur when those in the position of excess in regard to the wage-labour system disregard the fact that they have nothing to lose but their chains and take on the task of revolution anyway.

An uprising against the interests of capitalism by those excluded from it would almost certainly be shut down simply because of the ideological weighting of capital: there are no resources to organise such an uprising outside capitalism and plenty to defend it within it. An initial break might be made, but what matters is the future articulation of this break so that the kind of alternative explanation that would justify the inevitable subsequent extreme repression could not hold. In the following chapter I will identify this alternative as the 'communist hypothesis'. Local indiscretions, say the nationalisation of an oil company, can be tolerated to a certain degree, but without punctuating a substantial hole in our common-sense understandings of capitalism, this movement would be easily broken, mediated either through concessions in political management or through reactionary violence itself. As such, whilst we see that the basic elements of the act have a part to play in any radical politics, to successfully break with capitalism they must go beyond the resources provided by Žižekian theory.

Thus, it would be extremely naïve to hope for a collective formation of the excluded and exploited to take on a mass revolutionary action. Not only would such action be unable to slide under the radar and thus no longer be unrepresented (and therefore an element of the Real), but the degree of repression and state-sanctioned violence available means that any attack on the symbolic framework of capitalism would be hopelessly unsuccessful. Protests and workers' movements may achieve limited goals, but they will never achieve revolutionary progress on a wide scale under current conditions, and terrorism is simply akin to throwing eggs to break down a wall: lots of mess for no result.

Whilst recent riots and revolutions have provoked considerable anxiety amongst the agents of capital – a sure sign that we are tarrying with the Real – they have not been able to provide a sufficient puncture within the common sense of our time, nor the logic of profitability. Although the Arab Spring turned over authoritarian regimes, often in the name of the disenfranchised, economically nothing has changed, nor is it likely to. Certainly, NATO would not be supporting a specifically *communist* revolution in Libya. What concerns capitalists more are the uneasy flows of global finance. In order to break up capitalism, I will come to argue, we must prevent those points within our fantasmatic understanding of global justice that repress the anxiety of the Real from obtaining an unbearable foothold.

The remainder of this chapter considers two strategic positions that reproduce the aims of the act and its political direction, but focus upon provoking revolutionary change from 'above' rather than from the powerless below. The first of these can be described as 'subtractive politics'.

SUBTRACTIVE POLITICS

Žižek began to develop his notion of subtractive politics with *The Parallax View* (2006b), continuing with *In Defense of Lost Causes*

(2008) and, finally, *First as Tragedy, Then as Farce* (2009a). This mode of politics was initially characterised by the stubborn ethics of Bartleby, the central character in Herman Melville's novella *Bartleby, the Scrivener: A Story of Wall Street*. Žižek considers Bartleby's disciplined refusal to do his duty – 'I would prefer not to' – as a model for a withdrawal from the political co-ordinates of the capitalist matrix, one that has a potentially devastating effect. He holds that taking no position, actively not participating, or perhaps un-participating, in the capitalist order is the most powerful position possible. This patient strategy of withdrawal from action marks a strong distinction from the mad impatience of the act, particularly in its clinical form. This change stems not so much from theoretical developments within Žižek's work as from a strategic response to changing conditions within capitalism. Moreover, it signifies a shift of focus within Žižek's theory towards an explicit analysis of the shape and form of late capitalism.

For Žižek, contemporary capitalism's remarkable ability to combine resistance and power has meant that the most effective mode of politics is one which withdraws from visible forms of resistance-as-participation in order to provide a different kind of subversion. Consequently, Žižek's subtractive politics reverses Marx's famous Eleventh Thesis, in which he stated: 'The philosophers have only interpreted the world in various ways; the point, however, is to change it.' Instead Žižek argues (2006d: 238):

> The first task of today is precisely not to succumb to the temptation to act, to intervene directly and change things (which then inevitably ends in a cul-de-sac of debilitating impossibility: 'What can one do against Global Capital?') but to question the hegemonic ideological coordinates.

This subtractive strategy is the basis for Žižek's primary intervention into the Occupy movements. Arguing that no contemporary alternative to capitalism currently exists, Žižek rejects calls for the activists to engage with those in power, making use of the democratic mechanisms available and proffering an alternative that is bound to end up in debate over its particulars:

> We don't need dialogue with those in power. We need critical dialogue with ourselves. We need time to think. We effectively don't know. And nobody knows ... We don't know where we are. But I think that this openness is precisely what is great about these protests. It means that precisely a certain vacuum opens the fundamental dissatisfactions in

the system. The vacuum simply means open space for thinking, for new freedom, and so on. Let's not fill in this vacuum too quickly.

Here the goal of subtractive politics is to question the manner in which we understand our world in a mode that exposes and produces a crack in capitalism's disavowed foundations. As a consequence, subtractive politics focus not so much on the pressure of the Real from 'below' but, rather, on withdrawing from the ideological modes of fantasy that mediate against this pressure, such as our current fantasmatic belief in the unquestionable status of democracy. Where the politics of the act suggest a frantic urge for action at any cost, a subtractive procedure seeks to open up the space for action to occur. It is not, however, a matter of inactivity but, rather, a more strategic withdrawal: a politics of 'minimal differences' that seeks to identify those vital points which structure our ideological understanding of social life and remove their 'magical' quality. Thus, the hope of this 'active quietism' is that 'this minimal measure, while in no way disturbing the system's explicit mode of functioning, effectively "moves underground", introduces a crack into its foundations' (Žižek 2008: 391).

A modern day interpretation of Bartleby comes from the 1999 cult classic film *Office Space*. The protagonist, Peter, is faced with the ongoing agony of life as an IT worker in a 'cubical farm' in which, as he tells his hypnotist, 'I realised, ever since I started working, every single day of my life has been worse than the day before it. So that means that every single day that you see me, that's on the worst day of my life.' At this point he is accidently hypnotised into a relaxed state in which he calmly refuses to work. Politely declining to participate in the everyday activity of office life, Peter throws his workplace into chaos by revealing the pointlessness of his participation. Although the movie has something of a utopian ending as Peter repudiates office life to work outside 'with his hands', it nonetheless articulates the basic logic of subtraction: to reject those ideological devices that are maintained solely through our participation in the order. Breaking with this activity does not require a momentous act, but a refusal to participate in the forced choice.

Whilst the emphasis on subtraction and minimal difference appears quite divorced from the grandiose politics of the act, the aim remains the same: radical political change. What is different is the strategic positioning of the Real. By contrast to the 'miracle' of the act, in which the Real overwhelms the symbolic order, subtractive politics appears a much more subtle affair. The difference occurs through an interpretation of the relationship between the Real and the framework of understanding from which it is derived.

Moreover, subtractive politics relies upon a different understanding of our ideological circumstances. Today, Žižek argues, ideology within capitalism has reached an age of 'cynical fetishism' under which a traditional critique of ideology, exposing inconsistencies within ideology itself, no longer provokes a disturbance. He suggests that in today's 'post-ideological' world, ideology has more of a fetishistic shape. The traditional understanding of ideology is that it is threatened by symptoms that embody the contradictions of that ideology. By contrast, the fetish is an accepted lie that allows for the continued functioning of ideology (Žižek 2009a: 65). Žižek contends:

> The symptom is the exception which disturbs the surface of the false appearance the point at which the repressed other science erupts while fetish is the embodiment of the lies which enables us to sustain the unbearable truth. (Žižek 2007b: 251)

In the case of the symptomal functioning of ideology, when contradictions can no longer be repressed, ideology comes face to face with its disavowed truth and collapses. In terms of fetishism, ideology collapses when this fetish is no longer able to hold – a collapse which is often more total. Thus, it is not that Žižek proposes that 21st-century subjects are somehow more able to hold onto grisly truths – it remains the wager of psychoanalysis that 'the subject *cannot* openly admit and really assume the truth about what s/he is doing' (Žižek 2007b: 251, original emphasis) – but the structure of ignorance has changed. We know very well of the corruption of our political system and the false promises of consumerism, yet we act as if we do not. Instead, we withdraw to the safety of fetishistic *jouissance*, whether through ideological identification or consumptive *jouissance*.

This disjuncture between knowledge and belief has been a consistent tenet of Žižek's work, most strongly articulated in works such as *For They Know Not What They Do* (1991) in which he argues that although the subject may objectively know the truth, they are able to dis-identify themselves from this truth and continue to act as if they do not know. It is not, as in the traditional Marxist sense, that we do not know that our consciousness is false, and thus innocently comply with power. Instead, contemporary subjects are aware of their illusion and, although they distance themselves from this belief, continue to act as if they do believe. This distance allows the subject to separate themselves from any inconsistency within the big Other. We might privately believe that capitalism is corrupt but, by distancing ourselves from this institutional power we allow ourselves to continue to fulfil the demands of capital, perhaps working in a corporate role (Cremin 2011: 78).

This dynamic is both an inbuilt element of subjectivity – a potential reaction to the Real – and a historical consequence to an era when, in Colin Cremin's terms, 'the emperor has no clothes'.* As a consequence of this dynamic, speaking truth to knowledge and power has lost its effectiveness – the journalistic explorations of the likes of Noam Chomsky, John Pilger and Naomi Klein may reveal previously hidden truths, but they have lost the ability to shock and disturb. We are no longer outraged by political corruption or poverty, or, more importantly, if we are it has no effect of our actions. Marx may have believed that knowledge of their exploitation would be enough for the working class to throw off their chains but, today, not only is objectivity considered impossible, but truth itself appears to have lost its power – although the possibility of rupture remains.

A pertinent political example comes from American imperialism and torture. When the presence of Guantánamo Bay, Abu Ghraib prison and other images of the consequences of the 'War on Terror' emerged in the public domain, there was a degree of shock at the distance between these images and the official ideology of the American global project: the spread of justice, freedom and democracy. At one stage of the second term of George W. Bush's presidency, there appeared to be a genuine anxiety within the system, as hearings were held and debate raged about the role of torture and American global exceptionalism (*New York Times* 2008). At some point, however, the terms of the debate changed. The occurrence of these elements were no longer denied but, rather, cynically endorsed, as if there were no other option – this being the fetish that allowed the American public to largely accept the administration's sins against itself: contradicting the spirit of liberty was the *only* way to maintain it, and this was a burden that would have to be borne by the American people. This was not a miraculous occurrence but a targeted political strategy by the Bush administration to change the terms of the debate away from

---

* This disidentification from power is not unique to capitalism – much of Žižek's earlier work is replete with examples from late-era eastern European socialism.

this disruption, a strategy which succeeded because it allowed the discourse to move away from the anxiety of the Real.

Perhaps the most salient exemplar of the cynicism of social life today is the television show *The Simpsons*. Produced by the notoriously conservative Fox television network, the show regularly satirises many aspects of contemporary society, from religion to politics and popular culture. One of the most prevalent subjects of mockery is the Fox network itself, along with its arch-conservative owner, Rupert Murdoch. Rather than taking umbrage at this subversion, the network turns a blind eye. Whilst *The Simpsons'* subversive satire is taken to be a healthy – almost radical – aspect of American democracy, it holds no radical potential. Instead it signals the limitations of subversive politics today. Ultimately, the show is a source of profit for the network, who are content to be made fun of so long as money is made. Moreover, it signals the strong cynicism of the viewing public, who are aware of the failure of their institutions – it is not shocking to have *The Simpsons* openly display corrupt politicians or evil corporations, as we all *know* that this is the case.

Žižek's point in regards to this cynicism is that whilst we know of this failure, we continue to act as if we do not know. Furthermore, the kind of social commentary provided by *The Simpsons* allows the contemporary subject to believe that they are resisting (post) modern life, without having to change their compliant behaviour – it is as if society provides the critique for us, so no action is required. If the Other takes responsibility for its actions, then political action is not required. It is for this reason that the announcements of political inquiries or committees are so effective in quelling political discontent.

Moreover, perhaps the key point to note from the case of *The Simpsons* is the transcendental status of profit; all kinds of behaviour are tolerated, so long as profitability continues unabated. Tellingly, a dislocatory effect is most strongly felt at the moment that the efficiency of profit is disturbed.* No global problem is too big to ignore, except when it begins to threaten profit itself. No one expects aid promises to be delivered on, or climate treaties honoured (it is the promising, not the delivering, which provides the required servicing

---

* Particularly instructive in this regard are the actions of media corporations when a broadcaster has caused moral 'outrage'. The standard action is to apologise, whilst secretly happy at the attention brought to the network. Once advertisers begin to withdrawal their business, however, action *must* be taken.

of ideology), but once the financial sector was threatened during the 2009 crisis, a seemingly infinite amount of money was instantly found and used. The question, for Žižek, is how to subvert this process of cynicism and the rule of profit.

Žižek comes to suggest that we can no longer rely upon traditional ideological critique, in which the symptom is presented to ideology, but, instead, we must enact a form of subtractive politics which attempts to detach a fetishised defence from the Real. As such, those invoking a subtractive procedure actively seek to avoid the seductive appeal of these fetishistic points, refusing, for example, to engage in the kind of charitable endeavour that lessens the felt trauma of injustice. Here we can see why Žižek's politics are so often displayed as conservative: not only does his reading of the structure of capitalism often conform with that of its apologists (the pure operation of markets, the *need* for business to consider profit as the primary driver of its activities) but he refuses to actively posit any form of activity that would mediate against the harshest elements of capitalism. Although the direction of Žižek's politics are diametrically opposed to the likes of the Republican Party in the United States – and it would be extremely disingenuous to suggest that any kind of ideological alliance could be identified – in terms of a policy statement, it is difficult to see how the ideas of subtractive politics would be any different from a Republican manifesto.

The problem is then to discern the kind of activity that would most productively disturb capitalism under these conditions. The politics Žižek has in mind reject any acceptance of the ideological lens through which reality is understood and, instead, seek to disturb the relationship between an ideological horizon and the traumatic elements it fears. Glyn Daly calls this political art 'the subversion of subversion':

> the development of forms of subversion that do not condone or comply with existing logics of subversion but which seek rather to undermine and repudiate the latter and to thereby open up new spaces of political possibility and creativity. (2009: 294)

The question in relation to both subtractive politics and the act is whether successful transformative action depends on identifying points from which this overwhelming action might occur, or a more critical task of forcing open cracks within ideology itself from 'below', from the point of exclusion. The first appears to draw us back into a Marxist-communist revolutionary narrative in which the waste product of capital will eventually overwhelm the system in which it is produced. Not only can we reject the overt historical materialism inherent in this approach but, as I have previously emphasised in some detail, the state and power of capitalism is such that any 'naturally' arising resistance is already countered within the system. The act will not just suddenly occur without warning (although it might on 'their' side); we will not awaken to the overthrow of the White House and a communist utopia imposed by the urban poor.

Because of the strength of capital and in particular the manner in which it is able to disavow its own contradictions, any form of political intervention that insists upon revolutionary change must consist of a strategic reading of both sides of the symptomal knot. Political strategies that seek to unravel its grip upon shared social life must untie the ideological bounds that hold global capitalism together. The politics of the act do not appear capable of undertaking this task. Instead, the patient and strategic critique of ideology held in Žižek's notion of the subtractive procedure appears to be a more productive approach.

Nonetheless, subtractive politics has attracted as much criticism as the notion of the act. If the act appears too radical, asking for too much to be done, to Žižek's critics, subtractive politics, and in particular the image of Bartleby, appears overly patient at best and just lazy, ineffective and ultimately conservative at worst. If Žižek's work reminds us of the urgency of acting against capitalism – and this appears to be the central injunction of his demand to act – the suggestion of withdrawal appears quizzical. At worst, it appears to offer an excuse to withdraw to a critical distance and remain within the bounds of theory.

The key question as to the effectiveness of subtractive politics is how long the effect of the Real can 'remain alive' through strategic withdrawals from ideology. Ideological identifications and *jouissance* will always travel to the point of least resistance and, faced with the trauma of the Real, will grip onto alternative explanations for its presence. Without the Real continually pressing upon ideology, it is difficult to convince of subtractive politics preventing the reformation of a coherent and enjoyable ideological fantasy.

Let us take the case of global poverty. Subtractive politics relies not on any movements on behalf of the lumpenproletariat but, rather, a debunking of the mechanisms through which we keep the anxiety of their presence at bay. In this case, in applying a subtractive strategy to the Millennium Development Goals posited by the United

Nations, amongst which was a target to halve extreme poverty by 2015, politics would entail a rejection of the ideological terms of the debate, principally the narrative of the 'development ladder' whereby poverty is caused by political mismanagement rather than any exploitation. Here those actors involved would refuse to sign up for the goals or participate in the developmental measures, the wager being that such a refusal would expose the flawed logic of the United Nations and force alternative explanations into being.

This is, of course, an immensely risky political strategy, one that would place millions of lives in danger. The ultimate risk is that our political opponents would simply respond to this with a blackmail – fine, let's not recycle, give aid, respect democratic rights in our trading relationships – and alternative explanations that grip the public at large would become more powerful in subduing the effect of the Real. It appears that subtraction is most effective when all ideological resources can be exhausted, an extremely difficult notion under the multi-dimensional dominance of global capitalism. Subtractive politics appear like playing an off-side trap in football: a withdrawal of defence that can be highly effective when it works, but leaves the side extremely exposed when it fails.

Ultimately, the question linking the act, subtractive politics and the practice of concrete universality (to which we shall turn) remains how the Real foundation of global capitalism might be exposed. If the act relies too heavily upon the Real in its pure form and a revolutionary process that requires a miracle beyond the symbolic, subtractive politics focuses upon the shape of contemporary ideology that holds back the destabilising effect of the Real. This strategy is much easier to apply to ecological issues than poverty and labour, as the former appears to hold on a much stronger fetishistic structure: political responses to ecological degradation tend to focus upon technological solutions, even if there is political debate around the appropriate and effective means of their deployment. Here the subtractive strategy is not to posit an alternative approach, such as suggesting that technology is the root of the problem, but to actively attempt to undermine and subtract from the proposed solutions to remove the efficiency of the nodal points around which the discourse is structured. When a government announces the development of a new wind farm, a subtractive procedure would critique this development without positing an alternative, the goal being to expose the Truth behind the fetish without offering an alternative fantasmatic platform. In doing so the full disruptive effect of the Real is felt within ideology.

Unfortunately, however, the fetishistic structure of hegemonic ecological discourse does not hold any particularly strong disruptive *political* potential within capitalism. By contrast to the fate of the green movement, the lumpenproletariat – at least conceived as a consequence of class struggle – appears to have retained a symptomatic tension within capitalism. Although the presence of urban slums and unemployment has been documented on a level well beyond cynicism, its link to global capitalism, consumption and environmental problems remains disavowed. Importantly, Žižek signals this point in his previously noted consideration of the four antagonisms that currently haunt capitalism, in which he not only identified political exclusion of surplus populations as holding the most radical potential, but placed the emphasis on the exclusion of these populations through the production of new walls (whether physical or ideological) across the planet. It may be that a cynical acknowledgement of poverty is possible, but at this stage it appears that the blood of capital remains as the primary taboo point within global capitalism. We can acknowledge all sorts of political corruption, and cultural and commercial imperialism, but the blood of production is yet to fall at the feet of consumers. That these populations have to be excluded – rather than openly accepted by way of a fetish – suggests that tension remains.

Because of this tension, I wish to suggest that political activity that focuses purely upon the knot of ideology within capitalism may be needlessly limited. If the politics of subtraction focuses upon disrupting the efficiency of those nodal points which act as a fetish within ideology, allowing the force of the Real to be evoked, I suggest that 'wageless life' – as the inalienable remainder of capitalism – presents a potentially operable element of the Real. In relation to capitalism, the issue is whether the 'active quietism' of subtraction – seeking to disrupt our understanding of global capital by withdrawing from its points of ideological suture – is the horizon for anti-capitalist politics today or if there is something more to be said about the relationship between capitalism and its inherent contradictions.

PRACTISING CONCRETE UNIVERSALITY

In Chapter 4, I established that the moment of concrete universality occurs at the point at which the universal exception, the other side of the abstract universal horizon, comes to intrude upon that horizon. Here the abstract universal is the point at which ideology creates a sense of universal applicability, of cohesion and of fullness: the generalised point of 'common sense' by which we come to understand our shared social life. We might, for instance, posit that within Western societies the idea that our mode of politics is orientated around developing the universal (democratic) Good, rather than purely benefiting the elite, is hegemonic, regardless of whether it is true. For this reason, politicians who are caught embezzling public funds or working with special interest groups are considered to be unquestionably in the wrong: indeed to even argue so would be unnecessary.

If the abstract universal is constructed of a number of particular points, one of which stands in as the universal image of society, Žižek comes to argue that in order to create a universal set of this series of elements, one of these particular elements must be excluded. It is this point of exclusion which acts as the universal exception. Moreover, as Žižek states in regard to Lacan,

> not only is universality based upon an exception; Lacan goes a step further: universality is its exception, it 'appears as such' in its exception ... the exception (the element with no place in the structure) which immediately stands for the universal dimension. (Žižek 2006c: 30)

The gap forged by this exception acts as an embodiment of the Lacanian Real: it is the (necessary) point of impossibility that cannot be included within an imaginary set. As such, this exceptional point maintains the status of the Real – it has a presence only as an absence from ideology – but it nonetheless exists. What is important in this conception of universality, however, is that universality is neither this point of exclusion nor the generalisation of ideology, but is constituted by the tension between the two. The battle, not of particular signifiers to become the master signifier that dominates meaning, but between the abstract universal and its symptomal lie, is universality itself. To return to the previous example, if we were to posit that against the ideal of politicians acting in the general interest, this elite simply managed the state in the interests of the agents of capital and through the exclusion of the labouring masses, there comes to exist both the presence of an exception and the tension of the Real in the gap between this exception and the hegemonic ideological horizon.

Thus far in this book I have identified the universal exception of capitalism as the lumpenproletariat, which acts as the 'part with no part' or universal class within capitalism. The representation of this point which cannot be directly encountered is of vital importance, and has been discussed throughout this text. At this stage, however, it is enough to reiterate that the structural location of a population excluded from the benefits of production is the universal exception of capital. What is important here is not so much that this universal class hold any particular power over capitalism – they cannot withdraw their labour – but that they stand in contradistinction to the ideas capitalist consumers hold about themselves. Moreover, the rapid intensification of the lumpenproletariat through both the unjust expansion of capital and population growth is likely to make this incommensurability increasingly pressing.

The historical and structural presence of the lumpenproletariat dictates that global capitalism is unable to establish an egalitarian justice that applies equally to all humanity. The operation of capital is able to produce unprecedented levels of wealth for a minority of the population, a level of wealth that corresponds to previously impossible life expectancies and a potential for freedom from material need, but is constitutively unable to extend these privileges across the globe. Capitalism may not actively create (absolute) poverty in the majority of cases, but it does require it.

How does this hypocrisy translate to a form of politics? The ultimate wager is that we are unable to hold onto this Truth about the way we live and maintain a sense of ourselves as living in a just world in any manner. It may be that we are able to recognise that global capitalism requires an increasingly small fraction of the world's population to materially flourish at unprecedented levels through the absolute misery of others, and to continue to live under the guise of civilisation. It is just that this would be a different world from the one we live in today, not only one in which citizens consider themselves empowered – democracy allows for the idea that we decide the way we live – but also one with a sense of justice. This does not mean that Western subjects currently believe they live for the common good, without self-interest, but that they believe the big Other – our political systems – operates in this name. The institutions through which 21st-century civilisations are structured, whether the family, market, church or the state, are considered to work in the interests of all. Even the market labours under the fantasy that it is the most efficient system for all: our self-interest is thought to work for the common good. That the market and the flows of capital are necessarily greased with blood and despair lies in intolerable contrast with these ideas. The question is how to bring such a Truth into an unbearable contradiction with the ideological fantasy through which it is held. I propose that this is best considered as the act of practising concrete universality.

The practice of concrete universality involves the identification of the Real *qua* the universal exception and attempts to force its intrusion around its point of exclusion. This position has been best considered in *The Parallax View*. Through the notion of the parallax, Žižek suggests that we can 'practise' concrete universality by 'confronting a[n] [abstract] universality with its "unbearable" example' (Žižek 2006c: 13). This unbearable example is the universal exception which has an existence, although it is only felt as an absence within our ideological frameworks of meaning. That is, whilst a universal exception is excluded from ideology – it remains 'unthinkable' – it does have a material presence outside the predominant ideology. Nonetheless, it does also appear as the Real: a gap within the order of being. By taking a parallax view – in which both the exception and its point of exclusion are kept in sight, so that the gap between them is revealed – the presence of this excluded exception becomes clear.

What is important about the parallax view is not the positive existence of the exception. The exception always finds expression within the ideological form of the abstract universal in a palpable form. Poverty, for example, does exist within the ideological formations that support capitalism. Indeed its representation is often excessive, taking the form of meaningless statistics and images overridden with superego guilt. In this form it can be cynically acknowledged. What makes excessive forms of labour into a constitutive exception is the relationship with contemporary political horizons. These populations are ontologically excluded not because their presence cannot be acknowledged but, rather, because they cannot be acknowledged as an intimate (or rather, extimate) part of universality itself.

Thus, by identifying the universal exception as an element of the Real, the practice of concrete universality enables this point to be mobilised against the ideological realm in which it is externally housed. If the act relies upon a sudden revolutionary imposition of the Real and subtractive politics a rejection of the ideological minders of this point of trauma, practising concrete universality attempts to achieve both, using the pressure of the embodied Real to create revolutionary conditions within our ideological fantasies. Here ideology is directly confronted within its necessary nemesis, which exists as a symbolic element for the political opposition and an element of the Real for reactionary forces.

That is, the universal exception can be organised as a point of resistance, thrusting itself as a discursive element in contradistinction to our understanding of the Other. Movements such as the World Forum, for instance, can articulate their exclusion from global affairs as a necessary consequence of capitalism, thus pressuring the ideologies of power. Vitally, however, within these ideologies this pressure must be maintained as a point of the Real, a point that is incommensurable with the ruling logic: the lumpenproletariat as an intimate element of Western lives. In this sense, akin to the logic of subtraction, all attempts to 'understand' the point of anxiety within ruling discourses should be resisted, as should all dialogue. We are able to articulate what is an element of the Real within the hegemonic ideology, but it only remains Real to the extent that it cannot be included within that matrix.

Here those involved in anti-capitalist movements should not demand inclusion within capitalism but, rather, a recognition that suffering is dependent upon capitalism, forcing those on the side of capital to confront the contradiction between this position and the ideological narratives we embrace. This dual operation both threatens the consistency of the ideological fantasies we hold about ourselves and continues to evoke the presence of the Real.

Let us take the Occupy movements as an example of political strategy. At its core, the message of these movements is that a small elite – the '1 per cent' – is benefiting from the structure of political economy, while the majority – the '99 per cent' – are being exploited, or at least not enjoying the benefits of this system. Currently, this broad movement is using a Laclauian strategy, positing 'We are the 99%' as its slogan and empty signifier, inviting wide identification with their appeal. As such, the meaning of the movement is currently in flux. Variously described in the media as 'anti-capitalist', 'anti-corporate' or 'anti-banking', the movement has been criticised for failing to offer alternative positions or engage directly with democratic process. I have responded to this critique within this book, suggesting that both strategies are necessary to retain the energy of the movement.

The more pertinent critique is of the intentions of the protestors themselves. Some conservative critics have suggested that the motley collection of activists claiming to be the 99% are simply frustrated that they are not part of the elite. This appeal is certainly one discursive chain amongst the protestors, with many arguing that they are unable to gain access to education, mortgages or meaningful employment. A wider social-democratic appeal might hold that stronger democratic means must be applied to capitalism, returning it to a supposed time of baby-boomer equilibrium. This kind of movement would likely have some electoral success, primarily as a pressure group adjusting the terms of the debate in much the same way as the Tea Party movement in America.

As I have suggested throughout this text, however, this reform would hit a hard limit at capital. The problem is not with finance capital or runaway bankers, but with the systematic structure of capitalism. If the Occupy movement reduces its image of the 99 per cent to those suffering from the lingering effects of recession-era politics within the West, then it is doomed to compromise. What if we expanded this notion of the 99 per cent, considering how it could be applied globally?

Here the concern would not so much be mortgages and education, but infant mortality and slum populations. Although it is more difficult to draw a simple line between capitalism and these ills, it is only this strategy that would be effective in disrupting the hegemony of capital. To practise concrete universality in these circumstances would be to identify the grand contradictions of capitalism, specifically the mass exclusion of the lumpenproletariat and the ecological impossibility of including them within capitalism, with the systematic operation of capitalism. In doing so we break with the fantasy of democracy and the possibility of democratic mechanisms mediating against these excesses of capitalism, and draw a direct line between capitalism and these horrors, suggesting that this suffering is the necessary consequence of the way of life in which we participate.

Ultimately, the battle here is to avoid the Real anxiety of the direct association of our economic activity with horrific suffering being directed either towards ideological reform, or towards a disidentification from the system. As noted earlier, a cynical disidentification, where the subject knows but continues to act as if they do not, is a seductive position. Although the Occupy movement have done well to avoid the much of this cynicism by taking an active presence in cities and avoiding direct alternatives, an extension of their practice is required. Here the dislocatory power of the Real must be insistently associated with our economic activities, enforcing individual responsibility for the contradictions of a system which can no longer be considered 'just'. At this moment when the grip of capitalism on Western minds is slipping, it is time to reassert the impossibility of capitalism and our precise lack of imagination in the face of these difficulties, prompting not a militant overthrow of the system in order to fill the gaps, but a spirit of re-envisioning the politics of the future: it does not have to be this way.

Thus, I suggest that in response to the dark reign of global capitalism, the practice of concrete universality appears the most effective response from within Žižek's politics. This practice, one not far divorced from subtractive politics, or the act, involves actively insisting upon the repetitive presence of the exception, thrusting it into the face of ideology as an example of its failure and accepting no alternative, no positivisation, of the problem. In this regard, Žižek has suggested that

> this identification of the part of society with no properly defined place within it (or which rejects the allocated subordinated place within it) with the Whole is the elementary gesture of politicization, discernible in all great democratic events from the French Revolution (in which *le troisième état* proclaimed itself identical with the Nation as such, against the aristocracy and clergy) to the demise of East European socialism (in which dissident 'fora' proclaimed themselves representative of the entirety of society against the party *nomenklatura*). (Žižek 2008: 415–16)

Although Žižek has not significantly developed this identification with concrete universality – his interest quickly turned to subtractive politics and beyond – it holds much in common with his earlier notion of 'identifying with the symptom'. Illustrative of this approach has been the 'We are America' campaign in the United States, initially a protest movement which began as a response to a backlash against illegal, 'alien', immigrants. Against their representation as intruders, the group's protest emphasised their status as constitutive of the nation and its economy. Not only is the United States an immigrant nation but illegal immigration forms the backbone of the economy, operating as surplus of labour which takes the 'dirty' jobs that citizens are unwilling to take on. Without this labour, the US economy, and in particular the service and agricultural sectors, could no longer function – not only would wage prices rapidly increase but the underground economy of cleaning, maintenance and other such menial jobs would collapse.

This movement, however, signals the danger inherent in such protests. Rather than remaining as a dislocatory point, the tension inherent in their protest was disabled by liberal ideology which integrated the protest into a human rights discourse. It now exists as a 'get out and vote' alliance, well integrated into the system which keeps them at bay.* A more radical approach would have stemmed from a combination of subtraction and concrete universality. The protestors could have refused any such integration into the system, instead calling into question the system itself by way of their simultaneous necessity and exclusion.

Ultimately, the politics of this movement would have been more effective had they not revolved around establishing an ideological grouping, but had constructed the uneasy presence of this grouping within the governing ideology. The movement would have been successful if the likes of farmers, manufacturers and the other wealthy agents of capital who benefit from the presence of these aliens had come to acknowledge their necessity. The political battle would then revolve around a conservative acknowledgement of this injustice, 'we deserve their labour, their misfortune is not our fault, they choose to be here', liberal attempts to manage conditions, and the radical politics of forcing their inclusion within the discourse, thus changing its shape to permanently include the immigrants as Americans.

In regard to populations excessive to the needs of capital, every articulation of ideology and progress in the West should be strategically met by a reminder of this remainder, defying any notion that such surplus can be included in the global economy. The problem might be exclusion but the solution is inclusion in the sense of the impossible intrusion of this point into ideology. The art of the practice of concrete universality, therefore, is to mobilise the point or exclusion whilst retaining the anxiety of the Real. It is this anxiety, as caused by the presence of the Real, which offers the best prospect of destabilising capitalism.

The power and structure of capitalism is such that not only is the global economy fundamentally unsustainable within capitalism, but no form of alternative society is currently available. We cannot simply rally behind a new signifier, hoping in vain that a new world is possible. Nor can capitalism be bent in a new direction through a hegemonic battle for a new mode of being. Not only is there no alternative mode of subjectivity, but capitalism hits a hard limit with the impossibility of class structure such that any form of politics tackling the question of global sustainability must address the ideological knot of capitalist class relations.

In considering how to tackle this knot, I have suggested that the act – although forming the background for Žižekian political

* See www.weareamerica.org

engagement with capitalism – does not translate well to the collective sphere of global capital. The 'crazy' risk of transforming subjectivity found no equivalent outside the kind of all-out revolutionary approach long rejected by Marxist discourse. Alternatively, subtractive politics offers a more subtle approach to politics. Although the hope of grand transformation is not lost, it suggests that this can be achieved through smaller, more strategic, gestures. It particular, subtractive politics responds to the cynicism evident in ideology today. This response attempts to withdraw the fetishistic object to which we cling to prevent the anxiety of the Real. As such it is an effective approach but, because it does not speak directly to the Real, it is an approach with limitations.

Finally, in relation to the act and subtractive politics, practising concrete universality – an active contrasting of an exception with the system it constitutes – emerges as potentially the most effective strategic response to the contradictions of global capitalism. This approach embodies much of the wisdom of subtraction – the withdrawal from political action, the breakdown of fetishism – but seeks to utilise the tension provoked by concrete universality in a more productive manner.

Nonetheless, although this position is a powerful form of critique, it retains a negative form. This reading of Žižek's politics suggests that Žižek has been unable to reconstitute a Marxist image of shared social life and is instead stuck within a reconsideration of the politics of psychoanalysis within the Marxist tradition. Not only is there nothing in this articulation of Žižek's work which would excite policy wonks, but there is nothing that would inspire those on the street.

For much of Žižek's work this position appeared to be the limit of his work; a powerful critique of capitalism but nothing more. Žižek himself suggested that this was the necessary condition of both politics under capitalism and the work of a Lacanian philosopher – he conceived the limitations of his practice to be the provoking of new questions, not providing the kind of answers that would both satisfy his critics and provide a new horizon for the radical Left. As we have seen in this chapter, this has not made his work conservative but neither has it provided a response that has much life beyond academia.

Recently, however, Žižek has begun to identify, following Alain Badiou, the 'communist hypothesis' as the political horizon of our time. We must consider how this approach is different from any of the political positions Žižek has previously rejected; in the following chapter I shall consider how Žižek has been able to hold this idea as a reconstitution of Marxist politics without falling prey to the traps inherent in any normative expression of the Good. Firstly, I draw on the notion of the communist hypothesis, considering both Žižek's and Badiou's interpretations. In doing so I will suggest that Žižek's understanding of the communist hypothesis does provide a new horizon for the Left – not through its explicit content but, rather, by reference to Jameson's notion of utopia. This reference to utopia not only has the potential to allow the communist hypothesis to be used in a manner which avoids the difficulties of holding on to such a 'big idea' via the universal exception that produces concrete universality but, in doing so, provides the possibilities of going beyond critique and offering the kind of affective identification that avoids the cynicism which dominates politics today.

7

The Communist Hypothesis: Žižekian Utopia or Utopian Fantasy?

Although Žižek's work has always had a Marxist flavour and has hinted at an affinity with communism, his primary mode of political engagement has remained the critique of capital rather than the redevelopment of an alternative ideological platform. In the previous chapter I further developed this critique, positing a number of strategic modes of Žižekian politics in relation to the primary antagonism haunting contemporary capitalism, the lumpenproletariat.

These positions, however, remain purely strategic in the sense that they suggest no future normative conception of shared social life in themselves: one cannot attempt to institutionalise the practice of subtractive politics in the manner of Ernesto Laclau's suggestion that his theory of hegemony inspires radical democracy. This positioning of Žižek's politics resonates with both the impossibility of transposing Lacanian ethics into a substantive form of collective normativity and his insistence upon the historical limitations of political practice.

Parts of Žižek's recent work, however, have begun to overtly engage with communism such that he has been able to speak of it as 'our side' (Žižek 2009: 8). This commitment has come in the form of the 'communist hypothesis', developed primarily in his works 'How to Begin from the Beginning' (2009b) and *First as Tragedy, then as Farce* (2009a). Emerging initially from Alain Badiou's *The Meaning of Sarkozy* (2008), the resurgence of communism has resonated strongly with those involved in Leftist political theory, leading to a sold-out political conference on 'the Idea of communism' in 2009 – a conference which required speakers, as Badiou said, to agree that 'the word communism can and must now acquire a positive value once more' (Badiou 2010: 37) – and an ensuing collection of essays under the same name (Douzinas & Žižek 2010).

Badiou has subsequently produced a more focused text, explicitly titled *The Communist Hypothesis* (2010),* and in 2010 the *International Journal of Žižek Studies* published a special edition, entitled 'Žižek's Communism'. The latter, however, focused more upon Žižek's 2008 text, *In Defense of Lost Causes*, in which he sought to rehabilitate 'totalitarian' positions such as 'revolutionary terror' as a potential response to capitalism and the hegemony of liberalism amongst the Left. Nonetheless the critical and often polemic contributions to this special edition signalled the difficulty of Žižek's evocation of communism in any form: historically, critics' central rebuke of Žižek's politics has been that his Lacanian orientation prevents the development or acceptance of political positions that are alternative to capitalism. Moreover, because of this refusal Žižek's politics are often conceived to have an all-or-nothing logic that ultimately leads to a refusal to act indistinguishable from the most stubborn modes of conservatism.

Nonetheless, Žižek's reluctance to venture into ideological waters cannot be solely attributed to the limitations of Lacanian theory but also has a basis in his ontological grasp of the historical limits of subversion within capitalism. That is, Žižek has been reluctant to posit or support any particular ideological platform not so much because of the limitations of these positions – not that Žižek has been recalcitrant in examining these limitations either – but because they will inevitably be caught up in the logic of capital.

As such, Žižek's primary mode of engagement has been, in Glyn Daly's terms (2010: 15), to 'subvert the logic of subversion' within capitalism through his own dialectical triangulation of Hegel, Marx and Lacan. As such, in the previous chapter I suggested that it is by practising concrete universality that Žižekian politics is most effective as a form of political praxis against capitalism. Conversely, this practice makes no reference to the structure of the future other than a rejection of the capitalist present. Thus, Žižek's overt support for communism – an apparent ideological form of politics – marks a step-change from his form of political practice. We must consider, therefore, both the significance of the communist hypothesis for the practice of Žižekian theory and its value as a form of political strategy, particularly in regard to concrete universality.

In this chapter I will seek to consider this communist moment

---

* Interestingly, in keeping with much of the scholarship on the communist hypothesis, Badiou's explicitly titled work is a collection of essays and conference presentations, many of which have little or no relation with the title.

within Žižek's work, from its Badiouian origins to the apparent distance Žižek has established from Badiou's 'Idea of communism', arguing that although 'the communist hypothesis' marks a development within Žižekian theory, it can be considered confluent with his previous work in the sense that it proceeds only on the basis of an identification with points of antagonism within capitalism: the communist hypothesis is an extension of the practice of concrete universality. Moreover, I contend that Žižek's reading of communism can be productively extended via a utopian demand around the very limitations of capitalism, an extension that is quite distinct from the ideological contortions of Badiou's Idea.

Žižek's Communism and the Dictatorship of the Proletariat

Whilst Žižek's work is transparently directed as a response to global capitalism, his theoretical interventions have never settled upon an ideological platform which suggests a beyond to this critique. Žižek's commitment to the theoretical tenets of Lacanian psychoanalysis and Hegelian dialectics are readily apparent, as is his positioning within the Marxist tradition, yet the ultimate location of his political commitments has remained a point of academic speculation. Whilst some critics, such as Laclau, have come to suggest that Žižek's work is without political outlook because of his commitment to Lacanian analysis (Laclau 2000a: 289), others have come to argue that Žižek's work is replete with an implicit totalitarianism. The latter position was the predominant thrust of the special edition of the *International Journal of Žižek Studies* mentioned above entitled 'Žižek's Communism', in which a familiar collection of Žižek's critics* rounded on his intervention into totalitarianism in the 2008 text *In Defense of Lost Causes*.

Here Žižek provocatively flaunted his support for a number of 'lost causes' – primarily totalitarian politics, from Mao to Stalin and Heidegger, but also the theoretical lost causes of Marxism and psychoanalysis themselves. Yet, although he seeks to rehabilitate the 'kernel of truth' in totalitarian regimes, the central argument of the text is a rethinking of the limitations of liberalism and the end of global ambitions, rather than in detailed support for any ideological formation. The text produces a certain style of Žižekian

---

* The notable exceptions being Glyn Daly and Adrian Johnston, who produced generally positive contributions.

politics – provocative, polemical and aimed largely at destabilising hegemonic assumptions in the name of enabling more radical forms of subversion. Nowhere, however, does Žižek specifically refer to a communist hypothesis or engage in a direct endorsement of communism. Nonetheless, although Žižek does not directly associate terror, or indeed egalitarianism, with communism, Geoff Boucher and Matthew Sharpe's editorial introduction to the special edition says:

> In this edition of the *IJZS*, the contributors investigate Žižek's claim that his intervention is not a flamboyant posture masking the lack of a definite programme, but a serious contribution to the renewal of the emancipatory project of 'egalitarian communism'. (Boucher & Sharpe 2010: 2)

It appears that, for his critics, Žižek's communism lies in his apparent embrace of totalitarian values at the expense of liberal politics. This reading is not, however, at all congruent with his later and more direct consideration of communism, which specifically seeks to subvert any attempt to positively locate communism. Indeed, to suggest that Žižek's positions in *In Defense of Lost Causes* are communist is a retrospective reading, taking the emphasis of his later work and imposing it upon earlier arguments.

Nonetheless, the positions taken in *In Defense of Lost Causes* do establish the basis for Žižek's embrace of communism, which occurs not through an abstract, ideological commitment for communism but, rather, via political identification with the 'part with no part' of capitalism. Here, initially advocating the 'dictatorship of the proletariat' at the expense of liberal democratic values, Žižek suggests:

> The standard liberal counter-argument to those who warn about the 'invisible hand' of the market that controls our destinies is: if the price of being freed from the *invisible* hand of the market is to be controlled by the *visible* hand of the new rulers, are we ready to pay for it? The answer should be: *yes* – if this visible hand is visible to and controlled by the 'part with no part'. (2008: 419, original emphasis)

In this sense, Boucher and Sharpe's editorial contention that 'Žižek's program of egalitarian communism is to be actualized by a group dictatorship that will represent the interests of the radically disenfranchised worldwide and will implement policies aiming at material equality in the context of ecological sustainability' (2010: 3) is partially correct – Žižek is writing in support of material equality and ecological sustainability through the interests of the world's radically disenfranchised – yet entirely misses the point. Žižek has

168

no programme, let alone policies. Instead, his political intervention into communism is located in an entirely disruptive evocation of the globally disenfranchised and their association with capitalism. He has, for instance, suggested that one of the two sides of democracy – the other being the regulated process of electoral politics – is the direct imposition of those who are outside the polis (Žižek 2008: 417; 2009b: 45). Vitally, however, he does not imply any support for an alternative democratic programme: his consideration of the 'part with no part' lies only in terms of its (extimate) exclusion from capitalism.

In this regard, developing upon his consideration of the dictatorship of the proletariat, Žižek goes on to implicate the part with no part as the one antagonism (of the four noted earlier) with the most radical potential to disrupt capitalism. It is on the basis of these antagonisms that Žižek's reference to the communist hypothesis begins in earnest, although in *In Defense of Lost Causes* Žižek ends his discussion of these antagonisms by suggesting that not only do the first three designate the domain of the commons and thus justify a reference to communism, but that it is the fourth antagonism – exclusion – which is the site of universality within capitalism. The vital step from universality to communism is only taken in 'How to Begin from the Beginning', where Žižek prefaces his previous argument about the status of the four antagonisms by stating: 'It is, however, only the fourth antagonism, the reference to the excluded, that justifies the term communism'(2009b: 44).

However, Žižek does not begin to specifically refer to communism as a hypothesis until the publication of *First as Tragedy, then as Farce*. Here he introduces the hypothesis by way of reference to Badiou, who stated:

> The communist hypothesis remains the right hypothesis and I see no other . . . if this hypothesis is to be abandoned, then it is not worth doing anything in the field of collective action. Without the perspective of communism, without this kind of Idea, nothing in the historical and political future is of such a kind of interest to the philosopher. Each individual can pursue their private business and we won't mention it again. (2008: 115)

Žižek (2009b) repeats Badiou's argument, adding that one should not read the hypothesis as a 'regulative idea' of the kind that might lead to an ethical socialism with an *a priori* norm.* Rather the

* See Žižek's (2004a) previous debate with Boucher (2004).

communist hypothesis must be referenced to actual contradictions within capitalism. As Žižek states:

> If we conceive of communism as an 'eternal Idea', this implies that the situation which generates it is no less eternal, i.e. that the antagonism to which communism reacts will always be here. From which it is only one step to a 'deconstructive' reading of communism as a dream of presence, of abolishing all alienating re-presentation, a dream which thrives on its own impossibility. (2009a: 88)

As such, Žižek comes to suggest that the communist hypothesis comes into being specifically on the basis of one antagonism; the 'gap which separates the excluded from the included' (2009a: 97). Without this antagonism, Žižek suggests, the remainder of the set lose all subversive potential, becoming challenges and opportunities for the development of new markets; ecological degradation and the green dollar being the emblematic example. Instead, Žižek insists upon a rehabilitation of the Marxist problematic of locating a grouping which, precisely because it lacks a place in the social order, stands for the universal Truth of that order. Attempts to exclude the part with no part (as exemplified by the lumpenproletariat) whether through ideological mystification, the laws of private property or indeed physical walls themselves, constitute the struggle for universality within global capitalism. In the previous chapter I identified this struggle as the politics of practising concrete universality.

It is the necessity of maintaining barriers against the excluded within capitalism that justifies a specific reference to communism rather than to democracy or to fascism. Communism is not an innocent or arbitrary signifier but, rather – even if this conclusion has to be explicated from Žižek's position rather than directly read – signals a commitment to egalitarianism and equality not possible under capitalism. The question, Žižek asks (2009a: 99), is: if the demand of the part with no part cannot be answered within capitalism, is democracy 'an appropriate name for this egalitarian explosion'? Ultimately, his evocation of the communist hypothesis is a rejection of the liberal democratic horizon, suggesting that it is only a return to communism that would do justice to this demand. Yet, this form of communism is not guaranteed by history, rationalism or the big Other to be *the* form of political being but, instead, signals the point of impossibility within capitalism.

In this sense, Žižek's exposition of the communist hypothesis appears to be another iteration of the Lacanian dialectic in a Marxist context: an attempt to reinvent the communist mode of subversion within capitalism in a manner which capital cannot capture by practising concrete universality. Despite the mass of publications and positions Žižek has produced since his initial breakthrough in 1989, *The Sublime Object of Ideology*, the only elements that have altered since the opening chapter of that text (in which he extends on Lacan's assertion that Marx pre-empted the Lacanian symptom by detecting a fundamental imbalance within capitalism whereby a specific instance that appears heterogeneous to the operation of capital – selling one's labour – is universal to the operation of capital (1989: 21–2)) is the addition of the communist signifier and the specific reference to exclusion.

Yet this addition produces notable theoretical complications, as is witnessed by both the publication of *Living in the End Times* (2010) and Badiou's elaboration of his initial reading of the hypothesis. In the former, not only did Žižek not elaborate on communism as a hypothesis, returning instead to further analysis of the antagonisms that haunt late capitalism, but he also sought to distance himself from Badiou's 'Idea of communism', a proposition that has extended beyond its initial formulation. Badiou's Idea can be contrasted with Žižek's hypothesis in the sense that the former has sought to develop the ideological basis upon which it stands – ideology being in firm contrast to Žižek's evocation of the Real antagonisms of capital. Such a distinction signals the difficulty of Žižek's reference to communism. In his attempts to evoke the Real tension evident in the antagonisms of capitalism, the identification of this tension in a positive signifier threatens to undermine the disruptive effect of the Real within capital. The difficulties between representation and the Real are at the heart of Badiou's Idea of communism.

The Idea(l) of Communism

Badiou first introduces communism as a hypothesis towards the end of his polemic text *The Meaning of Sarkozy* (2008). Here he is less evasive as to the value of communism and the potential content of the communist hypothesis than Žižek, claiming that there have been two previous sequences of the hypothesis: the first from the French Revolution to the Paris commune (its establishment) and the second – its first attempt at realisation – running from the Russian Revolution to the end of the Cultural Revolution in China. For Badiou, our task today is to determine the yet-to-be-constructed content of the third sequence. There is, however, an ideological background to these sequences. Communism, Badiou suggests, will eliminate both inequality of wealth and the division of labour. Moreover, distinctions between manual and intellectual labour will disappear, along with differences between town and country. Naturally, the state itself will become unnecessary (Badiou 2008: 115–17). Thus, although Badiou does not specifically identify the shape of the programme that will come to embody this hypothesis, his initial emphasis has been upon the ideological imaginary associated with the signifier 'communism' and its relationship to equality and economy rather than the epistemological and ontological concerns that have preoccupied the Left since the discursive turn.

Nonetheless, in Badiou's follow-up exposition of the hypothesis in *The Communist Hypothesis* (2010), the hypothesis of the title is now distinguished as an Idea and a number of ontological concerns are reintroduced. In the chapter 'The Idea of Communism', Badiou seeks to develop what it means to hold to an Idea, attributing greater value to the form of the Idea than to the content of communism (2010: 254). Whilst this development gives greater consideration to the difficulties of representation in a manner confluent with the ontological basis of Badiou's previous work, it also provides additional concerns in regard to political practice within capitalism.

For Badiou, an Idea is generated by what he terms a Truth procedure. A Truth procedure comes into being in relation to a subject (as opposed to an individual) who becomes a 'militant of this Truth' (Badiou 2010: 234) in achieving subjectivisation. An Idea is thus the operation of a Truth procedure embodied by a subject within a historical state. In these terms, an Idea is the interplay between the singularity of a Truth procedure and a representation of history.

Nonetheless, for Badiou an Idea remains ideological in the sense that it not only imagines the emergence of a political Truth within a historical situation, but seeks to project that political Truth onto another historical situation (Badiou 2010: 238). Thus, whilst Badiou's second reading of the Idea of communism is not as openly ideological as his previous consideration of the 'third sequence' of the communist hypothesis, it still relies upon an imaginary identification.

Badiou is open as regards the ideological status of the Idea, simply stating that 'something can be said to be 'ideological' when it has to do with an Idea' (2010: 240). Nonetheless, the implications of invoking an ideological dimension to the practising of a Truth are significant. Whilst Badiou's Idea does not suggest that, to paraphrase

Laclau, 'communist society does exist', it does offer an imaginary horizon for subjectivised militants of communism to grasp in the anxiety-provoking face of Truth. That is, if the Real element of a Truth procedure grasps the subject, Badiou's Idea of communism implies that the militant subject of this Truth must be able to project the Truth onto an alternative imaginary, lest they be caught up in a reactionary appeal which lessens the anxiety of an encounter with the Real Truth.

Thus, for Badiou, the Idea of communism operates between the Truth held in the Real and the imaginary projection of this Truth onto an imaginary ideological idea. As such, even if revolutionary politics is ultimately a victory for those with no names – the part with no part – Badiou still insists upon the need for the finitude of proper names in politics (2010: 249–52). That is, whilst a political Truth is by definition excluded from the 'state', the vehicle through which that Truth becomes an event is an Idea based upon the nodal point of a proper name, whether of an messianic individual or an ideological movement.

For Žižek, Badiou's insistence upon the necessity of ideology and thus ideological illusion is evidence of his reliance upon a transcendental distortion and subsequent hidden Kantianism based upon a misreading of Hegel. In this regard, Žižek argued:

> One could also say that the Idea of communism schematizes the Real of the political Event, providing it with a narrative coating and thereby making it a part of our experience of historical reality – another indication of Badiou's hidden Kantianism. (2010: 185)

Without wishing to enter into Badiou and Žižek's longstanding debate over their respective understandings of Kant and Hegel, pertinently Žižek suggests that political practice organised around the tension of the Real, yet mediated by the narrative of the Idea and ideological solidification around a proper name, risks a short circuit between the Real and ideology. This short circuit cushions the anxiety of the Real and the possibility of a rupture within capitalism.

Thus, as much as the differences between Badiou's and Žižek's communisms can be identified as ontological, the primary distinction relates to political strategy in regard to the historical structure of capitalism and subsequent opportunities for radical subversion. Where Badiou contends that change can only come from a collective subject embodying the excluded truth of capitalism in the name of the Idea of communism, Žižek insists that there is no outside to capitalism within which an alternative node of ideology could flourish in a truly disruptive sense. Whilst Badiou's subject of communism is not specifically outside capital in the sense that it emerges from the internal failure of capital, any positive ideological movement stemming from this position becomes inherently linked with the structure of capital. In Badiouian terms, the ideological grip of capital is such that ideas only come to make sense in terms of the 'facts' of capitalism.

Certainly, Badiou's Idea offers the prospect of a powerful political movement, entailing a collective subjectification around the antagonistic points of capitalism. Yet severe doubts must be held over the effectiveness of such a movement. A movement of the part with no part, the universal exception, if successfully evoked in the manner Badiou suggests (and as proposed in the previous chapter), holds the possibility of providing substantive ideological disruption and anxiety provoked by an encounter with the Real.

The pertinent question, however, is what occurs after that point. The politics of practising concrete universality, I have suggested, acts to maintain the traumatic status of the Real, such that ideology cannot readily reconfigure itself. This process, however, cannot continue indefinitely: I am not proposing a return to the idea of permanent revolution, nor the early-Laclauian notion of a society constituted on the awareness of its own lack. Rather, the lesson of *jouissance* articulated in this book is that ideological fantasy is driven away from the anxiety of the Real. In this sense, it appears that the Left must necessarily engage in the development of alternatives to capital. Conversely, I have suggested that the effective development of these positions is impossible under the realm of capitalism.

In response to this problematic, I propose that, today, communism is best read through a utopian lens that resists the production of imaginary coherence and instead insists upon the drive of impossibility inherent in global capital. This lens, which involves a psychoanalytic rereading of utopia as well as communism, seeks to move Žižek's use of communism beyond the identification of the antagonisms of capitalism without establishing an alternative ideological fantasy.

Utopia: Demand the Impossible!

At its most basic, utopia can be conceived as an impulse or desire for something different from the existing. In this sense, utopianism has been referenced to the prospect of radical political change in the name of a perfect future society. The utopian urge, however, does not necessarily take the form of a desire for a radically different form of being. Today, the elementary utopian demand is embodied in the conservative hope that, ultimately, society does exist; that life could be managed in such a manner that the fullness of presence is possible within existing structures. We see this utopianism played out in discussion around environmental issues in which the threat of overwhelming ecological degradation is placated by the prospect of technological innovation, responsive markets and 'political will' (Sachs: 2008).

The utopian demand can be regarded as the desire for *jouissance*. Indexing utopia to *jouissance* means that at first glance, utopia – despite its radical pretensions – is a counter-intuitive position for any form of politics taking its orientation from a Lacanian-inspired psychoanalysis that has emphasised themes of lack, finitude and excess. Conversely, an alternate modality of utopia can be constituted around the very impossibility of its realisation, rather than the *jouissance* imagined in the ideological utopia of the ideal. This mode retains the demand for a better world but finds the drive for change in the limitation of imagination rather than its location in a specific ideal. If, for example, a dominant mode of contemporary environmentalism displays the tragic utopianism of the ideal harmony with nature, an alternative mode could momentarily exist in a discombobulation of ideology stemming from a collective and traumatic realisation that existing devices cannot prevent ecological disaster. This realisation – an evocation of the Real – has the potential to disrupt the consistently of capitalism in a way that new modes of understanding can flourish.

Utopia, considered in both these modes, is thus not to be divorced from the everyday but, rather, is at the heart of the human experience. It is a response to the operation that Ruth Levitas (2007: 290), following Ernst Bloch (1986), identifies as the fundamental utopian expression: that utopia is at its core an expression of the desire for a better way of being, a principle that Bloch designated as 'hope', or a desire for something that is missing. In this sense utopian thought does not require the wholesale imagination of new worlds, although this construction is an articulation of a utopian desire. Instead, these constructions are an expression of a larger demand for *jouissance* and wholeness before language.

Indexing utopia to *jouissance* suggests that, rather than taking the form of elaborate visions, a utopian urge appears in the everyday performance of social life. In this sense, utopia cannot be juxta-posed against ideology – utopia seeking to change society, ideology to maintain it – as Karl Mannheim thought (Mannheim, cited in Levitas: 2007: 289). Instead, this sense of utopia is entirely ideo-logical: utopia is an expression of *jouissance* that lies at the heart of ideology. The everyday performance of utopia, therefore, is the performance of *jouissance* in a variety of discursive forms – the elementary demand of the utopian/ideological position is that, contra Laclau, 'society does exist'.

It is the critique of this mantra that forms the basis of psycho-analytic criticism of utopianism. Suggesting that attempts to attain the fullness of *jouissance* or utopia must violently exclude a dysto-pian element that cannot be named, for many – and not limited to psychoanalytic theorists – utopian politics can be deemed idealisti-cally unrealistic at best, dangerous at worst (Gray: 2008). Barack Obama's presidential campaign and subsequent administration is one example of the inevitable failure (and danger) of the utopian imagination. Obama's campaign imagery of 'change' and 'hope' brought with it a wholesale imagination of a different kind of society. Yet, at the moment of his election, from his inauguration speech to the widespread restoration of Bill Clinton's political advisors, the desire and *jouissance* behind the Obama utopia collapsed. This col-lapse, despite being embodied by specific events, was not dependent upon these events but, rather, necessary: the utopian ideal collapses as soon as imagination is put into action. Equally, since this col-lapse a more potent movement has emerged, based largely around the ultra-conservative Tea Party, which seeks to restore the utopia of 'America' largely by way of associating Obama with an otherness that is threatening this imaginary.

The alternative mode of utopia, based around the impossibility of its instantiation, is more akin to the impulse of the Lacanian dia-lectic. Rather than seeking to extend or fulfil a utopian imagination, this modality locates the utopian moment at the very limits of ideol-ogy. Such a utopian moment lies not in the content of ideology but, rather, in the impulse for change that occurs when the symptoms of an order become overly traumatic so that they cannot be contained within ideology. The utopia of the Real – as opposed to the ideal – occurs when, unable to contain the trauma caused by exposure to the Real, new modes of being emerge.

As Žižek, discussing the lack of alternatives to capitalism, states in the documentary *Žižek!*:

We should reinvent utopia, but in what sense? There are two false meanings of utopia; one is this old notion of imaging an ideal society which we know will never be realised. The other is the capitalist utopia in the sense of new perverse desires that you are not only allowed but even solicited to realise. The true utopia is when the situation is so without issue, without a way to resolve it within the coordinates of the possible that out of the pure urge of survival you have to invent a new space. Utopia is not kind of a free imagination, utopia is a matter of inner-most urgency, you are forced to imagine as the only way out, and this is the utopia we need today. (Taylor 2007)

In this regard, a utopian drive lies in the impossibility of imagining an alternative future to capitalism, despite the inability to resolve its great horrors: such a demand is embodied in the oft-repeated remark that capital limits our imagination so that it is easier to imagine the end of the world than a change in the mode of production. Rather than attempting to suture the contradictions of capital, a utopian demand occurs when the subjects of capitalism are compelled to imagine a new mode of being in order to avoid the trauma of the breakdown of the ideological frameworks which have contained the horrors of capital.

The distinction between the two modes of utopia can be found in Thomas More's original conception, using Greek terms to bring together 'no place' and 'good place'. This suggests both a tragic and comedic face to utopia. Utopia can be tragic – a place we will never reach – or comedic; utopia lies in the constituent impossibility of its realisation. This latter form does not cling to an alternative conception of society but, rather, relies upon the build-up of energy around the very limits to our imagination. Imagination, of course, is not limited to the fancy of the individual. Rather, it is always a social creation; the limitations of our imagination are always the limitations of the ideological terrain.

A profound difficulty presents itself at this point: finding a way to imagine the prospect of an alternative future without foreclosing the possibility of it coming into being. What we require is not a utopian urge to fill out the failure of capitalism, either through capitalism itself or its cultural supplements, but a desire to move beyond capitalism on the basis of the traumatic impossibility of capital. This desire constitutes not only an approach to the Real but the *jouissance* of impossibility itself. That is, the impossibility of imagining utopia does not bring an end to *jouissance* but, instead, persists in the form of *jouissance*. This form of utopia does not dismiss *jouissance* as an illusion but, instead, suggests that *jouissance* drives every attempt to imagine utopia. The vital difference between the forms of utopia is that the positive mode attempts to locate this utopian place, whereas the impossible utopia plays upon the urge to go beyond the existing. The key distinction here is between the fantasy of full *jouissance* provided by utopia-as-content, and the subversion of alternative political imaginaries through utopia-as-form.

Whilst this form of utopianism leads itself to accusations of negativity and political quietism, positive forms are easily subverted. In relation to his reservations around the extension of imagination, Jameson argues that the designation of specific points of protest is contrary to the effectiveness of utopianism. It is for this reason that Jameson has previously suggested that utopia is at its most effective when it cannot be imagined:

> Its function lies not in helping us to imagine a better future but, rather, in demonstrating our utter incapacity to imagine such a future – our imprisonment in a non-utopian present without historicity of futurity – so as to reveal the ideological closure of the system in which we are somehow trapped and confined. (2004: 46)

When the specific contradictions become apparent, the tendency is to focus political demands upon these points. At this point the utopian imagination becomes limited and what might have been a revolutionary demand gives way to practical political programmes (Jameson 2004: 45).

If the utopian moment occurs when the limits of ideology cannot be sutured, the identification of this moment with a particular demand risks a positivisation of the Real and a subsequent reactionary appeal to *jouissance* and a wholeness of being. That is, if the trauma of the Real opens up a wound within ideology, this wound can equally and effectively be sutured by a renewed ideological movement which displaces the cause of trauma. A salient example of this process in these times is the green movement. Although green ideology at times suggests energy for widespread change that might be considered utopian, it has become too easy to divert this enthusiasm into smaller-scale demands that only serve to supplement the interests of capital and escalate ecological collapse.

Yet, if the Žižekian sense of utopianism – interpreted here through the communist hypothesis – takes its form from the expression of actually occurring antagonisms within capitalism, how does it avoid becoming particularised in singular demands? Whilst acknowledging that capital is able to include and pacify most of its symptoms, Žižek designates the 'part-with-no-part' as the specific contradiction that holds a vital, universal, status and thus cannot be subject to direct political demands. That is, whilst the utopian demand inherent in this necessary exclusion can be subverted in various ideological measures, such as charitable aid or the displacement of the antagonism to an exterior cause, the universality of the lumpenproletariat *qua* concrete universality cannot be integrated within capitalism and for this reason remains the impossible point of a utopian demand.

Nonetheless, as Jameson might suggest, indexing communism in relation to utopia is to mediate against the utopian demand by providing an object for the imagination, an imagination that will inevitably become caught up in the facts and consequences of capital. This is ultimately a question of the representation of impossibility and the signification of the Real. Jameson and Badiou, as presented here, represent two sides of this debate. Where Badiou attempts to animate an idea with an overwhelming ideological component, Jameson resists any temptation to suture the limitation of our political imagination. Žižek's brief evocation of the communist hypothesis, however, suggests a third alternative. Here the reference to communism does not seek to develop a new imagination but, instead, insists upon thrusting open the trauma into ideological fantasy via the practice of concrete universality identified in the previous chapter. This occurs, however, by identifying this trauma with both a specific antagonism – class struggle *qua* the lumpenproletariat – and with communism. The latter is read not through the positivity of ideology but rather, as an opportunity to insist upon the impossibility of capital and direct the interpretation of its collapse.

Communism and Utopia

Thinking communism in terms of utopia produces two alternative positions. Firstly, there is the fantasmatic utopia of communism without antagonism, a position Žižek has subjected to sustained critique, regarding it as the ultimate Marxist fantasy of capitalism without antagonism (see Žižek 1989: 49–53). This is the tragedy inherent in utopia as the image of the good place: an imaginary ideal that must fail and in doing so attributes this failure to an exterior cause. By contrast, the communist hypothesis lies in the utopian demand that the contradictions of capitalism are such that it cannot continue indefinitely. Specifically, the utopia of the communist hypothesis lies in capitalism's very failure to account for its own exclusions in the walls it is developing against the excess of humanity that builds around the globe: the universality of capital exists in this battle.

Badiou's Idea of communism has much in common with both readings of utopia. Read through the Jamesonian lens of utopianism suggested here, the utopian moment in Badiou's work occurs when the subject is grasped by a Truth such that they become a militant evangelist for this Truth, forcing the idea into being in the face of the facts of the situation. Nonetheless, the 'Road to Damascus' moment of Badiou's subject of Truth includes not only this moment but, also, the ideological path which provides the moment of Truth with political substance.

Although the emphasis lies upon the truth of a situation, such that it embodies the impossibility of capitalism, the mobilisation of this truth requires the subject to commit to an ideology. The Badiouian procedure thus enlists two utopian moments for its political power: one of the impossibility of the 'no place', the other of the 'good place' of the third sequence of the Idea of communism.

Yet Badiou's insistence upon the stabilising presence of proper names means we must question how this Idea could come into place without a reactionary *jouissance* and the fantasy of the utopian ideal. Indeed, Žižek contends that Badiou's notion of 'sequences' of communism signals the difficulty in his conception of it. Such an image of communism postulates the presence of an empty, universal frame that is altered under differing concrete circumstances. Instead of this abstract universality, Žižek's communism lies in the concrete universality evident in the failure of global capital (2010: 20).

Nonetheless, by contrast to Žižek's conception, Badiou's meaning of communism is clear in his notion of the Idea. Communism becomes both the interpretative procedure identifying Truth within facts and the ideology of a new world order; vitally, communism acts as a point of identification for the newly subjectivised individual. Žižek's communism remains more ambivalent. If his previous political positions have identified the tension and political power of those who are the 'part with no part', then we must consider how the addition of the communist signifier alters his politics. Through the reference to an impossible sense of utopia I have suggested that the traction provided by the utopian demand comes from an identification with the impossibility of capitalism. This identification owes itself to Žižek's

Lacanian reading of Marxism, rather than any historical reading of communist discourse.

Nonetheless, the difference between Badiou and Žižek on this point is much less marked than the contrast with Jameson. Where the latter insists upon the limitations of imagination as the place of utopia, both Žižek and Badiou seek to overtly politicise the moment of failure. The vital difference, however, is that where Badiou argues that an ideological platform is required for the subjects of Truth, Žižek seeks to politicise a potential rupture within capitalism by insisting upon its communist potential. This potential lies in the very impossibility within capitalism and is thus a utopian demand. Yet, even if Žižek does not himself postulate a consequential communist ideology, it is inevitable that the very spectre of communism would evoke images of the shape of the communist future. In this sense, we must insist on the vital distinction between Žižek's focus upon Truth and the Real and Badiou's collective subject. This distinction relates not so much to an abstraction of theory but, rather, an ontological reading of the conditions of possibility for subversion within capitalism. Where Badiou conceives of hope for a collective movement against capitalism, Žižek insists that capitalism can only be bought to its knees through an awareness of its own limits.

Here the Žižekian interpretation of communism is able to postulate this signifier without a corresponding ideological manifesto because it is not an abstract or ideal formulation but, rather, a reaction to existing conditions. In regards to Jameson's concerns around the possible subversion of utopian energy caused by the naming of this point, the communist hypothesis does not suggest a 'filling out' of the utopian space but, rather, signifies that point which cannot be filled out. In this way, through the impossibility of including the lumpenproletariat, the communist hypothesis does open up a new horizon for the Left but not one that will please many of Žižek's critics – it does not produce a new point of imaginary identification but, instead, opens up new space for these identifications to be formed.

Žižek's communism is not an empty treatise on political strategy but is dedicated to moving beyond capitalism. This commitment forms the basis of the 'communist' hypothesis rather than any reference to democracy as the driver of the future. Žižek justifies the use of communism as the named signifier of the transition from capitalism to the future by reference to the surplus of labour within capitalism itself, suggesting not only that capitalism is unable to provide any sense of global egalitarian justice beyond its own self-serving ideology, but that the communist horizon provides this hope. By utilising communism and the lumpenproletariat as the primary reference point to the end of capitalism, Žižek is signalling more than just a strategic intent to move beyond capitalism: he is implicitly suggesting a political commitment to egalitarian justice for which there is no requirement for further justification, but no possibility within capitalism.

Conclusion

Throughout this text I have argued that Žižek's work is a particularly effective response to the dark reign of global capitalism. Against the hegemonic critical reading of it as 'good theory, bad politics', Žižekian theory provides a radical continuation of the Marxist tradition through an approach that owes more to Lacanian materialism and Hegelian dialectics than the economism of classical Marxism and the political forms that followed. This continuation, however, comes without a manifesto, or indeed any significant detail. For this reason, the Žižekian politics produced over the past seven chapters will not satisfy many of Žižek's critics, nor inspire any party programme, although they can inform the burgeoning imagination of anti-capitalist action, most recently articulated in the Occupy movement.

What my interpretation of Žižekian politics does suggest is a return to the critique of political economy and class struggle via the Lacanian Real and the Hegelian universal. Identifying the global lumpenproletariat as the new universal class of 21st-century capitalism, I have argued that by reading this class through the Real, we are better placed to understand the potential for radical politics that lies within capitalism. This potential comes not from the possibility of an uprising of the disenfranchised but, rather, from the punctuation of the ideological ideas we hold about ourselves.

This punctuation suggests the ultimate wager of this book. I have argued that although Žižekian politics does not lend itself to a singular approach, the most effective political strategy that stems from his work in contemporary circumstances is the act of practising concrete universality, whereby the universal exception – a modality of the Real – is thrust onto the ideological horizon that excludes it. This punctuation, however, relies upon an implied contradiction between the suffering of the lumpenproletariat and the ideas we hold about ourselves as 'Good' animals living within a politically just system. These ideas relate not so much to our own subjectivity – the primacy of self-interest is well established here – but to the status of the big

Other, which works for the benefit of all, thus depriving individual actors of moral responsibility. If I have established, as a well-worked Marxist premise, that the operation of capital *necessitates* the death and suffering of those excluded from its benefits but included within its operation, the vital question is whether this suffering will come to impact upon our ideological fantasies so that we are forced to imagine a way of living beyond current forms.

It is a basic principle of psychoanalysis that the subject cannot simply accept Truth. Instead, the imposition of a Truth within ideological fantasy will destabilise the coherence of that fantasy. Conversely, subjectivity is also constituted precisely to prevent this kind of disruption: I have outlined these mechanisms in significant detail throughout this text, considering the nature of *jouissance*, fantasy and desire, along with fetishism and the perversity of the superego. The political struggle around the kind of politics proposed here involves subverting these mechanisms to keep alive the anxiety and trauma of the Real *qua* class struggle.

Undoubtedly, other responses to the Truth of capitalism are possible, even more likely. Conservative or reactionary forces may assert an acknowledgement of poverty and suffering as a necessary consequence of our lives, asking the Western subject whether they are willing to sacrifice their own well-being for the sake of others. It is this strategy we see in operation in the 'War on Terror'. Nonetheless, this approach does not sit easily, and is rarely seen in official politics. Instead, if for many the bald attacks on the survival and liberty of those said to be a threat to Western freedoms are unsettling, numerous discourses are available to quell this unease. Liberal action groups seek 'balanced' approaches that acknowledge the necessity of the horizon whilst comforting against the most disconcerting aspects of this strategy. Alternatively, either approach can be supplemented by the presence of fetishes about necessity, due process or the future. Finally, superego protest discourses work to infuse ideological narratives with a guilt that is hopelessly ineffective in producing political change.

What all these approaches avoid is an encounter with the Real, an encounter which is the basis of Žižekian politics. It is ultimately proposed that by evoking the Real in a manner that does not allow for an alternative identification, a utopian drive can be established that allows only the establishment of the communist hypothesis derived from the impossibility embodied by the lumpenproletariat.

If this political strategy appears needlessly complex, avoiding numerous more straightforward alternatives, this book has worked to establish the difficulties faced by the radical Left in re-establishing a political foothold against capital. These difficulties first became recognised in regard to the continual flourishing of capitalism and the contradictions of political movements associated with Marxism.

Recognising that political change has to be as much cultural as economic, Western Marxism came to reject historical materialism and the determinism and economism that came with it. In doing so it leant heavily upon the resources of the discursive turn which came to dominate Leftist politics in the latter half of the twentieth century. Whilst this turn to culture and language largely occurred as an attempt to explain the failings of Marxism, significant alternative readings of emancipation and Leftism came to reject the discourse altogether, regarding it as just another universalist grand narrative. These discourses remained primarily focused upon the role of culture and ideology rather than upon materialism, class struggle and the economy. If traditional forms of Marxism placed too much emphasis upon the historical unfolding of the economy and the destiny of the proletariat, the new forms of cultural or discursive Marxism appeared entirely impotent in response to the challenges posed by global capitalism.

Suggesting that Žižek's work should be read as a response to both the dominance of capitalism and the downfall of Marxism, I have nonetheless identified this relationship as complicated by Žižek's primary commitment to Lacanian psychoanalysis. Although psychoanalysis has often been combined with Marxism, Žižek's Lacanian reading of Marxism is strongly critical of both historical materialism and the cultural forms of 'post-Marxism' that have followed.

Primarily, Žižek suggests that in moving away from both the economy and the materialism of shared social life, contemporary Marxism is ill equipped to respond to capitalism. Nonetheless, whilst Lacanian approaches provide a particularly insightful reading into the dialectics of politics and enjoyment, suggesting that politics are not wholly contingent but instead rely upon the coherence of ideological fantasises that provide a material fixity, the prospects for a political alternative inspired by psychoanalysis appear grim.

Whilst psychoanalysis provides an intriguing reading of the prospects of the Good and of shared social life, it is incommensurate with the production of an imaginary notion of shared community which would match that suggested by Marxist communism. Through a critique of Stavrakakis and Laclau, I have suggested that the Lacanian dialectic cannot be institutionalised but that it offers an insight into the political that is best exemplified in the works of Žižek. Although I have rejected the postulation that there exists a singular form of 'Žižekian' politics, I have advanced a reading of Žižek that suggests his work provides a strategic form of politics based upon an alignment with the dislocating possibilities of the Real.

Moreover, I have come to identify Žižek's construction of capitalism as being at the core of his political work. Here, Marx's base–superstructure model can be reread through the Lacanian registers of the imaginary, the symbolic and the Real to produce a highly effective interpretation of capitalism. This understanding suggests that capitalism operates as a form of enjoyment, structured both through consumptive fetishism and through ideologies that reinforce our idea that we continue to live in a 'Good' society. Democracy is foremost amongst these ideologies, embracing the notion that all political demands can be met through democratic processes and, in doing so, rejecting any idea of popular protest or violent action.

This enjoyment means that capitalism has a degree of fixity, which, along with symbolic-structural feedback measures, means that capital can be productively interpreted as an articulation of the Real, whereby its dominance means that no alternative is currently possible: capital has hegemonised the place of hegemony. Conversely, against this symbolic-imaginary matrix, class struggle can also be understood as a modality of the Real, as every instantiation of the economy is based around the impossibility of class struggle – there is no class relationship.

Moreover, this understanding of class struggle can be extended through a Hegelian reading of universality and the Real, positioning the lumpenproletariat as the Real embodiment of the necessary failure of the class relationship within capitalism. As such, although capitalism can appear as an unbreakable matrix, the Real embodiment of class struggle within capitalism offers the prospect of a limit to its infinite reproduction.

This limit, however, does not suggest a natural form of politics. Instead, a number of strategic positions emerge from Žižek's work, each of which are an interpretation of the dialectics of *jouissance*, ideological fantasy and the Real. These strategies produce a potentially unique response to capitalism and the Real. Here I have considered the act and subtractive politics, as well as the practice of concrete universality. Finding the first two strategies limited in their appeal, given the circumstances in which they are to be applied, I have turned to the practice of concrete universality as the most effective strategic interpretation of Žižek's work in relation to capitalism.

By practising concrete universality and forcing a (discursive) intrusion of an exceptional element into the field of ideology which shields politics from the existence of that universal, capitalism can be dislocated so that a space would open for new forms of political practice. Specifically, I have recognised a recent development within Žižek's work – the identification with a communist hypothesis – as a guide to the shape of the future. This hypothesis does not suggest a particular discursive content for such a movement but, rather, holds the place of a utopian demand. This demand is not for a perfect society but for a recognition of the current impossibility of imagining such a society. In this regard, the communist hypothesis acts as an extension of the strategic positioning constructed in Chapter 6 – an attempt to thrust the exclusion of the lumpenproletariat to the ideological surface of capital.

Yet the question that has been largely foreclosed from this analysis thus far concerns the value judgements inherent in Žižek's work and this book. If this book has overtly worked towards a rejection of capitalism in the implied name of egalitarian justice, it has also tended towards the rejection of normative positions, in particular those based upon the transcendentalism of a moral signifier. Moreover, as well as the inherent commitment to the hungry of this world, I have hinted that Žižek's location of the communist hypothesis as *the* form of politics today suggests a normative positioning which is yet to be addressed. It is to this point that I shall now turn.

The Consequences of Žižekian Politics Today

The horizon opened up by the communist hypothesis allows for a new identification with the impossibility and injustice of capitalism, and a new direction for embodied political ambitions, but is without a programmatic political statement. Not only is such an approach incompatible with the politics of utopia, it is too much to expect from Žižek's work. Žižek is not the Master but, rather, a philosopher whose work has been able to open up new directions for political thought.

Nonetheless, we must carefully consider the consequences of practising this form of politics. Our age is not without proposals for responding to the symptoms of capitalism. There are a number of administrative approaches to poverty and environmental change that will potentially reduce the suffering of human populations in a very tangible manner. Programmes such as micro-finance for women in the Third World should be celebrated for the very real benefits they bring. Democracy in itself should not be jettisoned. Nonetheless, one of the primary assertions of this argument is that these movements will never be enough to relieve the suffering of all, or even the majority within capitalism. It is not that we should dismiss or discourage these moves but that we must be wary of their fantasmatic effects.

Yet if I have put forward a position that is too optimistic, implying that change will arise through the correct application of strategic theory, this has not been my intention. Circumstances are dire and our paths ahead will be difficult. There are some very real restrictions upon any movement for radical change. We cannot simply physically overthrow governments in this current state, as their power – whether military, monetary or ideological – is such that this kind of move would be instantly crushed. Instead, as was seen in the Arab Spring of 2011, regimes fall when they lose moral legitimacy, not from force alone.* Our time gives cause for a different kind of politics, a shifting of the ideological terrain by means of reconsidering the disavowed foundations upon which that power is based, so that overthrowing governments in the name of an egalitarian justice appears to be the only thing to do. It is only by confronting these unbearable foundations that a new imaginary energy will come into being, one that will push history beyond capitalism.

Thus, whilst we might admire the pragmatism of the likes of Jeffrey Sachs, or the moral imperatives at the heart of Greenpeace or Amnesty International, the circumstances of our time mean they are ultimately ineffective, if easily understood, solutions to the crises and contradictions of capitalism. If the Žižekian path outlined in this book appears to be a ridiculous risk – to demand a shift from a global society in which a part of that society is experiencing unparalleled wealth, life expectancies and freedom from direct want, to an undistinguished beyond identified only by its current impossibility – then this risk can be justified only by reference to the miserable plight of those who have no stake in the order yet remain as its foundations. For this surplus of humanity, such a demand is not a risk but, rather, their only hope.

---

* This text has not focused specifically upon the politics and strategies of revolution, considering the kind of street-level practices that might prove to be the most successful in the final movements of overthrowing a regime. Instead, the discussion has been directed at the foundational concerns of shifting the ideological terrain.

Conversely, the very notion of *communism* in the communist hypothesis is far from innocent, carrying with it the weight of a largely ghastly ideological history and strong ideological demands. Any form of politics that seeks to engage with this signifier will face battles on both sides: an administrative dismissal of communism as a failed and dangerously utopian ideology and attempts to fill the signifier with ideological meaning in the name of *jouissance*.

Furthermore, the power of capital is such that it is likely to continue for some time, despite our interventions. The shape of capital and its symptoms will morph and our responses must change as well. As urban slum populations increase and economic growth continues to put pressure on global ecosystems, it is likely that these symptoms, and the consequences of the capitalist mode of production, will become more apparent. Most particularly, it is likely that these symptoms will themselves become intrusions as climate change comes to the fore – increasing struggles over scarce resources – and the geographical distance between the 'haves' and the 'have-nots' lessens. This shift will occur not only through the spreading of slums – or the development of slums on the edge of previously wealthy cities – but through the increasingly prevalent trend towards illegal migration into the West. The strategic challenge is to avoid a reactionary hegemony, in which open power conflicts over resources and the dehumanisation of refugees and migrants become the norm. Rather, we must insist upon the contradiction between the consequences of capital and any remaining moral sense of ourselves. It is perhaps at this point that the wager that humans are 'Good' animals will be put to the test.

Nonetheless, at this time in history, in which capitalism reigns darkly supreme yet is plagued both by its own non-existence and by the tormenting presence of symptoms which prove its existence, Žižek's form of negative ontological politics is the one approach which provides the most hope for the kind of radical change that would drastically improve the material circumstances of the hungry by giving them a presence beyond their mere biological being.

Future Possibilities

If this book began with an explicit Marxist posturing, that position has been increasingly marginalised in favour of debate over the role and possibilities of psychoanalytic politics. Yet the value of Marxism as an intellectual and political resource should not be doubted and it is in this manner that Marxism ultimately informs Žižek's work. This is the most productive articulation of Marxist politics today – not as an explicit ideological position but, rather, as part of a renewed political practice that insists upon the excluded presence of the traumatic foundations of capitalism. Whilst the content of this political practice is distinctly Marxist – referring as it does to conceptions of class struggle, of exploitation, of communism and rejecting the primacy of democratic ideology – the form of its practice is dominated by a Lacanianism which overrides the traditional expression of these concepts. It is worth noting here that this is not the final word on Marxist politics. Although I have suggested that the most productive form of politics in response to capitalism is informed more by psychoanalysis than Marxism – without dismissing the restrictions on Marxist political practice after the signifier – it is quite possible that a future beyond capitalism will bring greater reference to the Marxist tradition.

On the other hand, the lessons learnt in understanding the negative ontological structuring role of language should not be dismissed: these are not limitations of capital but, rather, the ahistorical conditions of possibility for shared social life. Nonetheless, politics based upon a negative ontology, such as Žižek's, do appear to have a limited functionality, operating as a form of political intervention rather than suggesting any institutional content. These forms do speak to that institutional content, but whether an ethics of negativity can become the basis for community, and indeed the material reproduction of that community, remains an open question. What I have suggested in this book is that these forms of politics are essentially political and, through Žižek's reading of the politics of the political, can form the basis for radical movements. Conversely, the conditions of capital are such that there is no possibility for these alternative forms to gain the kind of traction which would allow any autonomous expression.

More than ever today we are provided with an opportunity to practise an active politics of the negative that operates through the deliberate exposure of the disavowed foundations of our order. These foundations offer the prospect of a dynamic and unsustainable disturbance in the prevailing socio-political order through the forced and embodied acknowledgement of the excluded as the foundations of our mode of being. To practise concrete universality is thus to cross the mode of fantasy that coheres the imaginary horizons of our civilisation, leaving ideology with no defence against that which must become unpalatable – if we have any sense of ourselves as a species of 'good animals'. This is Žižek's 'utopian impossibility', the practice of concrete universality such that we (as a people) are forced to imagine a new mode of being. This is utopia.

We must remember, however, that this political intervention remains academic. Not only is this book confined to the discourse of the university but the kind of political intervention which I have discussed relates to the advancement of ideas which, whilst a mode of political practice in themselves, are unlikely to resonate with the public as they are currently articulated. Instead, any movement which has the potential to provoke and carry through widespread change must engage with popular ideology, whether through ever-evolving forms of media or on the streets. Nonetheless, whilst there are limitations to the political reach of academic work, this work can and does play a vital role in informing various modes of political practice. Whilst the application of the strategies abstracted in this book would no doubt be rougher and more concrete, the identification of these approaches suggests a beginning to these processes.

Thus, Žižek's answer to Thomas Brockelman's (2003: 205) question 'What, after all, does it mean to be "against" capitalism if that suggests nothing about what one would change in it or substitute for it?', or to Laclau's almost hysterical demands (2000b: 206) for Žižek to reveal his alternative form of economy or radical imaginary, is not to produce an alternative horizon. It is, instead, to identify the exceptional and symptomatic points upon which ideological formations rest. Moreover, Žižek not only seeks to identify such points but, as I have discussed in Chapter 6 in relation to political strategy, to consider how the Real gap between ideology and its exception can be exposed.

Thus, in terms of the shape of the future, in this book I have not come to any conclusion except to state that if we are to have any true sense of egalitarian justice and global sustainability a new future is required. Moreover, following Žižek I have come to suggest that the most effective strategy for opening up space to forge this future is to practise the intrusion of concrete universality, a utopian practice which relies upon the communist demand of the lumpenproletariat. As such, Žižek's work is certainly not conservative, nor without a political basis.

But what form will the future hold? Certainly, utopia – in the sense of the fullness of being and the arrival of *jouissance* – will not occur. Instead, the future, like any other instantiation of human community, will be profoundly complicated and Žižek provides no suggestion as to what it might be. The consideration of these possibilities is beyond the scope of this text and more pertinently, beyond our current political horizon. Instead, what is required at this time in the history of humanity, when the morbid deadlock caused by global capitalism is becoming increasingly apparent, is the utopian practice of Žižekian psychoanalysis. The rest shall be history.

References

Adams, G. (2010), 'Golden times for global food chain'. NZHerald website, 15 May, http://www.nzherald.co.nz/business/news/article.cfm?c_id=3&objectid=10645043&pnum=0, accessed 9 November 2011.

Anderson, P. (1976), *Considerations on Western Marxism*. London: New Left.

Associated Press (2010), 'Alien life already on earth, says scientist'. Stuff website, 27 January, http://www.stuff.co.nz/world/3265741/Alien-life-already-on-Earth-says-scientist, accessed 9 November 2011.

Badiou, A. (2008), *The Meaning of Sarkozy*, tr. D. Fernbach. London: Verso.

Badiou, A. (2010), *The Communist Hypothesis*, tr. D. Macey & S. Corcoran. London: Verso.

Bank for International Settlements (2010), *Triennial Central Bank Survey: Report on Global Foreign Exchange Market Activity in 2010*. Basel: Bank for International Settlements.

Bauman, Z. (2004), *Wasted Lives: Modernity and its Outcasts*. Cambridge: Polity Press.

Bauman, Z. (2005), *Work, Consumerism and the New Poor*, 2nd ed. Maidenhead: Open University Press.

Bellamy, E. (1993), 'Discourses of Impossibility: Can Psychoanalysis be Political?'. *Diacritics* 23, 24–38.

Bloch, E. (1986), *The Principle of Hope*, tr. N. Plaice et al. Cambridge, MA: MIT Press.

Boothby, R. (2001), *Freud as Philosopher: Metapsychology after Lacan*. London: Routledge.

Boucher, G. (2004), 'The Antinomies of Slavoj Žižek'. *Telos* 129, 151–72.

Boucher, G. (2008), *The Charmed Circle of Ideology: A Critique of Laclau and Mouffe, Butler and Žižek*. Melbourne: Re.press.

Boucher, G. & Sharpe, M. (2010), '"Žižek's Communism" and *In Defense of Lost Causes*'. *International Journal of Žižek Studies* 4(2).

Boucher, G., Glynos, J. & Sharpe, M. (eds) (2006), *Traversing the Fantasy: Critical Responses to Slavoj Žižek*. Aldershot: Ashgate.

Bowman, P. (2007), 'The Tao of Žižek'. In P. Bowman & R. Stamp (eds), *The Truth of Žižek*. London: Continuum, pp. 27–44.

Bowman, P. & Stamp, R. (eds) (2007), *The Truth of Žižek*. London: Continuum.

Briggs, B. (2010), 'Britannia's balaclava gangs'. NZHerald website, 20 March, http://www.nzherald.co.nz/world/news/article.cfm?c_id=2&ob jctid=10633125, accessed 7 December 2011.

Brockelman, T. (2003), 'The Failure of the Radical Democratic Imaginary: Žižek versus Laclau and Mouffe on Vestigial Utopia'. *Philosophy and Criticism* 29, 183–208.

Bryant, L. (2007), 'Symptomal Knots and Evental Ruptures: Žižek, Badiou and Discerning the Indiscernible'. *International Journal of Žižek Studies* 1(2).

Butler, R. (2005), *Slavoj Žižek*. London: Continuum.

Butler, J., Laclau, E. & Žižek, S. (2000), *Contingency, Hegemony, Universality: Contemporary Dialogues on the Left*. London: Verso.

Connolly, W. (2002), *Neuropolitics: Thinking, Culture, Speed*. Minneapolis: University of Minnesota Press.

Connolly, W. (2008), *Capitalism and Christianity, American Style*. Durham, NC: Duke University Press.

Cremin, C. (2011), *Capitalism's New Clothes: Enterprise, Ethics and Enjoyment in Times of Crisis*. London: Pluto Press.

Critchley, S. (2007a), 'Foreword: Why Žižek must be Defended'. In P. Bowman & R. Stamp (eds), *The Truth of Žižek*. London: Continuum, pp. xi–xvi.

Critchley, S. (2007b), *Infinitely Demanding: Ethics of Commitment, Politics of Resistance*. London: Verso.

Daly, G. (2009), 'Politics of the Political: Psychoanalytic Theory and the Left(s)'. *Journal of Political Ideologies* 14, 279–300.

Daly, G. (2010), 'Causes for Concern: Žižek's Politics of Loving Terror'. *International Journal of Žižek Studies* 4(2).

Davis, M. (2007), *Planet of Slums*. London: Verso.

Dean, J. (2006), *Žižek's Politics*. New York: Routledge.

Dean, J. (2010), *Blog Theory: Feedback and Capture in the Circuits of Drive*. Cambridge: Polity Press.

Deleuze, G. & Guattari, F. (1977), *Anti-Oedipus: Capitalism and Schizophrenia*, tr. R. Hurley et al. New York: Viking Press.

Denning, M. (2010), 'Wageless Life'. *New Left Review*, November–December, 79–97.

Devenney, M. (2002), *Ethics and Politics in Contemporary Theory: Between Critical Theory and Post-Marxism*. London: Routledge.

Devenney, M. (2007), 'Žižek's Passion for the Real'. In P. Bowman & R. Stamp (eds), *The Truth of Žižek*. London: Continuum, pp. 45–60.

Douzinas, C. & Žižek, S. (eds) (2010), *The Idea of Communism*. London: Verso.

Drury, I. (2011), 'The "dirty secret" of British arms sales to Libya just months before Gaddafi slaughtered pro-democracy protesters'. *Daily Mail*, 5 April, http://www.dailymail.co.uk/news/article-1373444/Libya-The-dirty-secret-UK-arms-sales-Gaddafi.html, accessed 9 November 2011.

Eagleton, T. (1997), *Marx*. London: Phoenix.

Eagleton, T. (2003), *After Theory*. London: Allen Lane.

Eagleton, T. (2009), *Trouble with Strangers: A Study of Ethics*. Chichester: Wiley-Blackwell.

Eagleton, T. (2011), *Why Marx Was Right*. New Haven, CT: Yale University Press.

Economist (2011), 'Time to participate in democracy', 17 November, http://www.economist.com/blogs/democracyinamerica/2011/11/occupy-wall-street-0, accessed 7 December 2011.

Elliott, A. (2004), *Social Theory since Freud: Traversing Social Imaginaries*. London: Routledge.

Elliott, A. (2005), 'Psychoanalytic Social Theory'. In A. Harrington (ed.), *Modern Social Theory: An Introduction*. New York: Oxford University Press, pp. 175–95.

Evans, D. (1996), *An Introductory Dictionary of Lacanian Psychoanalysis*. London: Routledge.

Feldner, H. & Vighi, F. (2010), 'A Subject that Matters: Žižek's Ideological Critique Today'. *International Journal of Žižek Studies* 4(1).

Fink, B. (1995), *The Lacanian Subject: Between Language and Jouissance*. Princeton, NJ: Princeton University Press.

Fink, B. (1997), *A Clinical Introduction to Lacanian Psychoanalysis*. Cambridge, MA: Harvard University Press.

Fink, B. (2004), *Lacan to the Letter: Reading* Ecrits *Closely*. Minneapolis: University of Minnesota Press.

Fisher, M. (2009), *Capitalist Realism: Is There No Alternative?* Alresford: O.

Freud, S. ([1913] 1960), *Totem and Taboo: Some Points of Agreement between Mental Lives of Savages and Neurotics*. London: Routledge & Kegan Paul.

Freud, S. ([1930] 2004), *Civilization and its Discontents*. London: Penguin.

Geras, N. (1987), 'Post-Marxism?'. *New Left Review*, May–June, 40–82.

Gigante, D. (1998), 'Toward a Notion of Critical Self-Creation: Slavoj Žižek and the "Vortex of Madness"'. *New Literary History* 29, 153–68.

Gilbert, J. (2007), 'All the Right Questions, All the Wrong Answers'. In P. Bowman & R. Stamp (eds), *The Truth of Žižek*. London: Continuum.

Gouldner, A. (1980), *The Two Marxisms: Contradictions and Anomalies in the Development of Theory*. London: Macmillan.

Graham, J. & Amariglio, J. (2006), 'Subjects of Economy: Introduction'. *Rethinking Marxism* 18, 199–203.

Gray, J. (2008), *Black Mass: Apocalyptic Religion and the Death of Utopia*. London: Penguin.

Hall, S. (1977), 'The "Political" and the "Economic" in Marx's Theory of Classes'. In A. Hunt (ed.), *Class and Class Structure*. London: Lawrence & Wishart, pp. 15–59.

Hardt, M. & Negri, A. (2000), *Empire*. Cambridge, MA: Harvard University Press.

Harvey, D. (2008), 'The Right to the City'. *New Left Review*, September–October, 23–41.

Hawken, P. (1997), 'Natural Capitalism'. *Mother Jones*, March–April.

Homer, S. (1996), 'Psychoanalysis, Representation, Politics: On the (Im)possibility of a Psychoanalytic Theory of Ideology?'. Third Annual Conference of the Universities Association for Psychoanalytic Studies.

Homer, S. (2001). 'It's the Political Economy, Stupid! On Žižek's Marxism'. *Radical Philosophy* 108, 7–16.

Hunt, A. (ed.) (1977a), *Class and Class Structure*. London: Lawrence & Wishart.

Hunt, A. (1977b), 'Introduction'. In A. Hunt (ed.), *Class and Class Structure*. London: Lawrence & Wishart, pp. 7–14.

International Labour Organization (2011), *Global Employment Trends 2011*. Geneva : International Labour Organization.

Irwin, J. & Motoh, H. (forthcoming), *Žižek and his Contemporaries*. London: Continuum.

Jameson, F. (1991), *Postmodernism, or, The Cultural Logic of Late Capitalism*. Durham, NC: Duke University Press.

Jameson, F. (1996), 'Five Theses on Actually Existing Marxism'. *Monthly Review* 47, 1–10.

Jameson, F. (2004), 'The Politics of Utopia'. *New Left Review*, January–February, 25–54.

Jameson, F. (2005), *Archaeologies of the Future: The Desire Called Utopia and Other Science Fictions*. London: Verso.

Jameson, F. (2009), *Valences of the Dialectic*. London: Verso.

Johnston, A. (2005), *Time Drive: Metapsychology and the Splitting of the Drive*. Evanston, IL: Northwestern University Press.

Johnston, A. (2008), *Žižek's Ontology: A Transcendental Materialist Theory of Subjectivity*. Evanston, IL: Northwestern University Press.

Johnston, A. (2009), *Badiou, Žižek and Political Transformations: The Cadence of Change*. Evanston, IL: Northwestern University Press.

Kay, S. (2003), *Žižek: A Critical Introduction*. Cambridge: Polity Press.

Kovel, J. (2007), *The Enemy of Nature: The End of Capitalism or the End of the World?*, 2nd ed. London: Zed.

Kul-Want, C. (2011). *Introducing Slavoj Žižek: A Graphic Guide*. London: Icon.

La Berge, L. (2007), 'The Writing Cure: Slavoj Žižek, Analysand of Modernity'. In P. Bowman & R. Stamp (eds), *The Truth of Žižek*, London: Continuum, pp. 9–26.

Lacan, J. (1992), *The Ethics of Psychoanalysis 1959–1960*, tr. D. Porter. New York: W. W. Norton.

Lacan, J. (2006), *Ecrits: The First Complete Edition in English*, tr. H. Fink & R. Grigg. New York: W. W. Norton.

Laclau, E. (1989), 'Preface'. In S. Žižek, *The Sublime Object of Ideology*. London: Verso.

Laclau, E. (1990), *New Reflections on the Revolutions of our Time*. London: Verso.

Laclau, E. (2000a), 'Constructing Universality'. In J. Butler et al., *Contingency, Hegemony, Universality: Contemporary Dialogues on the Left*. London: Verso, pp. 281–307.

Laclau, E. (2000b), 'Structure, History and the Political'. In J. Butler et al., *Contingency, Hegemony, Universality: Contemporary Dialogues on the Left*. London: Verso, pp. 182–212.

Laclau, E. (2003), 'Discourse and Jouissance: A Reply to Glynos and Stavrakakis'. *Journal for Lacanian Studies* 1, 278–85.

Laclau, E. (2005), *On Populist Reason*. London: Verso.

Laclau, E. (2006), 'Why Constructuring a People is the Main Task of Radical Politics'. *Critical Inquiry* 32, 646–80.

Laclau, E. & Mouffe, C. (1985), *Hegemony and Socialist Strategy: Towards a Radical Democratic Politics*. London: Verso.

Laclau, E. & Mouffe, C. (1990), 'Post-Marxism without Apologies'. In E. Laclau, *New Reflections on the Revolutions of Our Time*. London: Verso.

Lebowitz, M. (2003), *Beyond Capital: Marx's Political Economy of the Working Class*, 2nd ed. Basingstoke: Palgrave Macmillan.

Lenin, V. (2002), *Revolution at the Gates: Selected Writings of Lenin from 1917*, ed. S. Žižek. London: Verso.

Levitas, R. (2007), 'Looking for the Blue: The Necessity of Utopia'. *Journal of Political Ideologies* 12, 289–306.

Levy-Stokes, C. (2001), 'Jouissance'. In H. Glowinski et al. (eds), *A Compendium of Lacanian Terms*. London: Free Association.

Lu, T. (2012), *Slavoj Žižek*. Durham, NC: Duke University Press.

Marcuse, H. (1956), *Eros and Civilization: A Philosophical Inquiry into Freud*. London: Routledge & Kegan Paul.

Marx, K. ([1867] 1999), *Capital*. Oxford: Oxford University Press.

Marx, K. ([1867] 2007), *Capital: A Critique of Political Economy*, vol. 1. New York: Cosimo.

Marx, K. & Engels, F. (1980). 'A Contribution to the Critique of Political Economy'. In K. Marx & F. Engels, *Karl Marx, Frederick Engels: Collected Works*. New York: International Publishers.

Marx, K. & Engels, F. ([1848] 2004), *The Communist Manifesto*. London: Penguin.

Miklitsch, R. (1998), 'Introduction'. *South Atlantic Quarterly* 97, 227–34.

Myers, T. (2003), *Slavoj Žižek*. London: Routledge.

New York Times (2008), 'The Torture Report', 17 December, http://www.nytimes.com/2008/12/18/opinion/18thu1.html, accessed 29 November 2011.

Özselçuk, C. & Madra, Y. (2005), 'Psychoanalysis and Marxism: From Capitalist-All to Communist Non-All'. *Psychoanalysis, Culture and Society* 10, 79–97.

Özselçuk, C. & Madra, Y. (2007), 'Economy, Surplus, Politics: Some Questions on Slavoj Žižek's Political Economy Critique of Capitalism'. In F. Vighi & H. Feldner (eds), *Did Somebody Say Ideology? On Slavoj Žižek and Consequences*. Newcastle upon Tyne: Cambridge Scholars.

Pappe, H. (1951), 'Wakefield and Marx'. *Economic History Review* 4, 88–97.

Parker, I. (2004), *Slavoj Žižek: A Critical Introduction*. London: Pluto Press.

Parker, I. (2007), 'The Truth about Over-identification'. In P. Bowman & R. Stamp (eds), *The Truth of Žižek*. London: Continuum, pp. 144–60.

Pound, M. (2008), *Žižek: A (Very) Critical Introduction*. Grand Rapids, MI: Wm. B. Eerrdmans.

Robinson, A. & Tormey, S. (2005), 'A Ticklish Subject? Žižek and the Future of Left Radicalism'. *Thesis Eleven* 80, 94–107.

Robinson, A. & Tormey, S. (2006), 'Žižek's Marx: "Sublime Object" or a "Plague of Fantasies"?'. *Historical Materialism* 14, 145–74.

Sachs, J. (2005), *The End of Poverty: Economic Possibilities for Our Time*. London: Allen Lane.

Sachs, J. (2008), *Common Wealth: Economics for a Crowded Planet*. New York: Penguin Press.

Schecter, D. (2007), *The History of the Left from Marx to the Present: Theoretical Perspectives*. London: Continuum.

Sharpe, M. (2004), *Slavoj Žižek: A Little Piece of the Real*. Aldershot: Ashgate.

Sharpe, M. & Boucher, G. (2010), *Žižek and Politics: A Critical Introduction*. Edinburgh: Edinburgh University Press.

Sheehan, S. (2012), *Žižek: A Guide for the Perplexed*. London: Continuum.

Stamp, R. (2007), '"Another Exemplary Case": Žižek's Logic of Examples'. In P. Bowman & R. Stamp (eds), *The Truth of Žižek*. London: Continuum, pp. 161–76.

Stavrakakis, Y. (1999), *Lacan and the Political*. London: Routledge.

Stavrakakis, Y. (2000a), 'On the Critique of Advertising Discourse: A Lacanian View'. *Third Text* 14, 85–90.

Stavrakakis, Y. (2000b), 'On the Emergence of Green Ideology: The

Dislocation Factor in Green Politics'. In D. Howarth et al. (eds), *Discourse Theory and Political Analysis: Identities, Hegemonies and Social Change*. Manchester: Manchester University Press, pp. 100–18.

Stavrakakis, Y. (2007), *The Lacanian Left: Psychoanalysis, Theory, Politics*. Albany: SUNY Press.

Taylor, A. (director) (2007), *Žižek!*. Hidden Driver / The Documentary Campaign.

Taylor, P. (2011), *Žižek and the Media*. Cambridge: Polity Press.

Tie, W. (2004), 'The Psychic Life of Governmentality'. *Culture, Theory and Critique* 45(2), 161–76.

Tie, W. (2009), 'Beyond the Dislocation(s) of Human Rights'. *Social and Legal Studies* 18(1), 71–91.

UN-Habitat (2011), *State of the World's Cities 2010/2011: Cities for All – Bridging the Urban Divide*. London & Stirling, VA: Earthscan.

United Nations Department of Economic and Social Affairs (2011), 'World population to reach 10 billion by 2100 if fertility in all countries converges to replacement level'. http://esa.un.org/wpp/Other-Information/Press_Release_WPP2010.pdf, accessed 4 December 2011.

Valentine, J. (2007), 'Denial, Anger and Resentment'. In P. Bowman & R. Stamp (eds), *The Truth of Žižek*. London: Continuum, pp. 177–96.

Vighi, F. (2010), *On Žižek's Dialectics: Surplus, Subtracton, Sublimation*. London: Continuum.

Vighi, F. & Feldner, H. (2007), *Žižek: Beyond Foucault*. Basingstoke: Palgrave Macmillan.

Wade, R. (2007), 'A New Global Financial Architecture?'. *New Left Review*, July–August, 113–29.

Wade, R. (2008), 'Financial Regime Change?'. *New Left Review*, September–October, 5–21.

Wood, A. (2004), *Karl Marx*, 2nd ed. New York: Routledge.

Wright, E., & Wright, E. (eds) (1999), *The Žižek Reader*. Oxford: Blackwell.

Žižek, S. (1989), *The Sublime Object of Ideology*. London: Verso.

Žižek, S. (1991), *For They Know Not What They Do: Enjoyment as a Political Factor*. London: Verso.

Žižek, S. (ed.) (1992), *Everything You Wanted to Know about Lacan (but Were Afraid to Ask Hitchcock)*. London: Verso.

Žižek, S. (1993a), *Enjoy Your Symptom! Jacques Lacan in Hollywood and Out*. New York: Routledge.

Žižek, S. (1993b), *Looking Awry: An Introduction to Jacques Lacan through Popular Culture*. Cambridge, MA: MIT Press.

Žižek, S. (1994), *The Metastases of Enjoyment: Six Essays on Woman and Causality*. London: Verso.

Žižek, S. (1997), *The Plague of Fantasies*. London: Verso.

Žižek, S. (1999), *The Ticklish Subject: The Absent Centre of Political Ontology*. London: Verso.

Žižek, S. (2000a), 'Class Struggle or Postmodernism?'. In J. Butler et al., *Contingency, Hegemony, Universality*, London: Verso. pp. 90–129.

Žižek, S. (2000b), 'Da Capo Senza Fine'. In J. Butler et al., *Contingency, Hegemony, Universality*, London: Verso, pp. 213–62.

Žižek, S. (2000c), *The Fragile Absolute*. London: Verso.

Žižek, S. (2000d), 'Holding the Place'. In J. Butler et al., *Contingency, Hegemony, Universality*. London: Verso, pp. 308–26.

Žižek, S. (2001), *Did Somebody Say Totalitarianism?*. London: Verso.

Žižek, S. (2002), *For They Know Not What They Do: Enjoyment as a Political Factor*, 2nd ed. London: Verso.

Žižek, S. (2003), *Welcome to the Desert of the Real: Five Essays on September 11 and Other Related Dates*. London: Verso.

Žižek, S. (2004a), 'Ethical Socialism? No, Thanks! Reply to Boucher'. *Teleos* 129, 173–89.

Žižek, S. (2004b), *Iraq: The Borrowed Kettle*. London: Verso.

Žižek, S. (2005a), 'Against Human Rights'. *New Left Review*, July–August, 115–31.

Žižek, S. (2005b), *Interrogating the Real: Selected Writings*, ed. R. Butler & S. Stephens. London: Continuum.

Žižek, S. (2006a), 'Against the Populist Temptation'. *Critical Inquiry* 32, 551–74.

Žižek, S. (2006b), 'The Fetish of the Party'. In S. Žižek, *The Universal Exception: Selected Writings, Vol. 2*, ed. R. Butler & S. Stephens. London: Continuum, pp. 67–93.

Žižek, S. (2006c), *The Parallax View*. Cambridge, MA: MIT Press.

Žižek, S. (2006d), 'The Prospects for Radical Politics Today'. In S. Žižek, *The Universal Exception: Selected Writings, Vol. 2*, ed. R. Butler & S. Stephens. London: Continuum, pp. 237–57.

Žižek, S. (2006e), *The Universal Exception: Selected Writings, Vol. 2*, ed. R. Butler & S. Stephens. London: Continuum.

Žižek, S. (2007a), 'Multitude, Surplus, and Envy'. *Rethinking Marxism* 19, 46–58.

Žižek, S. (2007b), 'With Defenders like These'. In P. Bowman & R. Stamp (eds), *The Truth of Žižek*. London: Continuum, pp. 197–254.

Žižek, S. (2008), *In Defense of Lost Causes*. London: Verso.

Žižek, S. (2009a), *First as Tragedy, Then as Farce*. London: Verso.

Žižek, S. (2009b), 'How to Begin from the Beginning'. *New Left Review*, May–June, 43–55.

Žižek, S. (2010), *Living in the End Times*. London: Verso.

Žižek, S. (2011a), 'Shoplifters of the World Unite: Slavoj Žižek on the Meaning of the Riots'. *London Review of Books*, 19 August, http://www.lrb.co.uk/2011/08/19/slavoj-zizek/shoplifters-of-the-world-unite, accessed 29 November 2011.

Žižek, S. (2011b), 'Slavoj Žižek Speaks at St Mark's Bookshop',http://www. lacan.com/thesymptom/?page_id=1539, accessed 7 December 2011.

Žižek, S. & Daly, G. (2003), *Conversations with Žižek*. Cambridge: Polity Press.

Zupančič, A. (2000). *Ethics of the Real: Kant, Lacan*. London: Verso.

Zupančič, A. (2006a), 'The Concrete Universal and What Comedy Can Tell Us about It'. In S. Žižek (ed.), *Lacan: The Silent Partners*. London: Verso, pp. 171–97.

Zupančič, A. (2006b), 'When Surplus Enjoyment Meets Surplus Value'. In J. Clemens & R. Grig (eds), *Jacques Lacan and the Other Side of Psychoanalysis: Reflections on Seminar XVII*. Durham, NC: Duke University Press, pp. 135–78.

Zupančič, A. (2008), *The Odd One In: On Comedy*. Cambridge, MA: MIT Press.

Index

EU representative:
Easy Access System Europe
Mustamäe tee 50, 10621 Tallinn, Estonia
Gpsr.requests@easproject.com

www.ingramcontent.com/pod-product-compliance
Lightning Source LLC
Chambersburg PA
CBHW050707280326
41926CB00088B/2860